# HUMANITY'S EVOLUTIONARY DESTINY

PETER LANG
New York • Bern • Frankfurt • Berlin
Brussels • Vienna • Oxford • Warsaw

*Seymour W. Itzkoff*

# HUMANITY'S EVOLUTIONARY DESTINY

*A Darwinian Perspective*

PETER LANG
New York • Bern • Frankfurt • Berlin
Brussels • Vienna • Oxford • Warsaw

**Library of Congress Cataloging-in-Publication Data**

Humanity's evolutionary destiny: a Darwinian perspective / Seymour W. Itzkoff.
pages cm
Includes bibliographical references and index.
1. Human ecology. 2. Humanity. 3. Ethics. 4. Human evolution.
5. Civilization. I. Title.
GF41.I89   599.93'8—dc23   2013047132
ISBN 978-1-4331-2545-4 (hardcover)
ISBN 978-1-4539-1256-0 (e-book)

Bibliographic information published by **Die Deutsche Nationalbibliothek**.
**Die Deutsche Nationalbibliothek** lists this publication in the "Deutsche
Nationalbibliografie"; detailed bibliographic data are available
on the Internet at http://dnb.d-nb.de/.

Cover design by Jules T. Itzkoff

The paper in this book meets the guidelines for permanence and durability
of the Committee on Production Guidelines for Book Longevity
of the Council of Library Resources.

© 2016 Peter Lang Publishing, Inc., New York
29 Broadway, 18th floor, New York, NY 10006
www.peterlang.com

All rights reserved.
Reprint or reproduction, even partially, in all forms such as microfilm,
xerography, microfiche, microcard, and offset strictly prohibited.

Printed in Germany

# Books by Seymour W. Itzkoff
## Smith College, Emeritus Professor

| | |
|---|---|
| *Cultural Pluralism and American Education* | 1969 |
| *Ernst Cassirer: Scientific Knowledge and the Concept of Man* | 1971, 1997 (2nd edition) |
| *A New Public Education* | 1976 |
| *Ernst Cassirer, Philosopher of Culture* | 1977 |
| *Emanuel Feuermann, Virtuoso* | 1979, 1995 (2nd edition) |
| The Evolution of Human Intelligence | |
|   1 *The Form of Man, The Evolutionary Origins of Human Intelligence* | 1983 |
|   2 *Triumph of the Intelligent, The Creation of Homo sapiens sapiens* | 1985 |
|   3 *Why Humans Vary in Intelligence* | 1987 |
|   4 *The Making of the Civilized Mind* | 1990 |
| *How We Learn to Read* | 1986 |
| *Human Intelligence and National Power* | 1991 |
| *The Road to Equality, Evolution and Social Reality* | 1992 |
| *The Decline of Intelligence in America, A Strategy for National Renewal* | 1994 |
| *Children Learning to Read, A Guide for Parents and Teachers* | 1996 |
| The Human Prospect | |
|   1 *The Inevitable Domination by Man, An Evolutionary Detective Story* | 2000 |
|   2 *2050: The Collapse of the Global Techno-Economy* | 2003 |
|   3 *Intellectual Capital in Twenty-First-Century Politics* | 2003 |
|   4 *Rebuilding Western Civilization, Beyond the Twenty-First-Century Collapse* | 2005 |
| Who Are the Jews? | |
|   1 *Soul of the Israelites* | 2004 |
|   2 *A Nation of Philosophers* | 2004 |
|   3 *Fatal Gift, Jewish Intelligence and Western Civilization* | 2006 |
| *The World Energy Crisis and the Task of Retrenchment* | 2008 |
| *The End of Economic Growth: What Does It Mean for American Society?* | 2009 |
| *Judaism's Promise, Meeting the Challenge of Modernity* | 2014 |
| *Liberty's Dilemma: America, Two Nations Dependent/Independent* | 2014 |

For
Benjamin, Aaron, Jules, Coleman, Nathaniel, Lucille, Zachary

In appreciation

Modern Philosophical: Karl Marx, 1818–1883; John Dewey, 1859–1952; Ernst Cassirer, 1874–1945

Scientists: Charles Darwin, 1809–1882; Francis Galton, 1822–1911; Carleton Coon, 1904–1981; Hans Eysenck, 1916–1987; Arthur Jensen, 1923–2012

# CONTENTS

Introduction     1

### Part I—Dynamic Progressions

Chapter 1.    Originating Adaptations of Animal Life    13
Chapter 2.    We Dominating Mammals    27
Chapter 3.    The Primate Pathway    41
Chapter 4.    *Homo*: Wherefrom?    51
Chapter 5.    Natural Selection of *Homo*    65
Chapter 6.    Cro-Magnon—*Homo sapiens sapiens*    77

### Part II—Evolutionary Outcomes

Chapter 7.    *Homo sapiens sapiens*: A Unique Animal Intelligence    93
Chapter 8.    Civilization: Symbolic Dynamics    105
Chapter 9.    Civilizational Dynamics: Exemplars    115
Chapter 10.    Symbolic Thought: The Universal, the Plural    123
Chapter 11.    Cro-Magnon's Progeny: The Modern Mind    135

| Chapter 12. | Dream of a Universal Humanity | 145 |
| Chapter 13. | Natural Selection of Humanity | 155 |
| Chapter 14. | Reality Suppressed | 169 |

### Part III—Our Twenty-First Century and Beyond

| Chapter 15. | Conditions of International Survival | 183 |
| Chapter 16. | Utopia Interdict | 195 |
| Chapter 17. | The United States in Transition | 205 |
| Chapter 18. | Catastrophe, Renewal, and Law | 215 |
| Chapter 19. | Destiny | 225 |

Index   235

| MYA* | Eon | Era | Period | Epoch | Events |
|---|---|---|---|---|---|
| 0.045 | | | | Recent | Modern humans worldwide distribution; sixth mass extinction event |
| 1.8 | | | Quaternary | Pleistocene | First hominines appear |
| 5 | | | | Pliocene | Origin of human family |
| 24 | | | | Miocene | Many grazing mammals; primate radiation |
| 37 | | | | Oligocene | First anthropoid primates; abundant birds |
| 58 | | | | Eocene | Modern mammals and angiosperms |
| 65 | | Cenozoic | Tertiary | Paleocene | Placental mammals diversify |
| 144 | | | Cretaceous | | Early mammals; first modern birds; first modern fishes; angiosperms appear and become dominant; climax of dinosaurs followed by their extinction at end of period; fifth mass extinction event |
| 213 | | | Jurassic | | First mammals; first birds; dinosaurs dominant; therapsids extinct; abundant bony fishes; gymnosperm forests |
| 248 | | Mesozoic | Triassic | | Reptiles diversify; first dinosaurs; many insect types; bony fishes diversify; abundant cycads and conifers; fourth mass extinction event |
| 286 | | | Permian | | Insects diversify; reptiles diversify; first therapsids; cycads and conifers expand; third mass extinction event |
| 320 | | | Carboniferous | Pennsylvanian | First reptiles appear; amphibians diversify; first conifers; abundant seed ferns; major coal deposits |
| 360 | | | | Mississippian | |
| 408 | | | Devonian | | First amphibians appear; terrestrial life diversifies; fishes diversify; first true bony fishes; fist sharks; second mass extinction event |
| 438 | | | Silurian | | Jawless fishes diversify; first jawed fishes appear; first terrestrial plants and animals |
| 505 | | | Ordovician | | All lifeforms still aquatic only; armored ostracoderm fishes diversify; invertebrates diverse and dominant; first mass extinction event |
| 543 | Phanerozoic | Paleozoic | Cambrian | | Aquatic life only; all modern animal phyla present; first vertebrates appear; trilobites common |
| 2500 | Proterozoic | The Proterozoic and Archean Eons are sometimes referred to collectively as the Precambrian. | | | Oldest eukaryotic fossils (algae) |
| 3800 | Archaean | | | | Marked by the beginning of geological history; first lifeforms evolved; oldest prokaryotic fossils |
| ~4500 | Hadean | | | | Solar System forms; molten Earth forms and begins to cool; no geological history during Hadeon (because there was no solid rock); when solid rock formed, geological history began and the Hadean ended |

1. **Evolutionary Timetable:** Always subject to revision given new scientific data.

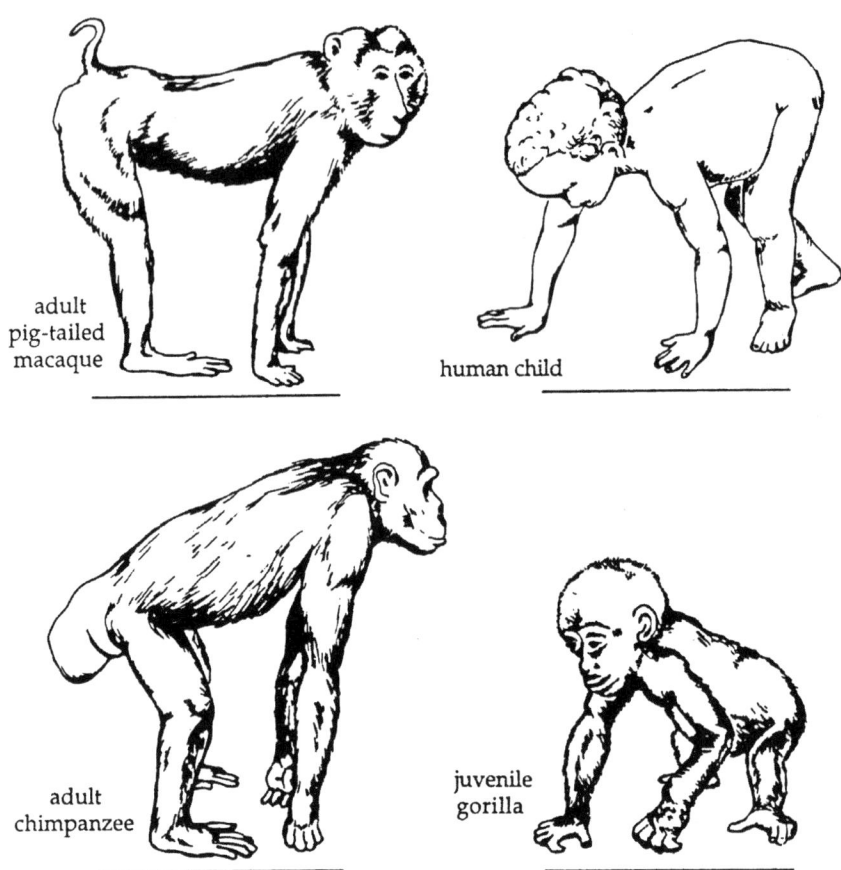

2. **Chimpanzee/Human Relationship:** The morphological relationship of chimpanzees and humans is distant. A critical example is the walking stance of young humans as compared to chimpanzees and gorillas. Young humans walk with their palms flat, as do monkey and orangutans. Chimpanzees and gorillas are knuckle-walkers requiring greatly different bone and muscle alignments, longer arms and shorter legs.

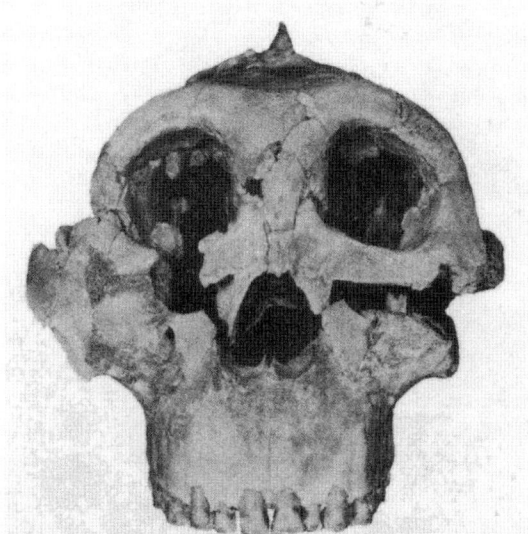
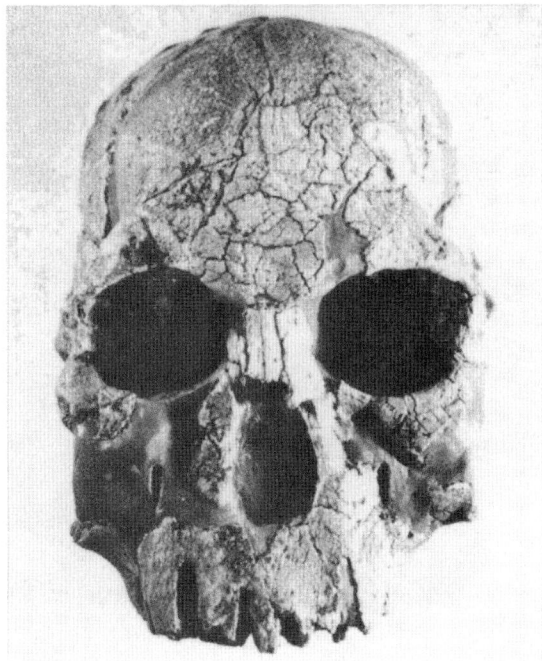

**3. Australopithecus and Homo:** *Paranthropus boisei* (Zinjanthropus) and *Homo rudolfensis* Both hominids lived in East Africa c. 1.8 mya. This robust Australopithecine as well as more gracile forms disappeared from Africa about 1 mya. *Homo rudolfensis* had a much larger brain and could have been an antecedent for more modern and recent humans.

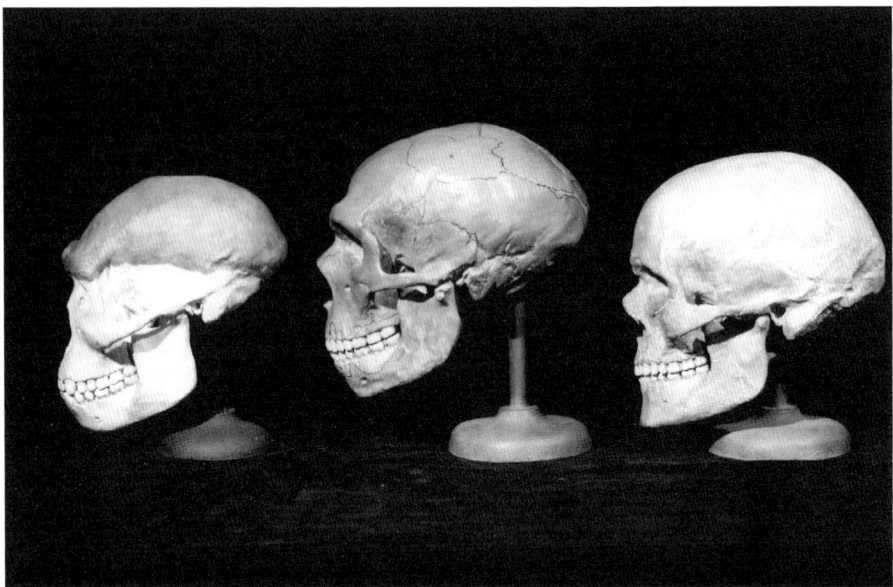

**4. Comparative Skulls**: (From left to right). *Homo erectus pithecanthropus*, c. 900k BP (Ancient Australid/Indonesia); *Homo neanderthalis*, c. 50k BP. (Caucasoid/Europe, West Asia); *Homo sapiens sapiens*, c. 35k BP Cro-Magnon, (Caucasoid/Europe). *(Neg. No. 323740. Courtesy Department of Library Services American Museum of Natural History)*

HUMANITY'S EVOLUTIONARY DESTINY    XV

5. **Evolution of Tools:** 1. Earliest erectine eoliths, from c. 1mya; 2–4 Evolved erectine tools, from c. 800k BP to c. 300k BP; 5–7. Mousterian Neanderthal tools; from c. 200k BP to 30k BP; 8–14. Developing Cro-Magnon tool kit, from c. 40k BP to c. 12k BP. *(Neg. No. 39685. Photo: Kirschner. Courtesy American Museum of Natural History.)*

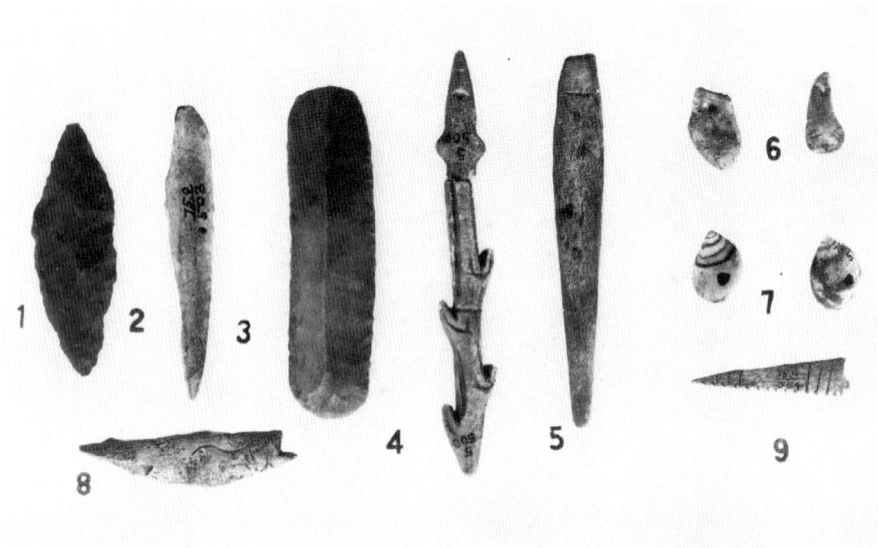

**6. Cro-Magnon (Hss) Tools and Ornaments:** Made of flint, bone, elk teeth, shells. Note: fragment 8, made of bone has a horse engraved on it. *(Neg. No. 39774. Photo: Kirschner. Courtesy Department of Library Services American Museum of Natural History)*

HUMANITY'S EVOLUTIONARY DESTINY    XVII

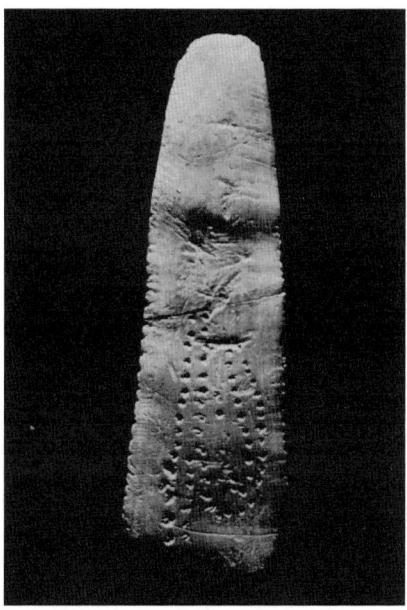

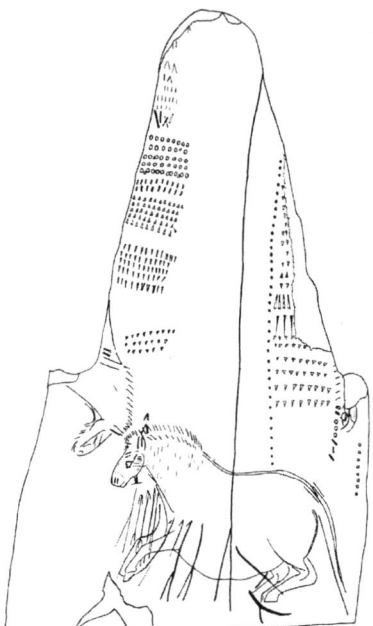

**7. Chronometric Markings by Cro-Magnon:** The modern mind seeks to understand the regularities of nature. (*top*) Engraved plaque, 9.7 centimeters, c. 25k BP. (*Neg. No. 2A17536. Courtesy Department of Library Services American Museum of Natural History*); (*bottom*) Sketch of notations on antler tool with drawing of pregnant horse. Notations may have attempted to record length of gestation by months of the moon. (France).

XVIII HUMANITY'S EVOLUTIONARY DESTINY

**8. Venuses of Cro-Magnon:** (*top*) Lespague, France *(Neg. No. 338394. Courtesy Department of Library Services American Museum of Natural History)*; (*bottom*) Dolni Vestonice, Czechoslovakia (fire hardened clay sculpture) *(Neg. No. 336871. Photo: Jim Coke. Courtesy Department of Library Services American Museum of Natural History)*. Both c. 25–20k BP. Some view these Venuses as hand or pocket held (9–12 cm.) memory tokens of traveling hunters. Notice the modernistic abstract, esthetic envisionment. Dolni Vestonice sculpture was made from an amalgam of clay and pulverized bone, then, fire hardened like pottery.

# HUMANITY'S EVOLUTIONARY DESTINY                                XIX

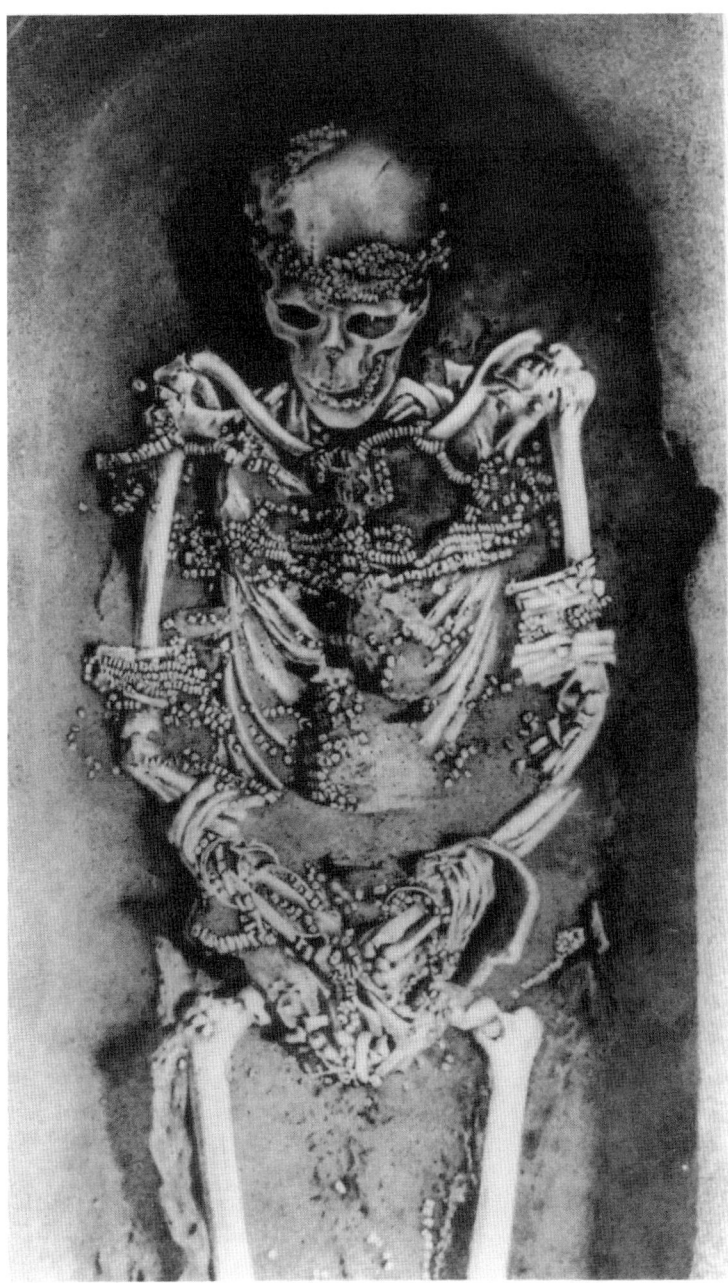

**9. Cro-Magnon Burial Traditions:** Buried near Vladimir northeast of Moscow, c. 28k BP this c. 60-year-old man's leather garments were decorated with mammoth tusk beads and pendants, bracelets, and necklaces of shells and animal teeth. Two juveniles in adjoining graves were also so decorated. Consider the work and skill required to commemorate these individuals.

**10. Remembrance Carving:** Miniaturized ivory carved head of a Cro-Magnon female. Possibly a token of love created for carrying while on the hunt. France, c. 25k BP.

**11. Relief Venus Sculpture:** An example of the variety of artistic techniques of Cro-Magnon sculptures. France, c. 22k BP. (© *Museum National D'Histoire Naturelle Editions d'Art Yvon— Imprimé en France 12 75 6033*)

XXII            HUMANITY'S EVOLUTIONARY DESTINY

12. **Carved Antler Bone:** Miniaturized carving, length, one inch, showing stags and salmon (note spinal cord), also diamond-shaped symbols. France, c. 12k BP.

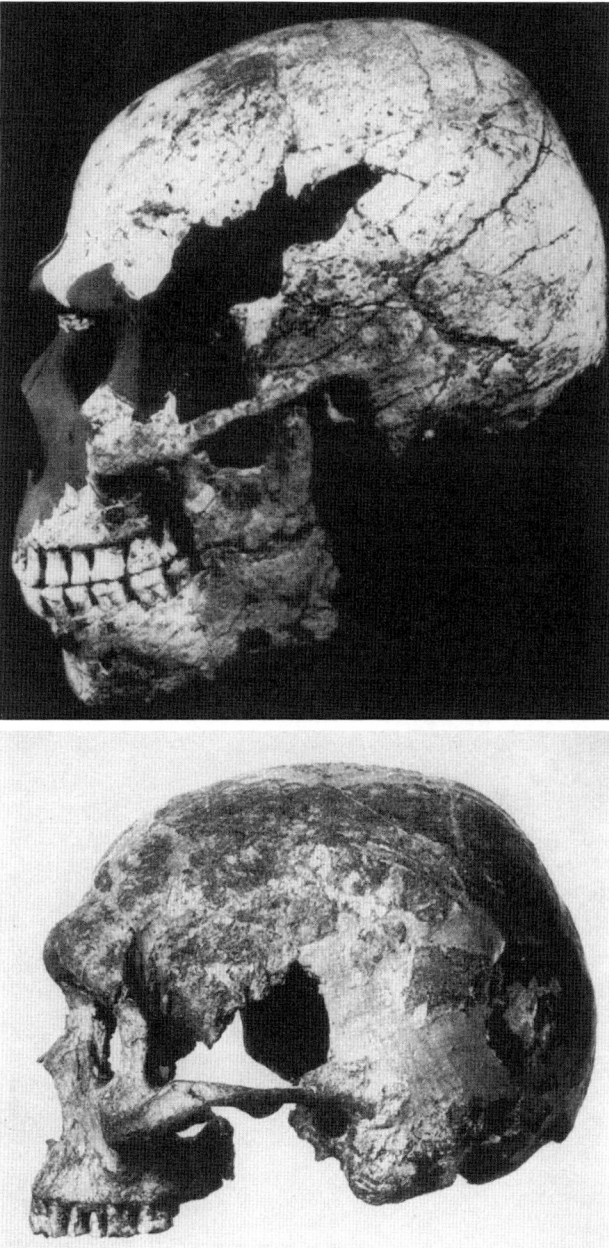

**13. Hybridization:** Skhul 5 (*top*), and Qafzeh 6 (*bottom*). Found in Israel (Mt. Carmel), both dating to c. 90–100k BP. Both fossils show Cro-Magnon and Neanderthal characteristics. But since they are found in conjunction with Mousterian (Neanderthal) tools they hint at a Cro-Magnon genetic intrusion into the Neanderthal community. Orthodox Neanderthal fossils dating more recently to 40k BP were found in the vicinity.

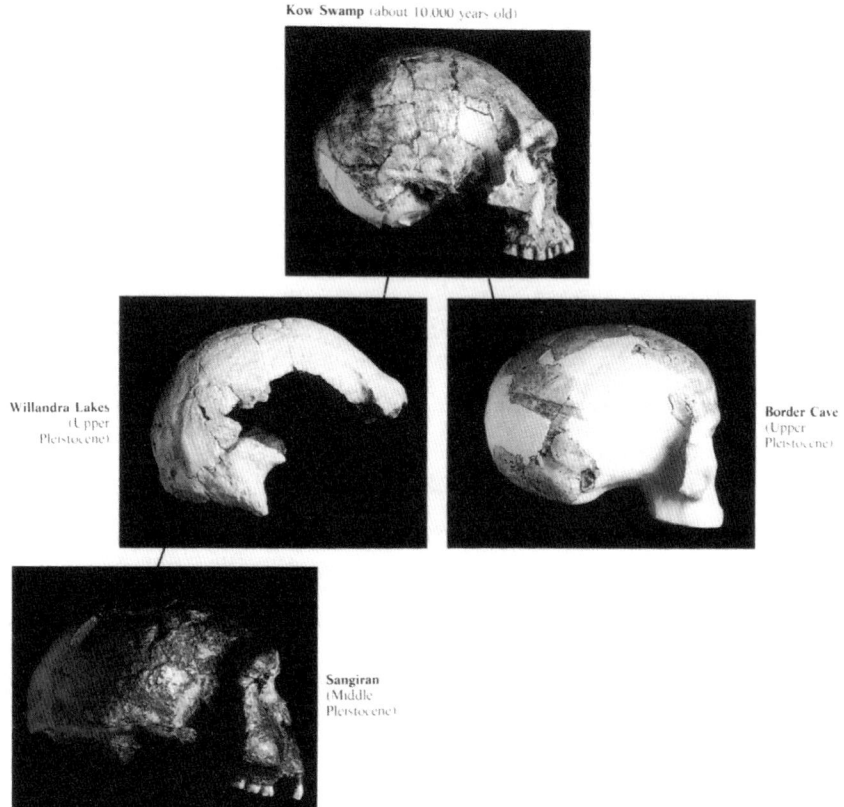

**14. Contemporaries?** Top: Kow Swamp, Australia, c. 10k BP; Mid-left, Willandra Lake, Australia, c. 30k BP (more modern than Kow Swamp); Mid-right, Border Cave, South Africa, c. 70k BP female? Capoid, hinting at Cro-Magnon intrusion; Bottom: Sangiran 17, erectine, Indonesia/Australid, Traditional estimates; one million to two hundred thousand BP. Recently, 52–27k BP. Recent discovery of *Homo florensis*, Indonesia, c. 18k BP (see figure 18), argues for the more recent Sangiran 17 dating.

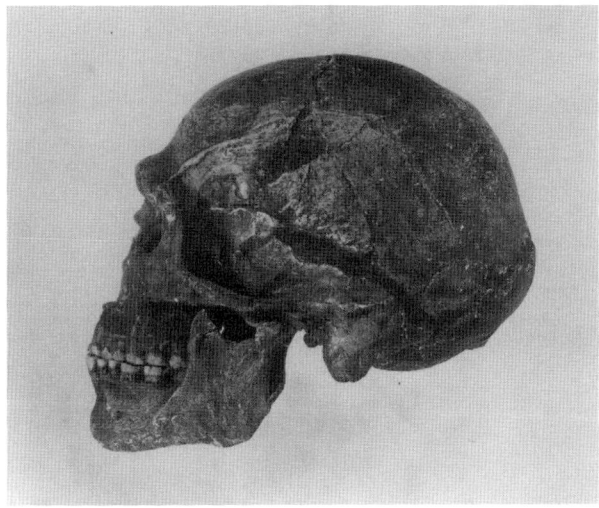

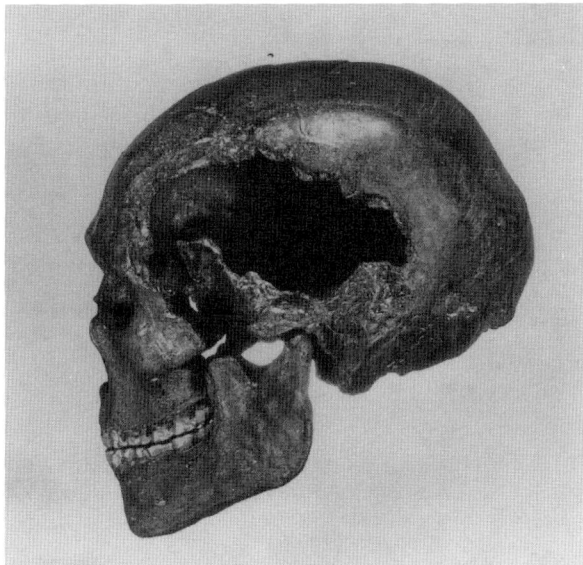

**15. Cro-Magnon Variables:** (*top*): Predmost, Czech Republic (*Neg. No. 310724. Photo: J. Beckett. Courtesy Department of Library Services American Museum of Natural History*); (*bottom*): Combe Capelle, France (*Neg. No. 310728. Photo: J. Beckett. Courtesy Department of Library Services American Museum of Natural History*). Both fossils date from c. 30k BP. and are associated with Cro-Magnon cultural tools and ornaments. However, Predmost like its associated Czech fossil skull, Mladec and the recently discovered Rumanian skull, Oases 2, seem little different than Qafzeh 6 (figure 12), which is dated to c. 90k BP. This suggests continual interbreeding of the Cro-Magnons with Neanderthals. However, after sixty thousand years the culture and brainpower argue that these primitive morphological remnants are relics. Current estimates put Neanderthal genes in modern Europeans at c. 5 percent.

XXVI HUMANITY'S EVOLUTIONARY DESTINY

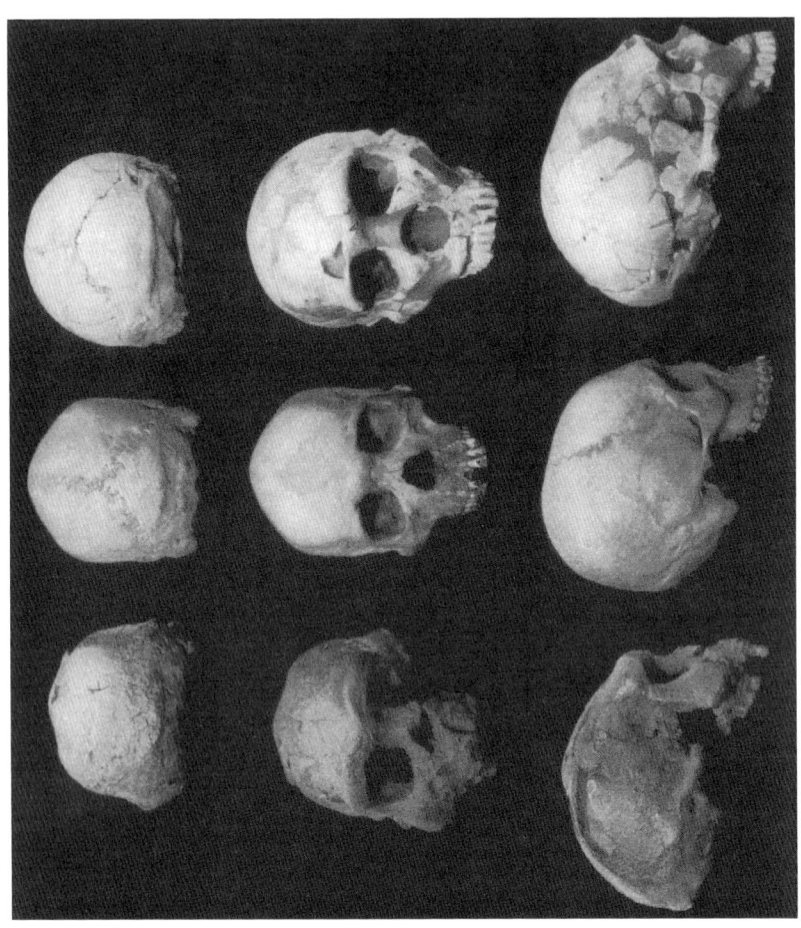

16. **Evolutionary Comparisons:** Left, Sangiran 17, erectine (Australid/Indonesia), a closer look, c. 52–27k BP; Center, Modern *Hss* Indonesian hybrid, mostly Mongoloid-Australid, with some Caucasoid admixture Right, Classical *Homo neanderthalensis*, Caucasoid, c. 60k BP, La Ferrassie, France.

HUMANITY'S EVOLUTIONARY DESTINY  XXVII

17. **Capoid Invasion of Europe:** The Capoid race includes Upper Paleolithic Boskopoids, here shown, as well as the disappearing Bushman in South Africa. This realization of a cave painting from Castellon in Spain shows typical art style of the Capoids, distinct from Cro-Magnon painting, engaged in a hunt, c. 20k BP. As with the Neanderthals, who disappeared from Europe c. 27k BP, the Capoids were driven out of Spain eventually into the South African desert (Bushman) by oncoming Caucasoid/Cro-Magnons and Negroids migrating out of West Africa. *(Neg. No. 336184. Courtesy Department of Library Services American Museum of Natural History).*

XXVIII     HUMANITY'S EVOLUTIONARY DESTINY

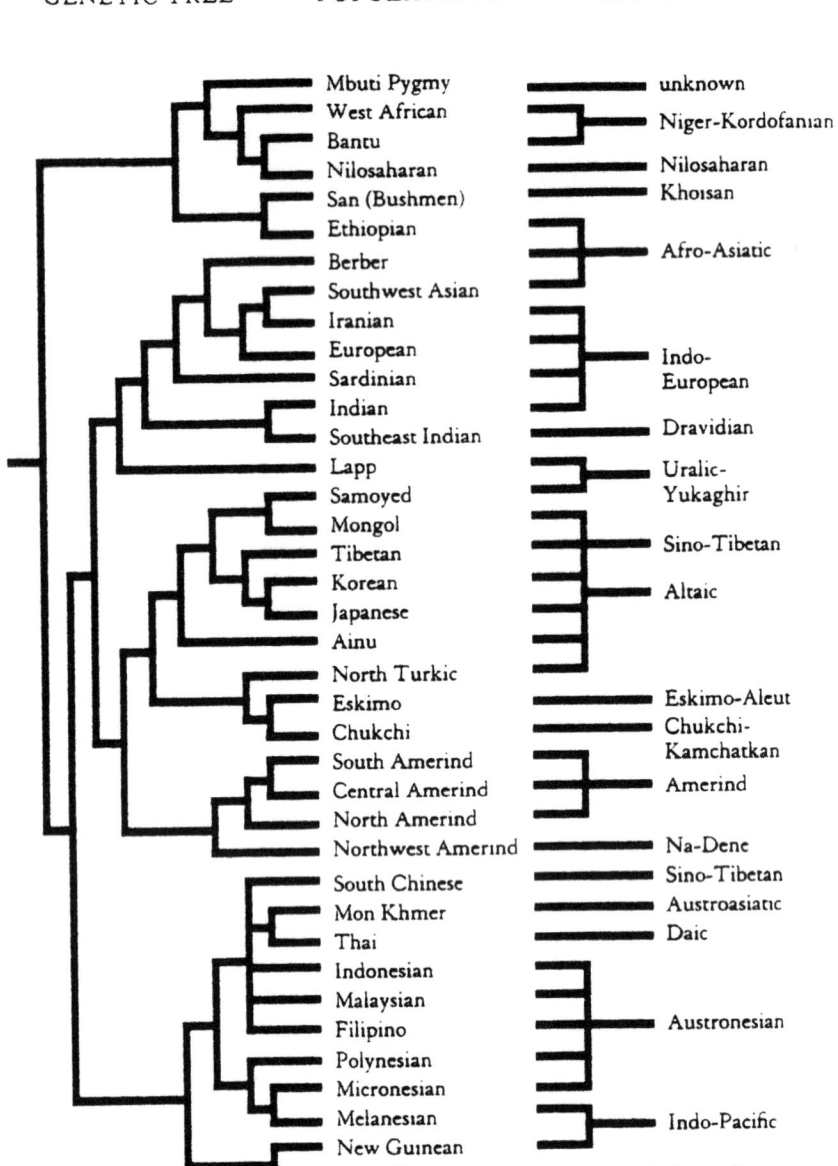

**18. Language and Genetic Relations of Humans:** This illustration reflects the work of Luigi Cavalli-Sforza. One of the obvious conclusions that this diagram suggests is that there is no relationship between Negroid language and genetic consanguinity to recent (100–10k BP, out of Africa humans.

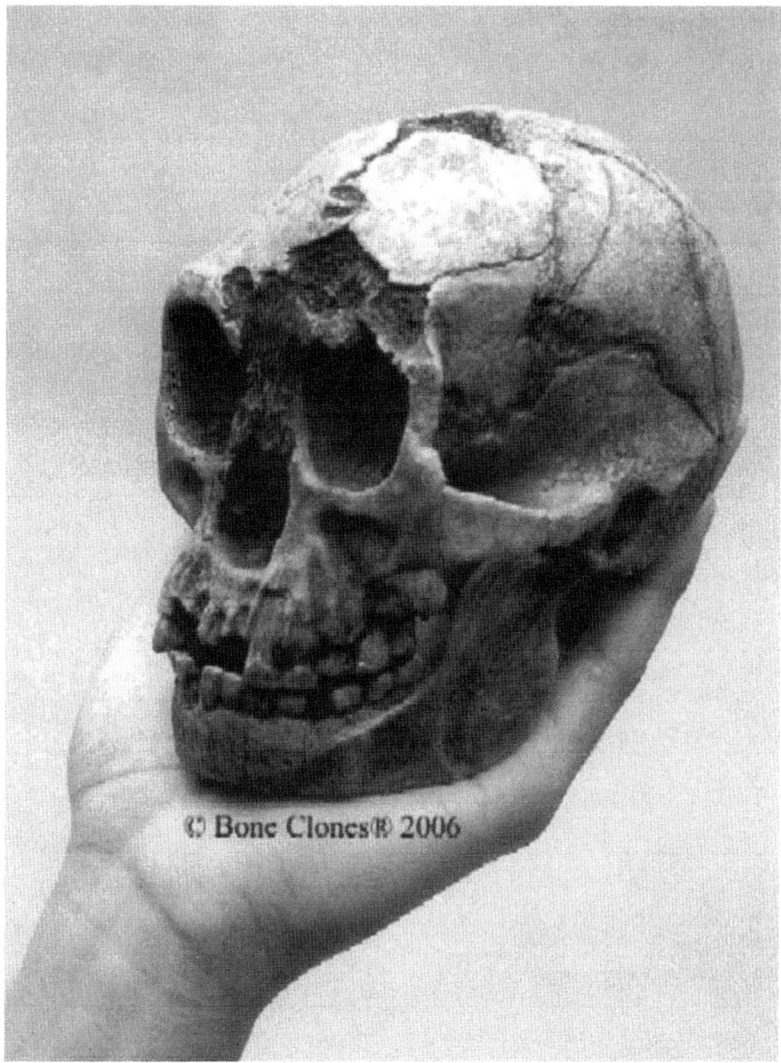

**19. *Homo florensis*, New Family on the Block:** An unprecedented fossil group of humans on a small Indonesian island, now dated to 18k BP. This human was a contemporary of Cro-Magnon, Hss. Its dwarfed size, 3.3 feet and tiny endocranial capacity, 400cm$^3$, equal to a Chimpanzee and close to *Australopithecus afarensis*, Lucy, 3.2 mya gives great verisimilitude to a view of separate lines of human evolution. It tells us that we are closer to the beginning of humanity's evolutionary integration on planet Earth than toward the end of our sojourn. (Model of Florensis skull by *Bone Clones Inc*)

# INTRODUCTION

## Perspective

*Humanity's Evolutionary Destiny* is an essay intended to integrate our biological heritage as a species with our current and future social embodiments of this evolutionary process. It is a product of many years of study, much writing, teaching, and lecturing. Above all this writing has been stimulated by the growing concern for the future of our own biological species. We are in this precarious situation together, and need a Darwinian perspective. Humans still are biological animals despite the social and political buzz to the contrary. All right, unique perhaps, but still subject to those classical principles of evolutionary dynamics laid down by the great Englishman and his worldwide scientific successors.

    The reader should first know that this writer is a liberal in its classic twentieth-century sense. Growing up in a semi-socialistic working-class family, the first thing I learned was the need to stay with factual reality, if only to keep our heads above water, to survive. Reality checking eventually forced us from socialism, with its ideological mirage, a product of tough times.

    The evolutionary perspective here being presented as both prolegomenon to and explanation of our ongoing international crisis is a result of my own movement away from satisfying youthful emotionally rooted ideologies. As one of my professors once said, quoting another: "If you are not a communist by the time you are twenty, you have no heart. If you are a communist by the time you are thirty, you have no mind."

In the latter parts of this book I will try to apply our Darwinian evolutionary knowledge of who we are as animals to our contemporary situation of perpetual crises. Sadly, our chaos of confusion is a product of an as yet undisciplined dimension of our human nature, religion/ideology. It has been very difficult to rein in these fantasies of mind whether theological or secular. Our contemporary world of science is still marred by enslavements, persecutions, wars, and genocides, now for well over a hundred years and ongoing. Perhaps several hundreds of millions of innocent *Homo sapiens* have been sacrificed in these most recent delusional carnages.

Thus while the exposition in the following chapters is factual and explanatory, the underlying vision is moral: to return us to a liberal vision of secular reality, so that we can deal practically and rationally with these accumulated, if unique evolutionary and historical circumstances, mostly of our own making. Using one's cortical capacities to distill reality from fantasy in order to act with practical world efficacy is in itself a deeply moral commitment. Perhaps in the process we could save the rest of the living forms that accompanied our species forward in time, and which have been decimated in kind and numbers in our ignorant thrust to momentary evolutionary power and dominance. These remaining vertebrate and non-vertebrate companions through time also need our consideration.

## Unfolding Reality

The reader should be helped to understand the context behind the words that follow in this book. How did the writer come to the views that he presents in summary and conclusion? What is the nature of this claim to be liberal? Many might see in these arguments a substantial deviation from what is today deemed "liberal," especially in these precarious times.

Growing to maturity in a post–World War II world, I was an activist for social equality, striving with unions and other "liberal" organizations to shed America of its racial, ethnic, social-class prejudice and deprivations, a supporter of the 1950s Civil Rights Movement's generation of new ideals of enthusiasm and hope. To rid all governmental impositions of inequality was the great dream of a Martin Luther King and of all his liberal contemporaries. Even into the '60s, with Lyndon Johnson's "Great Society" reintroduction of governmental activism in creating the more equal society hoped for by everyone, this novitiate academic was still on the bandwagon.

However, in spite of enormous efforts by the liberal community, governmental and voluntary, equality wasn't happening. The renewed institutional efforts to open the doors to opportunity weren't working. Here was the perennial hypothesis in the search for social equality. Stop the institutions of power from discriminating. Instead there now arose a steadily increasing cacophony of demonization. Supposedly, deeply ingrained prejudicial motives were subtly impeding these moral efforts. If so, only greater government intervention could reverse this majority incubus of hatred.

Naturally, in a free society all assumptions of power had to be analyzed and critiqued. By the 1970s the psychologists, psychometricians, had begun to analyze the mystery of the lack of success in equalizing minority achievement with the majority. Their analysis was built on over one hundred years of research concerning IQ. This earlier seminal work by scientists of the mind involved no racial and little ethnic analysis. It concerned itself with the existing majority Europoid populations of Europe and North America. Its aim was to relate educational and workplace achievement with presumed bio-genetic diversity in intellectual potential. But this new 1970s research, because it now discussed majority/minority IQs, quickly became anathema to those arguing for purely societal causations. Such analysis thus became "politically incorrect," and finally subject to institutional interdict. Most researchers, psychologists, anthropologists, and geneticists quickly scurried to the sidelines to save their careers.

But why would not a factual analysis promulgating a non-societal causation be warranted, at the least as legitimate intellectual inquiry? We needed to know the truth. The vendetta against these researchers also smacked of totalitarian-like ideological intimidation. After all, other policy routes might lead to human equality rather than the one that led to the demonization of a society and then the tremendous ideological political pressure to introduce massive socioeconomic redistribution.

To this writer, the purely psycho-genetic explanations fell short of the necessary explanatory structure that might allow for a more rational set of social policy initiatives. Then began a decades-long study into the origin and meaning of what really was a world of inequality. Viewed within this 1970s context it was clear that the issue was not necessarily a racial one. The

Japanese, Koreans, and the Chinese were demonstrating very clearly that they could emulate and even outrun the dominant Europoid ethos (even if the Japanese could not win its mid-twentieth-century world war).

My graduate training was in the philosophy of science (physics) and in epistemology, a neo-Kantian analysis into the workings of the human mind as the mind constructs knowledge from its sensory origins. Parallel with this study was a deep curiosity about evolutionary theory itself. There had to be answers here, to allow us to understand the clear differences in human civilizational and cultural attainments throughout human history and into the realities of the twentieth- and twenty-first-century world.

These differences ought not stimulate the angry rhetoric that had now spread into what once was the liberal intellectual community. There were enough evil doers in this twentieth century to explain its horrible events, without creating pseudo-demons. Any research that would attempt to clarify the realities of such human differences in general intelligence, IQ, ought not to exclude the further step and question, why? Certainly nature could tell us something about our heritage and destiny, of both evil and good.

Thus, over the past three-plus decades I have been researching and writing about humanity's evolutionary push into contemporary reality. My most comprehensive and recent analysis of our evolutionary journey, *The Inevitable Domination by Man* (2000), summed up the purely evolutionary forces that brought modern humans to the fore. This present essay takes the argument and much of its substance from this earlier work. It adds new materials, as well as a significant expansion into the historical and contemporary circumstances of the United States and the world around us. Evolution has consequences, even into our own day.

While some of the research conclusions of the earlier work were controversial, both theoretically and concretely, I am gratified to note that in every case these hypotheses, after more than a decade of third-person scholarly research, have in the main been substantiated and in no instance have they been factually countered or refuted.

## Creationism: Right and Left

The ultimate contemporary concern of this book is that the western European/ North American leadership has been led astray by the emotional pulsations of the lower brain now blurring the critical cortical functions of factual analysis.

This is understandable given the avalanche of scientific, technological, economic, and demographic change and expansion hurled at us by the past several centuries.

We are a species that behaves not as militarized ants. On the contrary we are specialized vertebrates now with very diverse non-instinctual symbolic enthusiasms, desires, and skills. For all of civilized history we have seen conflicts even among closely related ethnicities and nationalities that have attempted to annihilate each other for reasons of social difference. Our horrifying civil war, which set ethnic whites against each other because of moral concerns about slavery, freedom, and equality, is but one recent example.

Perhaps Karl Marx codified this most recent intellectual malaise in his theory of history, his revolutionary predictions of European class warfare, again, "like against like." Indeed this happened in World Wars I and II, with many genocides and the *Holocaust* for good measure. The modern ideological embodiments of this perception of human difference and inequality are revealed in the horrors of modern fascist and communist totalitarianism—here, punishment of those who succeed. These same demonological views about talent differences may be more latent in the West. However the effect of those policies—which do not encourage and treasure intellectual and social accomplishments, which on the contrary encourage social dependency—places the so-called democratic world on the road to national suicide.

To explain this intellectual perversion of reality one can invoke the term "creationism." Oddly in one of the most advanced societies on our planet, the United States, we have seen official attempts in the various states to outlaw Darwinian perspectives on evolution and at the least institute for parental choice the Judeo-Christian Bible's perspective on the origin of humans as set forth in Genesis. Most of these individuals in power able to shape the education of the young, either in the lower schools or in state-run higher education, find no difficulty in functioning in the modern world, probably applying in their own practice mass media versions of Darwin's supposed fang-and-claw "selectionism." One might call these creationists of the "right" quaint atavists. But, they have too much power.

Fortunately, the rational scientific community has rallied in the varied states to forestall the complete misshaping of young minds. However, in vast portions of the world such ideologies dominate the education of the masses. In only a few Islamic nations do we see any attempt to limit the religio-obscurantist controls of the imams over the minds of young and old alike.

An even greater insidiousness lies in the creationism of the left. It should be said that Marx himself was a devotee of Darwinism, and in many ways shaped his argument in terms of the selective powers inherent in evolving modern economic systems. But his totalitarian followers reshaped the argument to assert that humans had no inherent biogenetic social needs. Stalin, following the work of the theorist Michurin, allowed his lackey, Trofim Lysenko, to try to reshape Soviet agriculture, this to enable him the more easily to collectivize the kulaks, functioning Soviet farmers, mostly in the Ukraine. Ultimately Stalin subjected them to genocide.

Unfortunately, environmentally reshaping oats into wheat and barley into corn or whatever fantasy Lysenko attempted to realize in his Lamarckian anti-Darwinian and anti-Mendelian crusade, created an agricultural disaster. Lamarck, an eighteenth-century French visionary naturalist, thought that changes to the phenotype (external characteristics) of an individual or species during its lifetime could be transferred to progeny. But that was interesting and innocent eighteenth-century speculation. By dint of Stalin's purges, many great Russian biologists and geneticists were eliminated; most died in the gulags. The idea that humans had no inherent biogenetic characteristics that could make their way into the social arena was anathema to an ideology that despised and feared inherent human diversity of mind.

National Socialism went one step further by ideologically translating the high social and cultural accomplishment of the tiny Jewish minority in the German states into a presumed pathology of ethnic/religious domination. The Nazis could not accept such differences in their own German/Jewish ethnics and feared the Jewish populations to the East. In the end they engaged in the most titanic abhorrence, the *Holocaust*, six million innocents poison-gassed, burned, shot, and shoveled into ravines. Naturally, they explained this destruction of their intellectual betters with the word "eugenics." And this locution shook the world.

The great increase of wealth that emanated from the Western world after 1945, the uniting in communication and transport of the human species, the supposition that the wealthy could spread this sea of surplus to change the social structure of humankind led to a new, hopefully benign, vision of creationism. This was built upon the same intellectual edifice as were the totalitarian constructions, but now modified into a social welfare philosophy. It did attempt to balance the values of human freedom with the altruism of giving, redistributing this wealth to change history.

It was "creationist" because it explicitly denied any references to the biology of the human mind when it considered the variability of cultural outputs given the vast scale of aid that was poured upon the recipients. No matter how ineffectual the results of this philanthropy, the commitment was always, ever more, an endless effort to eliminate the supposed environmental blockade. We are social creatures. We all are of the same intellectual potency, are we not? So went the ideological sureties of this era, the latter half of the twentieth century.

Today, the failures are emblazoned across all media. The wealth has disappeared, absorbed into a mountain of debt. The condition of humanity, 1.8 billion in 1900, 6.2 billion in 2000, and growing, has not improved in the recent half century during which trillions of dollars have been expended in the philanthropic redistribution of this momentary wealth.

And our intellectual leaders still wonder why. *Humanity's Evolutionary Destiny* is an attempt to turn our thinking away from a religiously motivated, if indeed secular ideology of sociological creationism. We do have a biological origin, as a species. Were we to fully understand the concrete meanings of this biological, evolutionary heritage, we might yet turn our world onto the path of rationality in dealing with our humanity, of all ethnic and racial backgrounds.

## Darwinian Perspective

Charles Darwin knew little of the specifics of human evolution when he published his masterwork, *Origin of Species*, in 1859. A few years later, 1868, in south central France, the building of a railroad line had accidently uncovered the skull of a Cro-Magnon, the archetypal lineage of modern humans. The development of modern genetics was yet to come, first in the solitary research of the priest, Gregor Mendel, his work first published in 1865–66.

Yet, the basic structure of evolutionary dynamics that Darwin proposed still stands as the foundation of our understanding of the processes by which lines of animals, plants, fungi interact with nature and with each other such that a steady process of new forms of life appear. At the same time other, less adapted lines disappear into evolutionary history.

So it has been with the human lineage. As I point out in the following chapters, a shift has occurred in our understanding of human evolution, with the uncovering of new concrete exemplifications of the ancestors of modern humans. Instead of a linear sequence of one or two ancient hominid forms developing into *Homo sapiens*, the evolution of humans seems more like a bush-like phenomenon. Human-appearing fossil parts can be found at about eight my (million years) before the present (BP). By three to two my BP, a wide variety of human types were roaming the forested plains of Africa.

As we go forward in time new forms appear, all with successively larger skulls and accompanying brain power, tools. The older forms have disappeared; here and there a few recidivists seem to have survived into the recent past in outlier domains. The important point is that from even as long ago as eight my BP it is probable that these precursor human types had no real competitors. The ancient competing apes had disappeared or migrated (orangutans). Existing African apes, chimpanzees and gorillas, had long been pushed into the recesses of the west African jungles. The only explanation that fits reality is that humans themselves engaged in the sharp selective struggle to maintain themselves in their conjoint environmental redoubts.

The result of this selective struggle for reproductive efficacy was an ever-brainier human. Ultimately we witness the victory of the human hyper-cortex, now ensconced in a creature called *Homo sapiens sapiens*. Here is simply explained the coming of the literate civilizations of the past, and, today, modern science and technology. Hidden as yet is the fact that this struggle for dominating brain power continues on today. The hopeless philanthropy to maintain the weak will shrink. Sadly, the international disaster that is going to hit us will result in a triage sure to uncover this reality of evolutionary change.

The key element in Darwinian selection as it factors into human evolution has been and always will be human intelligence and its cultural emanations. We may try to disguise this reality because we do not fully understand its meaning nor its dynamic in such a complex multicultural and multiethnic world. But in the long run of centuries, not decades, it will reveal itself. The adaptive and selective dynamics of ever-increasing brain power in humans has been going on for many millions of years. This process is not over for this very variable super-species, *Homo sapiens*.

Sociobiologists have been attempting to confront the problematics of the Darwinian teachings. As we discuss in later chapters, they have attempted to give contemporary concreteness to human behavior in terms of supposed selective psycho-social processes in our lives today. Many of these scholars point to manipulations of power, the way in which groups and individuals favor their own kind in terms of reproductive efficacy, one example being the often sad evidence of foster fathers protecting their own but killing the children of a wife or companion, those young sired by another male. Male lions tend to act so.

Other more recent experiments have attempted to negate the brutal implications of such sociobiological models by focusing on supposed innate human altruistic behavior. Neurological research has supposedly shown tangible brain reactions indicating pleasure and happiness when defined altruistic charitable actions are engaged in, even to the financial detriment of the giver.

On the other hand, one could for example propose that a similar brain reaction of altruistic joy could have taken place in the neurologies of the Islamic terrorists of 9/11 as they guided those planes towards the World Trade Center, sacrificing their mortal lives and killing thousands of innocents, all for the pleasure of their altruistic sacrifice, for *Allah*. Unfortunately there is much of such nonsensical pseudo-science today being proposed, stimulated by the as-yet formidable intellectual challenges presented by Charles Darwin's vision.

In the chapters that follow it is hoped that the proposed conceptual evolutionary model as applied to our ongoing human evolutionary pathway will be considered in both its theoretical and concrete postulation.

## The Moral Vision

It is clear that the moral impetus behind our attempts to bring about a unified socio-economic level of life for all humankind, here by the sociological creationist ideology of the democratic West, was rightly perceived. The human world through the dint of modern technology, communication, and transport had truly brought humanity into "one world." The evolutionary and historic separations of *Homo* into widely disparate races with their varying cultural levels of life could no longer be consciously tolerated. It was an inheritance of a past that evolution always rejected, subspecies competing for life support within one ecological setting. These earlier pathways of separation had now become an especial moral contaminant; it had precipitated the brutalities of slavery and colonialism within the larger human clade.

The question underlying this state of affairs, always imminent and never clearly debated, was how might the modern world gather itself together to right this now historical and evolutionary anomaly. From evolutionary near history alone we learned from the fate of the European/Caucasoid Neanderthals that no two related subspecies could inhabit the same ecology without inherent competition and conflict. Naturally the Neanderthals contributed some of their genetics to the oncoming Cro-Magnon competitors. But the latter did not reciprocate substantially. The Neanderthals disappeared as an ethnic subspecies some forty thousand years ago.

If we cognitively desire that the human species should be relatively uniform in intellectual competency and thus forever leave behind historical racial inequalities, even the intra-ethnic divisions of social class, we must ask how we can accomplish this goal. The current model has failed. First, it led in the twentieth century to horrible genocidal destructions of the most intellectually and socially talented classes. Second, it set off a wildly enthusiastic but irrational attempt at environmental amelioration which has finally run out of steam and money, creating a more recalcitrant set of problems than those existing when this misguided ideological crusade began.

So, we need ideas as to how we can successfully achieve this moral goal of social unification without the destruction of the best of our species that has taken place over the past several centuries. We want human equality of opportunity. We treasure ethnic differences without endless ethnic suppression. Today we see racial differences as an irrelevant spoke in the wheels of progress inherited from our past, eventually to be distanced from the future of the human species.

This book should be seen as a contribution to this discussion, hopefully to promote analysis and debate.

# PART I—DYNAMIC PROGRESSIONS

# · 1 ·
# ORIGINATING ADAPTATIONS OF ANIMAL LIFE

## Adaptive Pathways

Our planet has existed as an independent celestial body for c. 4 by (billion years). As with all physical entities in the universe, it was subject to the observed principle of entropy—that is, that a heated body gives off its energy into a cooler external environment. High-energy bodies dissipate their energy, here expressed as heat into the larger and cooler (energy) environment in which it is located.

Life probably began not too long after the earth's first cooling stage, a time yet of great energy activity and transfer. Now, the as yet mysterious and epochal counter-entropic set of events began to take place. That is, certain chemical compounds and interactions amongst these chemical compounds began to accumulate energy from the surrounding environment, taking other compounds, or chemical elements that could be metabolized, and forming them into new energic potencies. This whole as yet inchoate set of events taking place over the first billion or so years fills numerous textbooks of hypotheses, experiments, and visionary postulations.

Several distinct advanced forms of life, counter-entropic processes, energy metabolizing machines were formed: fungi, plants, animals. These also originally divided into single and then multicellular structures. The adaptive advantage of the simpler unicellular entities, translated selectively over several billion years, is the unstated selective postulation that the basic parameters of the external environment would remain broadly stable. This stability of the external environment allowed them to continue to mobilize the necessary energy to reproduce, divide, and "die" as long as the planet remained basically non-hostile to these basic parameters of energy production.

Unicellular life forms could even metabolize nonorganic metals and chemicals, distinct from the majority of other such autotrophs, uni- and multicellular forms that lived off the energy of the sun. This great and later biological innovation transformed the light of the sun into photosynthetic energy. In consequence of giving off the resultant free oxygen into the environment, it created enormous metabolic potencies within the living environment, made dynamic the expansion of heterotrophic animal life.

The proliferation of multicellular (metazoan) forms of life gave potency to an adaptive pathway that was more adventurous. Instead of the ability to live and die doing more or less "one thing," multicellular forms, especially heterotrophic animal types, thrived on their biochemical ability to live off other organic molecules and living forms. Early on, these heterotrophic forms took on the adaptive pathway of movement. Here we imply the ability, again made possible by the basic adaptive receptivity developing on planet earth, that would smile on this complexity of metabolic processing. It furthered the need and ability of these heterotrophs to move around, to find through predation what could satisfy the energic requirements of the animal types. A developing metabolic repertoire of functions would also help to maintain internal homeostasis over time and subsequent challenges. Bulk and an energy bank account had its adaptive advantages in an external world that was always changing in climate and ecological balances.

By c. 2 by BP, the great kingdoms of animals, plants, and fungi had differentiated. By 1 by BP, oxygen had reached its present proportions in the atmosphere and in the seas, which by now were teeming with living forms. It is interesting to note that the larvae of the starfish, sea lilies, and other echinoderms, now largely rooted and sessile filtering animal life, were free swimming, as with proto-chordates, lancelets, also free swimming, even showing signs of a notochord, indicating a stiffening body form able to self-direct. But these animals' categories thence took a more conservative safe and stable adaptive route, as compared to the now more adventurous, if still an ancient, adaptive pathway represented in vertebrate morphology and behavior. The evolving vertebrate lines might have been instrumental in forcing the "others" into this conservative turn to security.

A whole series of living adaptations had by now taken place in these three or so billion years of life experiments: 1) the gigantic self-maintaining complex "eukaryote" cell and its slower rate of genetic change; 2) sexual reproduction in the major kingdoms, plants and animals; 3) bilateral structure in animals and the beginnings of frontal lateral distinctions, mouth and anus functions, here in primitive worms, by c. 700 mya (million years ago). From this time on, it is thought that a very slow period of evolutionary specialization led gradually to the shaping of our ancestral phylum the chordates/vertebrates, not to be fully realized until c. 550 mya, as seen in the Burgess Shale deposits, *Pikaia gracilens*: mouth, gill slits, discs of muscle for movement, a tadpole-like tale. Here was an animal with the beginning sensory structure that would later fully evolve into the paradigmatic frontal vertebrate brain.

It is possible that these seemingly *advanced* vertebrate characteristics may have originally been provoked by a heterochronic/neotenized (retention of infantile traits into adult forms) series of environmentally pressured genetic and selective events which turned a seemingly opportunistic line of creatures, probable "mud burrowers," back into their more ancient and infantilized free-swimming adaptive forms. This presumably had positive adaptive results, which led to a later breakthrough as an animal phylum, predominantly adapted to sensory reactivity and heterotrophic predation.

Indeed, all the non-vertebrate chordates (deuterstomes), in their mature forms, turned into sea bottom-dwelling sessile filter feeders. Among the protostomes (embryological development of mouth first, then anus): brachiopods, cephalopod mollusks, tiny calcareous ostracods, all represent adaptations in which food is passively filtered into their systems, either through tentacles or body muscle flexing, both of which could move water and food through their nutritive systems.[1]

Clearly, the fixed passive way of life must have been a recurrent genetic and adaptive option for animals of varying structural and evolutionary heritages. The shift from the presumed bilaterality of the free-swimming larval form in the echinoderms (sea urchin, starfish) regressing to the equally ancient reminiscence of radial nerve net "symmetry," specialized in by sponges, jellyfish, and corals, may flag in these lines of animals an equally hoary past. The three taxons (echinoderms, chordates/vertebrates) all are deuterstomes (blastospore becomes the anus).[2]

## Vertebrate Brain

It was in the selective shaping of a bilateral, slimly elongated worm-like creature either free swimming or ground adapted, as in the various worm phyla, that the vertebrates gradually obtained a concentration of neuronic material in the anterior or frontal part of the animal wherein reception of information could be integrated into behavior.[3]

Now defining the vertebrate subphylum is the nerve cord that runs front to back just above the notochord, later to become a fully evolved spinal column. This elastic rod functioned primarily to protect the major neuronic communication link between head and tail. However, neural arches roofing the nerve cord and connected to the musculature, called myomeres which functioned by way of nerve relays from the spinal cord and the sensory organs, act as propelling contractions for propulsive force—for movement forward, sideways, and for braking. A series of at first cartilaginous, then inverted bone arches under the nerve cord, with the neural arch above the protective vertebrae, served also as anchor for the musculature of the fish.

The spinal cord connected to the nervous center at the front of the fish. A variety of sensory messages would be received from all the surfaces of the animal. Three systems in addition now clustered: a) The olfactory system, with receptor cells in the nasal capsule, through which water flowed. These messages were transmitted to the olfactory bulbs at the front of what would become the brain (the forebrain). b) Light-sensitive cells arranged in a sheet (retina), located in two lateral eyes and one pineal eye at the top of the head, this later to be lost. These messages were received in the brain by the optic tectum located in the roof of the midbrain. c) The acoustic system, which received messages through hair cells that were located in grooves of the head and down the sides of the animal, the lateral set of acoustic receptors on either side line system. These latter signaled vibrations in the immediate vicinity of the fish. In addition, the rear portion of the brain detected distant sounds. Other detectors sending messages to the hind brain noted turning motions and other bodily adjustments. These served to transmit this information via fluids in semicircular tubes that were connected to the hind brain.

Cerebral integration of all sensory information was located on the upper surfaces of the olfactory centers in the forebrain. A cerebellum on the roof of the hind brain controlled motor coordination.[4] It is suggested that the olfactory system in the basic vertebrate design gave rise early on to the amygdala and hippocampus, indeed, then still primitive components of the rhinencephalon, the nose brain. Modern descendants of the ancient jawless fish, the so-called cyclostomes, possess a well-developed hypothalamus, thalamus, rudimentary hippocampus, and almost mammalian amygdala. These are all part of the so-called limbic system memory structures, critical to the basic responsive survival functions working in the brain.[5]

Since life is always opportunistic, and since a presumptive case can be made for the possibilities for eking out a living in relatively shallow waters or close to the surface, where oxygen was plentiful and a light-sensitive eye would come in handy early on, the sudden appearance in the fossil record of true vertebrates 470–420 mya should not fool us into erring on the side of a macro-evolutionary creationism. The enormous time spans that are now estimated for the evolution and development into modern fungi, plants, and animals of the large eukaryote cell ought to warn us about the necessity for "time," in which molecular, genetic, and then selective processes created not only the evolved vertebrate body plan, albeit in constant process of modification and specialization, but also an already highly articulated brain and neural structure.

So decisive was this evolutionary innovation, the vertebrate brain, that by the time we meet it in the Ordovician, c. 470 mya, it is clear that an adaptive breakthrough had already been made. Not only the mere carving out of an ecological niche by an organ that allowed for the successful and mobile exploration of the environment, then the exploitation of the inert and vulnerable prey at the sea bottom, but an organ that would not significantly change either in structure or size for over 250 my.[6]

Clearly, the neurological structure developing in these proto-vertebrate creatures, as they struggled to secure their oxygen supplies either close to the surface or in deep water environments, demanded as part of their adaptive passage, and made possible in their basic body plan, more interconnected neurons in the anterior regions of the body permanently cementing the frontal/posterior organization of the animal. Whether from the basic requirements of securing food in this niche, given the basic body structure available to them, or through some kind of "red queen" to keep up with the competition of similar forms in the lee of the continents, free-swimming arthropods, or perhaps intraspecific competition with other fish, the selective demands, in contrast to the many Cambrian (550 mya) bottom dwellers, were shaped not to acquire, for example, massive defensive calcite shields, but rather a brain sufficient to move as a predatory master of the ecology.[7]

## Ecological Mastery

Once the vertebrates attained a generalized capacity for sensory information processing to meet the demands of their mid-water ecological niche, c. 450–400 mya, and a size and predatory capacity that clearly made them relative masters of their domain, further mutation in terms of accommodation to specialized morphologies, behaviors, and capacities for environmental exploitation, became necessary. It may have been a return to the bottoms, now feeding on equally, if defensively, adapted and still competitive mollusks, worms, and echinoderms. Or they gravitated to the more oxygenated surface ecologies. At the water bottoms, they were not now filtering microbes and organic detritus. Rather, they were uprooting and crumbling into food morsels the defensive morphological bastions of the echinoderms, arthropods, and mollusks.

The early vertebrates had mysteriously attained an adaptive *rubicon* of behavioral competence that did not require more than the shifting around of these various brain structures and sensory and muscular connections to meet micro-needs, rather than a more expansive macro-growth of the brain. That this growth was still theoretically possible is evidenced by the relatively empty and beckoning cranial cavity. However, some 250 my later, significant growth of the brain would begin again in two widely dispersed successor "reptile" lines, birds, and mammals.[8]

One wonders why a process of orthoselection (evolution in a straight line) for continued brain expansion did not earlier occur. Here, growth in this set of organs, sensory inputs, and muscular and behavioral outputs, leading to successively more adaptive behaviors, and therefore issuing in positive selection, did not continue beyond a general radiation of the three classes of early fish.

Could further growth of the brain have then been maladaptive, causing internal physiological dysfunction? Or would a larger brain have been mal-selective in a competitive and mechanical sense, precipitating a shift to a narrow and precarious adaptive plane? In summary, the aqueous and earthly world of the early vertebrates, into which they successively penetrated, did not as yet require greater sensory integration and the larger brain that this would have produced. What seems to have been necessitated was raw body restructuring, ever more streamlined for immediate competition, movement, biting, breeding, each in their respective and existing ecological niches.

Considering that from the late Silurian to the early Devonian, 410–390 mya, we already have a geographical distancing of their various fossil lines, those fish phylogenies exhibiting air-breathing pre-adaptations must have had an even more ancient originating moment, (Ordovician, 500 mya). It tells us once more of the role of genetic and morphological/behavioral preadaptations in enabling the dynamics of new evolutionary solutions.[9]

This particular and presumptive preadaptation, which made possible a transition from a classic design of a surface-to-peripheral-mid-water vertebrate to one that allowed juicier adaptive pickings at the bottoms, was now made even more selectively powerful by this long-evolving and modernizing morphology which now included a lung. "Enjoy the nourishment at the bottoms, but up you go for a gulp of that fresh oxygenated air."[10]

For 300 my—from the Proterozoic "Riphean," 700 mya, to the Devonian, 390 mya—the relatively shallow waters in which metazoan animal life evolved maintained an inviting luxuriance of food supplies and numerous secured ecological niches. It did so both for the comfortably adapted shelled filterers and scavengers, as well as for the more adventurous bilateral animal forms evolving in other and various peripheral environments. These, like so many other animal phyla, were tempted to return at a more evolved structural/behavioral level (lancelets, agnathans, placoderms) to the abundant bottoms and their seeming security.[11]

## Transition to Land

> A key evolutionary event may have been the development, in some fish, of an air-filled pouch communicating with the pharynx. The air in the pouch came from the gills by way of the blood, which circulated through an increasingly rich network of capillaries surrounding the pouch. An advantage the fish derived from such a pouch was adjustable buoyancy the main function of what is now the swim bladder. Another advantage was that the fish, in the manner of a scuba diver, carried a reserve of oxygen it could use in case of emergency, when its blood oxygen fell to a dangerously low level. In such an event, oxygen would diffuse in the reverse direction from the pouch into the blood. The adaptation opened the way to breathing, the pouch acting as a primitive lung. We can watch this in our fish bowl when a goldfish surfaces to take a breath of fresh air and, more dramatically, during the dry season in many a tropic lake of Africa, South America, and Australia, where lungfish survive for months in the drying mud, awaiting the next rainy season.[12]

The lure for successful animal life on land was the possibility of extracting the rich trove of oxygen from the atmosphere, a supply which was only modestly dissolved in water, 0.0451 grams per liter, as compared to 6.70 grams of oxygen in a liter of air, approximately 150 times greater, both at room temperatures.[13] In time this greater availability of oxygen-metabolizing potential would offer important selective advantages for those creatures sporting an adaptive valence of larger-than-average brain size and thus facility in information-processing.[14]

A rich oxygenated environment combined with an available supply of food at the water's edge, or on land, would become the great adaptive beckoning that would be held out to a line of creatures structurally preadapted to make a move out of the mainlines of water specializations.

Recall that, to serve the metabolic needs of the metazoans, especially those still-exploring bilateral predators above the sea floors, the extraction of oxygen from water must have been perfected early in animal evolution. The larval sea squirts, urochordates, have gill slits, mouth, a primitive eye, a long thin tail with a notochord that traverses their body front to back. They propel themselves through the water much like the ciliated eukaryotes, 500 my earlier, which absorbed their oxygenating sustenance through their cell walls as they moved toward and ingested their food near the water surfaces. In the adult stage, the sea squirt, now fixed on the sea bottom, still absorbs its food and oxygenating water through a large pharynx with gill slits.[15]

Recently Siwalla has argued that the sea squirts or lampreys, rather than reflecting the earliest originating line of vertebrate forms, should be seen as an outlier pattern in early vertebrate evolution. Instead, the originating vertebrate forms can be traced through developmental genetic analysis to a "benthic worm with a mouth, and pharyngeal gill slits supported by cartilaginous gill bars."[16]

The generative and generalized swim bladder that provided a pathway out of the water, as well as back into deeper waters, for the different lines of fish, reflects a shallow watery world of intense richness and violent and sharp selective pressures. This ecology increasingly shaped its denizens into specialized niches. But the genetic variability must have been there to allow for the flourishing of complex and evolving mobile and predatory forms, as well as to allow for new lines of adaptation for the successors of falterers, once both specialized and successful.

Thus it is that the early chordates and the even earlier proto-echinoderms, themselves probably early bilateral swimmers, ceded the open waters. So, too, the jawless fish, their domination thence to be shunted aside by the *placoderms*, both forms now fairly specialized gill breathers, with no hint of an air-breathing sub-specialization. The spiny-finned acanthodians are also gill breathers who succumbed to the competitive pressures of the sharks and the bony ray-finned fish. Only the early failed lancelets, sea squirts, and then the hagfish and lampreys, the latter descendants of the jawless *agnathans*, produced descendants into the present.[17]

It is probable that the ancestors of both the *dipnoan* lungfish and the *crossopterygian* lobe-finned fish, both equipped with swim bladders that could access atmospheric oxygen, were developing their morphological and physiological specializations in parallel with these variously evolving lines, the failures as well as the winners.[18]

Both the above lines seemed to have been extremely successful predatory machines during their relatively brief period of florescence. The thick limb-like stabilizing adaptations of the crossopterygians, as compared to the ray-finned lines that would go on to evolve into the *teleost* (fast moving, highly visual contemporaries in the seas and lakes) explosion of the Cretaceous, some 300 my down the line, give evidence for this shallow-water specialization, one that would lead either to death for all but a very few forms of air breathers, or migration into a totally new adaptive plane.

We bear in mind the comment of C. de Duve with regard to the air-breathing needs of goldfish (carp). This characteristic of air-breathing under conditions of oxygen distress in polluted or overheated water, as well as a widespread need to take a periodic breath of air, can be found in a wide variety of fish, from catfish to cichlids to gouramies, as any aquarium devotee will note. It is clear that the *actinopterygians*, who inherited the mid-waters as the crossopterygians and dipnoan lungfish waned, must have retained that ancient capacity for air breathing, either through direct adaptive retention or within the genetic memory of the line, to be extruded into adaptive reality under conditions of changed oxygenation levels in the waters within which they lived.

Perhaps it is true that the air-breathing adaptation in the evolving swim bladder came into use for this line (*crosspterygians*) some 70 my before the development of feet.[19] Yet it is also persuasive that the lobe-finned organs that were used for stabilization and for facilitating rapid predatory movements near the water bottoms contain the same basic bone structures that would be subsequently adapted for support of a now extremely "heavy" body in the much thinner atmospheric density of the air. The density of air is .001 g/cm$^3$, as compared with water, which is 1 g/cm$^3$. Muscle has a density of 1.05 g/cm$^3$; bone's density is 3 g/cm$^3$.

The always-changing landscape and climate on the planet made the emergence of the proto-amphibians both possible and necessary. Additionally, this move was made as part of a general thrust of life above the water line. Both plant and animal forms (insects, scorpions) preceded the proto-amphibian *crossopterygian panderychthyids*, creatures who had probably been adaptively and selectively pressed to survive in ever more dangerously desiccating marine environments. For reasons unknown—chance opportunism or pressured specialization—they had been shunted *out* of the deeper, safer pools, and ever closer to that point of no return, the *rubicon* of life on land.

For a few lines of panderychthyid crossopterygians, the probably forced exploration of land was, with any luck, a halfway path back to the waters. The pathway back into the seas has been a tempting adaptive solution for a wide variety of subsequent vertebrates, reptiles, birds, mammals. Evidence is that a number of lobed finned fish did not take that crucial step onto land, early on returning to the depths. The *coelacanth* is an example: "It behaves more like a gymnast than a fish, with unusual twists and turns…its ears are similar to ours … it now bears live young."[20] One wonders whether these morphological characteristics were typical of other Devonian (c. 400 mya) exemplars with the equipment to perdure and proliferate.[21]

## Perspective

The vertebrate adaptive plan, like the vertebrate body plan, needed much time for its eventual perfection and proliferation in the Ordovician, some 500 mya. As in so many subsequent evolutionary transitions, the late success of one line should not necessarily suggest or imply its sudden revolutionary coming into being. Rather, the success of the vertebrates, given the embryological evidence of evolutionary affinities and origins, argues for an ancient and steady, if precarious, adaptive tack. The survival of the line, and its gradual perfection of body plan, amidst the quick and distinct successes of other animal lines and their own particular adaptive pathways, tells us about the very variable and relatively open ecological possibilities existing on our planet during the metazoan animal expansion, after 1 by.

Evidence now tells us that the vertebrates were survivors. Long hidden on the peripheries, they eventually burst into a form of dominance that has lasted for some five hundred million years. It is a dominance characterized by the occupation of an adaptive ecology heretofore uncontested, the mid-and upper ranges of their aqueous environment, an environment open to aggressive predatory exploration. The innovative character of the vertebrate design is its long-run ability to broaden and expand on the environmental limits of its life ecology.

Indeed most of animal life—major phyla such as Porifera, sponges; *Cnidaria*, corals and jellyfish; nematoda, round worms; mollusks, snails, clams; echinoderms, starfish, sea urchins; even ancient Hemichordata, acorn worms; and chordates, lancelets—have remained unchanged adaptively and morphologically for hundreds of millions of years. Nestled in the security of their working adaptive niche, mutations that could alter the security of this adaptive pattern have been ruthlessly suppressed by a variety of genetic strategies selectively established within the respective chromosomal structure. As a result, these forms have been subject to successive and major extinction events when the security of their adaptive niche has been threatened by external events. They had heretofore secured their adaptive niche; genetic variability had been selectively discouraged over the eons. In the end they had surrendered their reservoir of genetic, morphological, and behavior plasticity for efficiency within the niche.

On the other hand, the vertebrates have long taken an evolutionary road premised on the selective reality of ecological and environmental variability, having made their living out of an adaptive fitness predicated on modest external changes, and in turn constant genetic change and much intra-specific variability to maintain the possibility for selective "good luck," even in the face of major external catastrophes.

What we are not observing, as we dig deeply into the geological record of physical as well as organic evolution, is the full range of variability that exists at any one slice of time within any clade. Much of this variability cannot be observed in the limited available fossilized exemplifications of these ancient forms. Taxonomic categories are an imposed classificatory device helping to organize the concreteness of what we observe at any one time. Too often we reify these categories and miss the relevant concreteness of unknowability in the fossil exemplars.

Within the major portion of vertebrate history observable to us from the evolutionary record, no "pure" or monophyletic lines of vertebrates exist. Each species (our own definition of evolutionary consanguinity) constitutes a mosaic of variability.[22] The adaptive niche may seem to require a delimited range of behaviors and aptitudes. However, the broad fitness encompassed in the vertebrate body plan requires a versatility of behavioral and morphological response that needs to be reflected in all lines. There does exist from the dawn of eukaryote sexual reproduction the selective imprint for genetic variability as well as in its phenotypic, day-to-day embodiments. This variability allows for the existence of outlier forms at the fringes of the adaptive range.

Ernst Mayr long emphasized the evolutionary importance of peripheral outlier populations for the future fortunes of a line:

> Evolution progresses rather slowly in large, populous species, while most rapid evolutionary changes occur in small, peripherally isolated founder populations. The more populous a species is, the more epistatic interactions occur and the longer it will take for a new mutation or recombination to spread through the entire species and therefore the slower evolution will proceed. A founder population, with less concealed variation because of having fewer individuals, can more readily shift to another genotype, or to use another metaphor, to another adaptive peak.
>
> The genetic reorganization of peripherally isolated populations permits evolutionary changes that are many times more rapid than the changes within populations that are part of a continuous system. Here, then, is a mechanism that would permit the rapid emergence of macro-evolutionary novelties without any conflict with the observed facts of genetics.[23]

## Notes

1. Sepkoski, J. (1993). Foundations: Life in the oceans. In S. J. Gould (Ed.), *The book of life* (pp. 58–59). New York, NY: Norton.
2. Wray, G. A., Levinton, J. S., & Shapiro, L. H. (1996, October 25). Molecular evidence for deep precambrian divergences among metazoan phyla. *Science, 274,* 568–573. Also see Vermeig, G. J. (1996). Animal origins. *Science, 274,* 525–526.
3. Joseph, R. (1993). *The naked neuron* (pp. 15–18). New York, NY: Basic.
4. Radinsky, L. (1987). *The evolution of vertebrate design* (pp. 25–27). Chicago: The University of Chicago Press.
5. Joseph, R. (1993). *The naked neuron* (pp. 54–56). New York, NY: Basic.
6. Jerison, H. J. (1973). *Evolution of the brain and intelligence.* New York, NY: Academic Press; Jerison, H. J. (1982). The evolution of biological intelligence. In R. J. Sternberg (Ed.), *Handbook of human intelligence* (pp. 723–791). Cambridge: Cambridge University Press; Jerison, H. J. (1977). The theory of encephalization. *Annals of the New York Academy of Sciences, 299,* 146–160; Jerison, H. J. (1983, March 11). The evolution of the mammalian brain as an information processing system. In J. F. Eisenberg & D. G. Kleinman (Eds.), *Advances in the study of mammalian behavior, special publication no. 7.* Shippensburg, PA: The American Society of Mammalogists.
7. Jerison 1982, *op. cit.*, pp. 746–748; Van Valen, L. (1973). A new evolutionary law. *Evolutionary Theory, 1,* 1–30; Van Valen, L. (1974, November 22). Two modes of evolution. *Nature, 252,* 298–300.
8. Benton, M. (2005). *Vertebrate paleontology.* Malden, MA: Blackwell Publishing.

9. Long, J. (1995). *The rise of fishes* (pp. 135–136, 186). Baltimore, MD: The Johns Hopkins University Press; Hildebrand, M., & Gonslow, G. (2001). *Analysis of vertebrate structure* (5th ed.) (p. 33). New York, NY: Wiley: "The problem of identifying sister group relationships".
10. Erwin, D., & Krakauer, D. (2004, May 21). Evolution: Insights into innovation. *Science, 304,* 1117–1119.
11. Long 1995, *op. cit.,* p. 102; Liem, L., & Walker, W. (2001). *Functional anatomy of the vertebrates: An evolutionary perspective* (p. 277). New York, NY: Harcourt.
12. de Duve, C. (1995). *Vital dust* (p. 205). New York, NY: Basic.
13. K. Hellman, Smith College, personal communication, c. 1995.
14. Aboitiz, F., & Montiel, J. (2007). *Origin and evolution of the vertebrate telencephalon, with special reference to the mammalian neocortex.* New York, NY: Springer; Striedter, G. (2005). *Principles of brain evolution.* Sunderland, MA: Sinauer.
15. Long 1995, *op. cit.,* p. 31; Benton, M. (1993). The rise of the fishes. In Gould 1993, *op. cit.,* pp. 66–67.
16. Siwalla, B. (2007). New insights into vertebrate origins. In S. A. Moody (Ed.), *Principles of developmental genetics* (pp. 114–128). New York, NY: Academic Press.
17. Stock, D., & Whitt. G. (1992, August 7). Evidence from 18S ribosomal RNA sequences that lampreys and hagfishes form a natural group. *Science, 257,* 787–789.
18. Nicholls, H. (2009, September 9). Evolution: Mouth to mouth. *Nature, 9/10 461,* 164–166.
19. Stebbins, G. (1982). *Darwin to DNA, molecules to humanity* (p. 279). San Francisco, CA: W. H. Freeman.
20. Nisbet, E. (1991). *Living earth* (p. 257). London: HarperCollins.
21. Stebbins 1982 *op. cit.,* pp. 282–285.
22. McKinney, M. (1993). *Evolution of life* (pp. 38–43). Englewood Cliffs, NJ: Prentice Hall.
23. Mayr, E. (1954). Change of genetic environment and evolution. In J. Huxley, A. C. Hardy, & E. B. Ford (Eds.), *Evolution as a process* (pp. 206–207). London: Allen and Unwin. Mayr, E. (1997). *This is biology* (p. 195). Cambridge, MA: Harvard University Press.

## · 2 ·

# WE DOMINATING MAMMALS

## Hidden Evolution

The further down the study of evolutionary history digs the more conjecture is added to our presumptive knowledge. As noted in the previous chapter, the sparse empirical data, fossils, and the implications of climatic and geological change catapult us into controversies born of scant information. It seems the greatest errors that have been generated over time, then corrected by subsequent empirical evidence, are imputations of causality–the hypothetical jumps from one seemingly new and critical piece of fossil evidence, placed in hoped-for chronological sequence, in a straight line to the next exemplar.

The theoretician Richard Goldschmidt became famous in the field by his postulation of the concept of "hopeful monsters" as a way of explaining a sudden fossil appearance that is a radical advance or deviation from the existing assumed sequence of fossil forms. Stephen Gould, a Harvard-based evolutionist and writer on psychological matters, his work now discredited for his political misshaping of controversial matters, was a convert to this view, e.g., "punctuated equilibrium."[1]

More thoughtful readings of the evolutionary problem have more or less come to the rational conclusion that a sudden fossil appearance does not necessarily mean the creature was suddenly created by some marvelous creationist force in nature. Rather, and most probably, considering the long distances in time that we are attempting to resurrect in theory and evidence, we have not as yet found the precursor forms that would give us an evolutionary sequence fitting the Darwinian and genetic orthodoxy of small changes leading over time to major branch displacements and shifts in the evolutionary tree.

This issue is of great importance in the path of understanding with regard to the mammals, and our own human evolutionary pathway. As we will note in future chapters, hidden evolution can characterize the ultimate creation in our own pathway into the present *Homo sapiens sapiens*.

## Roots of Dominance

From the standpoint of the present taxonomic class of mammals, their major adaptive shunting into evolutionary dominance is defined adaptively by their relatively large brain/body ratios. The originator of this type of analysis, Harry Jerison, stuck to his guns for many years, even while a few detractors argued that structural differences in the brain should also account for the relative position of mammals in their adaptive intelligence quotients.[2]

But as we have noted in chapter 1, the transition to land of the vertebrates reveals in the morphology of these early proto-amphibians a large skull cavity with a relatively small brain, pointing evidently to the lack of adaptive need to fill these open spaces.[3]

But there are also other adaptive morphological and physiological pointers in shaping the destiny of the mammals and then their joint adaptive co-relations with brain and neurological structures to have moved the mammals into their position of relative dominance on the land surfaces of our planet. Fundamentally, placental reproduction and endothermic heat and metabolic regulation were key elements in this evolutionary pathway into creating the current human shadow over the planet.[4]

The contemporary evidence is that the transition onto land was begun c. 400 mya and certainly completed within 50 my. The evolutionary assumption has been that the pathway towards the present was treelike, amphibians developing out of the crossopterygians, then the reptiles and birds, finally from some as yet hypothetical mammal-like ancestor into the fully formed mammal precursors, placentals, marsupials, monotremes, the now extinct multituberculates. This originating exemplar, perhaps Morganucodon, a rat-sized creature, from about 225 mya.[5]

The fossil record of mammal-like reptile precursors is impressive—the names, in temporal sequence, being the synapsids and therapsids, of which the cynodonts derived from the latter line. These reptile forms flourished from c. 325 to c. 200 mya.[6] By the above more recent time frame, the ancestral crocodile and dinosaur (archosaurs) reptile forms dominated. The hints of mammalian origins given in the four-legged locomotor positioning, the possibly homeothermic metabolism for dry land flourishing, and the radical jaw restructuring, from the major reptilian lines, all hint at this therapsid heritage of the mammals. The fact that mammals were appearing in the fossil record at the presumed time of the decline of the classic therapsid/cynodonts adds to this evolutionary connectivity.[7]

## Ancient Mammal Origins?

*Placental* reproduction is one of the most important evolutionary developments leading to the dominance of the mammals. Other lines of mammals were pushed aside, adaptively, in the process of modernization: multituberculates, whose young were expelled from the birth canal at an extremely undeveloped stage, given the fossil evidence, the Monotremes, with their very reptilian pattern of egg laying, the young lapping milk from modified sweat glands rather than from nipples. These latter also are not fully homeothermic. The marsupials are closer taxonomically, part of the so-called Therian evolutionary plan. Their reproductive structure is quite different from the more primitive eutherian/placentals, leading in the marsupials to the birth of larval-like young who migrate into the marsupial mother's pouch for long-term nourishment.[8]

Over one hundred years ago, H. F. Gadow of Cambridge University noted that " … many lizards, some chameleons and many snakes … retain their, in these cases very thin-shelled, eggs in the oviducts until the embryo is ready to burst the egg-membrane during the act of parturition or immediately after it. Such species are usually called ovoviviparous, although there is no difference between them and other viviparous creatures, for instance, the marsupials."[9]

This reproductive resemblance of both reptile and fish to the marsupials, as well as the existence of true placental-like reproduction in ancient and modern sharks, argues for a proto-mammal line of air-breathing fish-amphibian-synapsid reptiles that might eventually be traced to the earliest stages of the tetrapod invasion of the land surfaces.[10]

Important adaptive strategies of marsupial and placental therians: in times of extreme danger placentals would have to abort, whereas marsupials could eject their young from the pouch, implying for the latter a less threatening adaptive pattern to the life of the mother. Once born, however, placental young grow faster; also placentals have a quicker reproductive cycle. There is also a better nutritional advantage for the young to receive nutrients across the placenta. Again, forelimbs of placentals can evolve in numerous ways, while marsupial young must be specialized to climb into the mother's pouch, and at an undeveloped stage.[11]

The innovations inherent in placental reproduction should therefore not be thought of as a unique evolutionary development. In all likelihood it was experimented within the tetrapods at some early point in their transition from the water. Viviparity, the intimate circulation of nourishment from the mother's placenta to the embryo within her body, occurs in various fishes, a number of cyprinodonts, the four-eyed fish, Anableps, and a wide variety of hammerhead and carcharhinid sharks.[12] Ovoviviparous rays, which lack placenta, the young at first depending on their yolk sac, produce a "milk" rich in protein and lipids, quite similar to mammalian breast milk. This they channel from the uterine wall into the mouths and gill chambers of the embryos.[13]

What is additionally interesting about the placental mode of viviparous reproduction in sharks is that, as Jerison notes, a Permian (c. 275 mya) shark fossil similar to the contemporary living horned shark, Heterodontus, is reported to show a brain size similar to modern sharks; these latter are at the mammal-placental rodent level of brain/body encephalization.[14] Early in the Silurian, as the jawed fishes expanded, some 420 mya, the cartilaginous sharks radiated into their own tenaciously held ecological niche and with this move seem to have developed an unusually large fish brain, viewed by Jerison as intermediate in size between most lines of fish (except the visual modern teleosts) and the amphibians-reptiles in terms of their brain/body encephalization quotient.[15]

The clue to the unique future dominance of the placental morphology lies in the presumed ancient connection with viviparity in the fish (sharks). It is thus highly suggestive that the contrast between the marsupial benign adaptive morphology, the marsupials' similarity to many extant reptile lines, and the placental patterns of true viviparity and birth could lie in the paedomorphic retention of an ancient fish/shark/tetrapod adaptation for the protection and nourishment of the unborn young. Further, this argues for the hidden evolution of the placentals, which protected their way of life by nurturing these ostensibly defensive morphological adaptations, until their morphologies had played out their latent selective power.

Recall that sharks, primitive in their cartilaginous structure, separated from the ancestral bony fish, c. 500 mya. Even in the bony fish we find a variety of birthing solutions which, while not viviparous, tell us that animal life was, early on, engaged in a search for the best adaptive solution of protecting the young at their most delicate point of origin. We find in aquarium "live bearers"—guppies, mollies, platys—the male actively penetrates and inseminates the female, whose eggs develop internally. At parturition the young are expelled and at a greater size than comparable egg-laying fish.

An important evolutionary hint lies in the fact that a relatively primitive group of fish, sharks, early on developed placental modes of reproduction, here linked with a larger-than-average-sized brain, and extraordinary predatory skills. Proto-mammalian evolution may therefore be traced back to that critical juncture of the transition from the seas to land. A true mammalian ancestral form may very well be lurking fossilized in some ancient sand pit or in the sea bottoms, some 500–400 mya, thus not necessarily evolved from a therapsid reptilian ancestor, 300–225 mya.

*Endothermy* is hypothesized to have been developed in the therapsid/cynodont line of mammal-like reptiles, c. 300 mya. Possibly, this was at the time of the Permian climatic crisis, which saw the desiccation of the land, the drying up of the seas, and a period of colder continental-like period of climate.

Leonard Radinsky, in discussing the slow evolution of the mammals from their first appearance, 220–190 mya, to their radiation at the end of the Cretaceous, c. 65 mya, and thus their relatively slow evolution into dominance, cites the following reasons: a) Endothermy was only advantageous in relatively cold climates or in climates of great variation. Most of this period was quite warm and less seasonal. One could ask of Radinsky why the proto-mammals did seem to develop endothermy as an adaptive characteristic. It was a fairly early adaptation, with internal viviparity the final placental adaptation. Possible reply: the Permian, from which the cynodonts radiated, may have been colder than we now generally concede. b) Energy-wise, it is costly to be endothermic and maintain a constant internal metabolic rate.[16]

Mammals require ten to thirteen times as much food energy as reptiles and amphibians to maintain the same body mass. Early on, this meant that less energy was available for growth and reproduction. Mammals, then, were small. Radinsky argues that it was more advantageous for mammals and birds to be endothermic rather than ectothermic for the past 65 my than for the 160 my of the age of reptiles.[17]

The largely equable climate of the Triassic, 245–208 mya, on the other hand, enabled the ectothermic and still highly visual archosaur line to make the most of its demanding daylight and visual energies, gradually taking over the mainline land adaptive niches, where size and food bulk reinforced each other.[18] The gradual redirection of therapsid-eucynodont evolution was toward the diurnal way of life. Endothermy demands a steady supply of food at all hours in the day, ten times more than similar-sized reptiles. It also allowed the latter in the cool of the evening to slowly digest the vast amount of daytime food in their gut. Endothermy in the mammals was in all likelihood a preadaptation stimulated by the Permian (250 mya) variability of climate, not a later accommodation away from a reptile dependence on the warmth of the sun for energy renewal. It was a preadaptation for life in the cool of the night.

However, consider the fact that birds are endothermic. Birds first evolved from a precursor archosaur (dinosaur) line certainly, not later than 200 mya. Were these first reptilian forms endothermic? At any rate, modern birds have nothing to do, evolutionary-wise, with the mammals. The conclusion has to be that, way back at the origins of the reptile line, or even before, endothermic experiments were being placed into the evolutionary "crap game" as an adaptive solution. If in the earliest reptiles, why not in the earliest mammals, both to be perfected in the further genetic and selective honing, as per the demands by the outside world.

## Therian Morphology and Behavior

Therian mammals, placentals and marsupials, have modern tribosphenic molars that are adapted to crushing foods. The coracoid bone in the shoulder, jointed to the breastbone in reptiles and early mammals, differs in therians. Now a collarbone, also scapula and shoulder muscles, allows creatures to move limbs so as to cushion jumps or falls when they land on their front legs, it also facilitates bounding movements, especially in the dark. All marsupials except wombats and anteaters are nocturnal.

Janis believes that early marsupials were tree-living, with grasping tails and forepaws to hold food. Their metabolism was slower than that of the placentals. Placentals were more terrestrial in the earlier stages, burrow dwellers that buried their feces.[19] The internal carriage of the unborn young over a relatively long period of pregnancy probably allowed for more behavioral flexibility, and thus an ability to move from ground to tree living, as the need arose.

The typical retinotectal visual dominance that is hypothesized for the basic sensory orientation of the stem reptile line was thus redirected in the post-Permian therapsid/cynodonts, as intrinsic to the ancient proto-mammals. Having survived a period of great climatic temperature instability, this evolving homeothermy created metabolic requirements seven times that of the equivalent-sized reptile. Here was necessitated change in sensory dominance. Here, also, is the clue to the steady reduction in size of the eucynodonts and the extant tiny mammals that inherited the late Triassic, early Jurassic landscapes, 220–200 mya.

Leonard Radinsky stipulates that in going from reptiles to mammals there was first a five-to tenfold increase in brain size relative to body size. The cerebellum was relatively enlarged, reflecting greater motor coordination. Unlike birds, early mammals, as stated above, had a fairly small brain-centered visual system, the olfactory bulbs were relatively large. Mammals also expanded the outer layer of the cerebral hemispheres of the forebrain into a major higher information-coordinating center, the neo-cortex.

> Many groups of later mammals experienced a further increase in relative brain size that was correlated with the increased size of the neo-cortex, compared with the early mammal condition. Most workers consider the increased brain size an indication of increased "intelligence." However, while such a conclusion may seem to be intuitively correct, there are virtually no scientific data to support it, and the functional significance of increased relative brain size remains an unsolved puzzle. The puzzle is particularly intriguing because increased brain size occurred dozens of times independently among various groups of birds and mammals.[20]

The adaptive split was further heightened by the morphology of the palate that the mammal-like reptiles were evolving: a palate that allowed for simultaneous chewing and breathing, on the run, as it were, and the development of increased audition, as the jaw bones were gradually rearticulated. Too, there was an increase in olfactory sensitivity and organization in the brain, vibrissae in the nose area for additional tactile sensitivity.[21]

The brain is metabolically demanding. Natural selection tended, over many millions of years, to link brain and behavior metabolically. Along with an additional adaptive direction toward feeding on smaller animal and insect forms, the incipient mammals thus carved out a new division of land adaptations, negotiating an adaptive balance with competing reptiles.[22]

The reptile neural retina contains millions of neurons. The auditory system plays a much smaller role, with a few hundred neurons in the area of the middle ear. By contrast, mammals have about thirty-five thousand neurons in the spiral ganglion of the inner ear. Processing this new information source, the product of the reconstruction of the various bone ossicles of the jaws, was gradually taken up by the brain itself, in contrast to the reptile information processing system, in the neural retina. "Encephalization in the earliest mammals was probably an adaptation in response to a packing problem: where to put the neurons from non-visual systems that had evolved to do the kind of processing that is done by retinal neurons in 'normal reptiles.'"[23]

What the brain required for the mammals, which was not involved in simpler retinal visual behavior in reptiles, was the integration of the various sense organs, the newly specializing auditory, tactile, and olfactory inputs, as well as a restructured scotopic, rod-based retinal visual system that was useful in dim light, as compared to the cone structures of the lower vertebrates. Cone system vision responds rapidly to light with high photic energies, often a thousand times as strong as that required for the activation of the rod system. Later, according to Walls, the cone system that modern mammals utilized, "redeveloped" in a homologous manner to the reptile system, when most mammals began to invade diurnal ecological niches.[24] The adaptive response from the information provided from these variously located sensory input systems would have had to be integrated.

The first step would be the recognition within the brain that the information was, for instance, visual or tactile. Since information came in momentarily from these various sources as well as from the body's more autonomic emotional and physiological markers, there thence came the beginnings of a hierarchical marking and organization of this information for adaptive behavioral responses. Here began the recognition of an outside world in which the sensory and integrative dimensions of experience created images of "objects" outside of the body, none of which were without impact on the internal valences of the mammal's semi-spontaneous behavior system: fear, flight, appetite, desire. Both information systems, the sensory and the emotional/physiological, required their integration in a larger brain. A number of researchers view the earlier creation of the vertebrate brain itself as having the capability for "chunking" such information from the senses into an object-rendered "real world of experience."[25]

## Brain Dynamics

Pursuing this seemingly surprising fact of slow mammal evolution, even while they were presumably under the survival gun of the dinosaurs, thus supposedly under some form of selective pressure from above, we come to *Didelphis virginiana*. This is the common opossum. Colbert and Morales compare this living marsupial with the dawn opossum, *Eodelphis*. They find little difference in the brain, skull, and body structure in these two examples of one line of mammals, some 100 my apart.[26]

A nocturnal prowler, the modern form feeds on insects, vegetation, small animals, worms, grubs, insects, and slightly larger vertebrates. Its threat posture is much like that of reptiles—uptilted snout, and mouth opened wide. It also attacks with a reptile-like downward slashing movement of the teeth.[27]

This modern opossum is "at first strangely similar to that of one of the mammal-like reptiles of the far-off Triassic."[28] Jerison confirms this odd bit of evolutionary stagnancy in a table comparing the body/brain weight and volume of endocranial "olfactory bulbs" of animals that he believes to have inhabited similar ecologies in the Mesozoic and in more recent times. They are a) *Triconodon mordax* from the upper Jurassic, early Cretaceous, 140 mya; b) *Ptilodus montanus*, an extinct multituberculate from the Paleocene, some 60 mya; c) *Didelphis marsupialis*, the contemporary Virginia opossum; d) *Rattus norvegicus*, the contemporary wild rat.

Jerison's encephalization quotient—the relative level of brain to body size in these creatures, given the average fossil and living mammal to be at Encephalization Quotient, or EQ, of 1.0—is as follows: a) 0.28; b) 0.26; c) 0.22; d) 0.42 (average of many singulars). This means that it is possible that triconodont, one of the final representatives of the extinct morganucodontid line (monotremes?), itself relatively unchanged from the upper Triassic, c. 210 mya, and its successor form from the upper Jurassic, lower Cretaceous, c. 140 mya, had more brainpower (0.28) than a Cenozoic multituberculate (0.26), and a contemporary marsupial opossum (0.22). The clear winner in brainpower, and apparent adaptive survivability, is the contemporary and ubiquitous wild rat (0.42), almost double the opossum's encephalization quotient.[29]

It is thus possible, if not likely, that once precipitated into dominance from the generalized post-Permian cynodont radiation, or from ancient elemental mammal forms, brain size and relative encephalization of the early mammals remained static for at least 100 my, from c. 220 mya to 120 mya.[30]

"[T]he expansion of the brain event in '*Triconodon*' [c. 140 mya] had probably occurred as part of the transition between mammal like reptiles, cynodonts, and the true mammals, [even] before the appearance of the [earlier-Monotreme-like] '*Sinoconodon*' [c. 210–195 mya]."[31]

The two ends of the mammal evolutionary continuum first reveal a five to ten times increase in average mammal brain size over the reptiles.[32] At the other end of the comparative evolutionary spectrum is the small relative size of this average Mesozoic mammal brain, 10–30% as compared with modern mammals, given similar body size.[33]

## Heterochrony and Hidden Evolution

Gregory and de Beer early noted that in evolutionary processes, "rate gene" developmental changes (heterochrony) more often than not secure the survival of a threatened animal type. It has resulted in behavioral adaptive shifts, often covert, by moving the particular phenotype out of the ongoing selective crucible, often as an adult behaving and looking like a juvenile. And because this genetic tradition of variability has given a new lease on life to many different phenotypes, it has been a mainstay dimension of evolutionary dynamics for hundreds of millions of years.[34]

Larval echinoderms hint at an incipient notochord before they bury their roots into the sea bottom. Indications are that developmental retention of the larval state into the mature animal could have been a key to the creation of the chordates.[35] The earliest amphibians hint at the paedomorphic retention of juvenile crossopterygian physical features, giving them the plasticity to adapt to a mixed water and wetland environment.

So, too, the diminutive modeling of the mammals, both in their first mouse-like realization in the late Triassic, early Jurassic, c. 225–200 mya, and then again in the late Cretaceous, could have involved sequences of developmental gene mutations that dredged up a heritage of such successful options from their evolutionary history. Summoning the genetic resources involved in producing highly variable adaptive patterns, both structural and behavioral, was made possible by a hundreds-of-millions-of-years-old heritage that is largely unknown to us today.

The subjects of this fortuitous reservoir of variability were tiny, furtive, diverse in behavior and location, and small in number. The subsequent explosion in the Paleocene (c. 55 mya) became the phenotypic expression of an adaptively repressed genetic heritage of evolutionary change, heretofore under overt selective restraint. The distinction to be made here lies in the fact that new external ecological opportunities suddenly presented themselves for the existing evolutionary potential to express itself, now in expanding demographics and widening geographic expression. Not only could the mammals now grow larger; they could take their micro-variability of phenotypic potential into an exploding diversity of ecological opportunity.

## Issues in Mammal Evolution

1. Significant gaps exist in the fossil record both at the beginning of evidential mammal evolution, Upper Triassic/Lower Jurassic, 220–190 mya, and later in the Upper Jurassic/Lower Cretaceous, 160–130 mya. There is always the temptation to fill in such blanks with pre-existing candidates, and then to draw straight lines. Such speculative temptations ought to be resisted.
2. Comparative brain size of mammals: a) *Triconodon mordax*, c. 140 mya, had a larger brain than the contemporary *Didelphis marsupialis* (Virginia opossum). b) *Sinoconodon*, c. 220 mya, and *Triconodon*, c. 140 mya, the latter a probable descendant of the former, had equal brain size, even after 100–80 my of evolutionary change. Evolution takes time.
3. Contemporary monotremes reveal many reptilian features, not the least of which is their egg laying, which places them on an evolutionary grade close to the earliest known stages of mammal morphology, c. 220–190 mya.
4. Placentals with marsupial-like epipubic struts present hints about the earliest stages of therian (placentals and marsupials) evolution and separation. These recidivistic placentals were still extant toward the end of the Cretaceous, 90–65 mya. This suggests both the branching character of the evolutionary process, as well as the probably recessed time origins of many seemingly suddenly modern forms.[36]
5. It is essential to keep an open mind about the mammalian developmental patterns over time as well as other evolutionary dynamics, including that of the hominids. The growing awareness of hominid bush-like, rather than treelike, taxonomic causal relationships over time should educate us to the fact that origins tend to be ever pushed back in time, as new evidence appears.[37]

## Notes

1. Goldschmidt, R. (1940). *The material basis of evolution*. New Haven, CT: Yale University Press; Gould, S. J., & Eldridge, S. (1977). Punctuated equilibria: Tempo and mode of evolution reconsidered. *Paleobiology, 3*, 115–151.
2. Jerison, H. J. (1973). *The evolution of the brain and intelligence*. New York, NY: Academic Press; Jerison, H. J. (2000). The evolution of biological intelligence. In R. J. Sternberg (Ed.), *Handbook of human intelligence* (pp. 216–244). Cambridge: Cambridge University Press; Jerison, H. J. (1983, March 11). The evolution of the mammalian brain as an information-processing system. In J. F. Eisenberg & D. G. Kleiman (Eds.), *Advances in the study of mammalian behavior, special publication no. 7*. Shippensburg, PA: The American Society of Mammalogists.
3. Rowe, T., Macrini, T. E., & Luo, Z-X. (2011, May 20). Fossil evidence of the origin of the mammalian brain. *Science, 332*, 955–957.
4. Kemp, T. (2005). *The origin and evolution of mammals*. New York, NY: Oxford University Press; Luo, Z-X. (2007, December 13). Transformation and diversification in early mammal evolution. *Nature, 450*, 1011–1019.
5. Janis, C. (1993). Victors by default. In S. J. Gould (Ed.), *The book of life* (p. 172). New York, NY: Norton.
6. Benton, M. (1993). Four feet on the ground. In Gould 1993, *op. cit.*, p. 103.
7. Kielan-Jaworowska, Z., Cifelli, R. L., & Luo, Z-X. (2004). *Mammals from the age of dinosaurs*. New York, NY: Columbia University Press.
8. Szalay, F. (1993). Metatherian taxon phylogeny. In F. Szalay, M. J. Novacek, & M. C. McKenna (Eds.), *Mammal phylogeny* (pp. 234–240). New York, NY: Springer.
9. Gadow, H. (1911). Reptiles-anatomy. *Encyclopaedia Britannica* (11th ed.) (Vol. 23, p. 170). New York, NY: Cambridge University Press.
10. Clack, J. (2002). *Gaining ground: The origin and evolution of tetrapods*. Bloomington, IN: Indiana University Press.
11. Nisbet, E. (1991). *Living Earth* (pp. 198–199). London: HarperCollins; Janis 1993, *op. cit.*, pp. 174–176.
12. Bone, Q., Marshall, N. B., & Blaxter, J. H. S. (1995). *Biology of fishes* (p. 178). London: Blackie Academic & Professional.
13. Bone, Marshall, & Blaxter 1995, *op. cit.*, pp. 180–182.
14. Jerison 2000, op. cit., p. 775; Deacon, T. W. (1990). Rethinking mammalian brain evolution. *American Zoologist, 30*, 629–705, esp. p. 652.
15. Jerison 1973, *op. cit.*, p. 100.
16. Radinsky, L. (1987). *The evolution of vertebrate design*. Chicago: The University of Chicago Press; see also Bininda-Emonds, O. R. P., Cardillo, M., Jones, K. E., MacPhee, R. D. E., Beck, R. M. D., Richard Grenyer, … Purvis, A. (2007, March 29). The delayed rise of present day mammals. *Nature, 446*, 507–511.
17. Radinsky 1987, *op. cit.*, p. 148.
18. Crompton, A. W., Taylor, C. R., & Jagger, J. A. (1978, March 23). Evolution of homeothermy in mammals. *Nature, 272*, 333–336.
19. Janis 1993, *op. cit.*, p. 176.

20. Radinsky 1987, *op. cit.*, p. 148.
21. Jerison 2000, *op. cit.*, p. 777.
22. Raichle, M., & Gusnard, D. (2002, August 6). Appraising the brain's energy budget. *PNAS, 99*, 10237–10239.
23. Jerison 1982, *op. cit.*, p. 777.
24. Jerison 1973, *op. cit.*, pp. 272–273; Walls, G. (1942). *The vertebrate eye and its adaptive radiation*. Bloomfield Hills, MI: Cranbrook.
25. Griffin, D. R. (1976). *The question of animal awareness*. New York, NY: Rockefeller University Press; Humphrey, N. K. (1978). Nature's psychologists. *New Scientist, 78*, 900–903.
26. Colbert, E., & Morales, M. (1991). *Evolution of the vertebrates* (pp. 245–247). New York, NY: Wiley-Liss.
27. Evans, L. T. (1958). Fighting in young and mature opossums. *The Anatomical Record, 131*, 549.
28. Gregory, W. K. (1967). *Our face from fish to man* (p. 48). New York, NY: Hafner; MacLean, P. (1990). *The Triune brain in evolution* (pp. 251–252). New York, NY: Plenum.
29. Jerison 1973, *op. cit.*, p. 212, table, 10.2; Jerison 1977. *op. cit.*, pp. 156–57.
30. Jerison 1983, *op. cit.*, p. 131.
31. Jerison 1973, *op. cit.*, p. 314.
32. Radinsky 1987, *op. cit.*, p. 148.
33. Jerison 1973, *op. cit.*, p. 216.
34. Gregory, W. K. (1937). Supra-specific variation in nature and in classification: A few examples from mammalian paleontology. *American Naturalist, 71*, 268–276; de Beer, G. (1958). *Embryos and ancestors* (3rd revised ed.). Oxford: Oxford University Press; Gregory 1967, *op. cit.*
35. Garstang, W. (1928). The origin and evolution of larval forms. *Report of the British Association for the Advancement of Science for 1928* (p. 77).
36. Kumar, S., & Hedges, S. B. (1998, April 30). A molecular timescale for vertebrate evolution. *Nature, 392*, 917–920; Wilson, G. of the University of Washington in *Nature*, March 2012, argued for an early multituberculate diversification from about 90 mya. He puts their origins as at least 165 mya, else Morganucodon, c. 225 mya, see above.
37. Nishihara, H., Maruyama, S., & Okada, N. (2009, March 31). Retroposon analysis and recent geological data suggests near simultaneous divergence of the three superorders of mammals. *PSAS, 106*, 5235–5240; Luo, Z-X, Yuan, C-X, Meng, Q-J, & Qiang, J. (2011, August 25). A Jurassic eutherian mammal and divergence of marsupials and placentals. *Nature, 476*, 442–445.

# · 3 ·

# THE PRIMATE PATHWAY

## Evolutionary Theory: Knowns and Unknowns

In April 1996, Christopher Beard of the Carnegie Museum of Natural History, Pittsburgh, reported on his continuing research into primate origins in China: fossilized jaw and teeth of *Eosimias centennicus*, discovered in May 1995 along the banks of the Yellow River in Shanxi Province. Weighing 3.5 ounces, *Eosimias* had many monkey-like traits—deep chin and dagger-like canine teeth—but small-sized, blunt molars suggesting a fruit and insect diet. However, Beard suggested that this primate, at c. 55 mya (late Paleocene-early Eocene), still resembled a rodent-like lemur more than a modern monkey.[1]

The discovery of primates seemingly different from other forms yet discovered—both ancient and extinct as well as early modern forms—suggests the depth of evolutionary levels from which this radiation of human placental mammal ancestors derives.[2]

Yoder has also reported on the fact, heretofore unrecorded, of prosimian, strepsirhine lemurs originating in Africa at an even earlier Paleocene level, c. 62 mya. Heretofore the prosimians were thought to have radiated to Africa from Northern Hemisphere origins. In her phrase, "... early primate evolution was characterized by rapid divergence and diversification that nearly simultaneously (in geological terms) produced both the fossil and the living lineages, sometime before the late Paleocene."[3]

When we include the molecular genetic research of Hedges and Janke, also Luo, who place the divergence of the placental mammals and their incipient modern families well back into the Cretaceous (c. 100–90 mya), and possibly into the Jurassic, well prior to the total Cretaceous/Paleocene extinctions of the dinosaurs and the disappearance of many marsupial lines (c. 65 mya), we realize that what we know today about evolutionary origins and separations leads almost unfailingly ever further back in time.[4]

This is true of the origin of eukaryote metazoan animals, and probably true also of the origin of the phylum Chordata and the vertebrates, and, as recently argued by Wray et al., the amphibian invasions of the land, the discovery of the earliest reptiles.[5] It underlines the fragility of dating, especially those based on the existing paleontological record, what we have up to now dug up from the ground. Molecular analysis, although still fraught with newly discovered and modifying variables—for example, the real possibility that rate changes over time in mitochondrial DNA, ribosomal RNA, and in other parts of the genome—can skew interpretation, constitutes a sobering check on both phylogenetic as well as chronological sureties.

The cytogenetic evidence seems to indicate that the modern genetic and chromosomal structure of animals has been in place for at least five hundred million years. This means that the number of chromosomes and genes has remained stable; the kind of rapid phenotypic impact of mutations on structure and activity to be found in bacteria was no longer possible in metazoa. The buffering against rapid genetic change in animal forms by the preponderance of non-coding genes within the chromosomes has acted to slow down mutational changes that have an impact on the adaptive behavior of animals. In addition, the great heterogeneity in the number of chromosomes within a variety of animal lines argues against seeing, at least in contemporary forms, a pattern in which supposedly more recent animal lines have more chromosomes and genes than supposedly atavistic forms that have not changed over many hundreds of millions of years.[6]

Genetic variability is indeed the stuff of evolutionary change, and modern Darwinian theory. The question then is how do we understand the process of change in the lines of animals of greatest interest to us, namely the placental mammals, the primates, and indeed the particular evolutionary forms that led to *Homo*? What probably strikes the mind with ever greater force as we observe the constant readjustment in scientifically established chronological patterns of evolutionary origins and diversification, ever toward more ancient derivations, is the contrast between observable fact and those hidden evolutionary processes yet waiting to be discovered, i.e., covert evolution.

## Major Preadaptations

As yet we do not know the genetic or chemical pathways that led to the establishment of the preadaptations of endothermy and placental reproduction. The seas' more equable temperature consistency, especially in those hundreds of millions of years of swampy warmth, seems not to have selected out such an adaptation. Yet as we know, great geological as well as temperature changes have taken place over these billions of years during which life on earth has been evolving. The selective sieve is ever ongoing, and the great majority of life forms have disappeared. The major cause has to be ecological and environmental change, rather than direct competition from other life forms.

Endothermic regulation must have lurked in the background in semi-maladaptive vertebrate forms for many a millennium. The great Permian extinctions, c. 250 mya, thence or simultaneous with the breakup of the super-continent Pangaea into the more recent geologic constellations, seem to coincide with a more variable continental climate and thus the positive selective opportunity for creatures living on the survival's edge to begin to come into their own, here, pre- and post-reptilian flying machines, mammalian homoeothermic regulation, animals requiring high caloric inputs to maintain their energy levels in nighttime as well as in daylight.

Placental reproduction, as we have already noted, was part of a very variable and ancient reproductive tradition in the vertebrates, fish, reptile snakes, and proto-mammals. It revealed its usefulness for mammals only much later in its time of adaptive service to the survival of this taxonomic class and, probably adventitiously, again the variability of the environment, competition with other mammals, even with the lurking dinosaurian hegemony, 200–65 mya.

Another preadaptive specialization was the particular visual-brain system that would be selected for in an animal line that was probably left on the margins of early placental radiations. As the proto-mammals entered a more nocturnal life, the older visual-tactile system, the optic-tectum (retino-tectal system of the proto-archosaurs) had become reduced in efficiency, c. 240–210 mya. The thalamus, receiving direct retinal projections and already in contact with the cerebral cortex through the olfactory system, reinforced a newer association of visual stimuli (rod system) with this older reptilian olfactory-cortical system.[7]

Much later, 110–80 mya, as the evolving mammals reentered a diurnal mode of life, the most efficient structural readaptation was to reassociate the visual (now the newly-appearing cone system) and motor pathways with the cortical system rather than to redirect it to the older mid-brain (optic tectum or superior colliculus) visual brain centers of the reptiles. The reciprocal growth of the cortex in organizing and integrating this visual information was selectively stimulated by the newly adaptive arboreal life of the primates. These environmental adaptations continued to further incorporate the diverse sensory inputs and modalities now as part of cortico-cortical connectivity.[8]

It should be noted that bird evolution has paralleled the evolution of the mammals in that both classes have developed divergent visual and metabolic patterns from their supposed reptilian ancestors. Both endomorphism and visual/cortical connectivity, as well as color vision, served powerful adaptive and selective evolutionary purposes when nature brought them together, in need, c. 200 mya.[9]

## The Placental/Primate Adaptive Zone

The proto-primates plesiadapids, c. 100–65 mya, probably were both frugivorous and insectivorous. This implies the shifting of a way of life from a more ground-dwelling nocturnal existence to a life both in the trees and on the ground. This versatility almost surely heralds an existing change in the brain structures for behavior, the return to the cone system of vision (possibly derived from another, more ancient mammalian line), from the earlier rod vision developed for life in the dark. It reflects the changing adaptations, and dominance, of the earliest insectivores/primates as they began to move around an environment that now allowed for more day as well as night exploration and feeding.[10]

The lone Cretaceous tooth of *Purgatorius*, the primate or plesiadapiform, also ought not surprise us for its presumed dating, considering recent molecular evidence arguing for a much earlier Cretaceous separation of placental mammal lines, still hidden from archeological eyes.[11]

The sequence of placental separation and expansion is implied in the mitochondrial data developed in Munich by Axel Janke and Svante Pääbo et al., in which the rodents are viewed as diverging early on from the placental evolutionary line, the primates and ungulates/artiodactyls grouped as a sister taxon. In addition, Janke and Pääbo view the ungulates and carnivores as derived from a common ancestor (*Oxyclaenus*—arctocyonids), placing whales and seals with the cows.

Their divergence schema for the placentals is: a) rodents, ungulates, and primates, c. 114 mya; b) primates, ungulates, c. 93 mya; c) carnivores, artiodactyls, c. 55 mya; d) cows, hippopotami, whales, c. 41 mya; e) mice, rats, c. 35 mya. Their schema of phylogenetic relationships based on mitochondrial data jibes significantly with those of G. G. Simpson, made over sixty-five years earlier on the basis his paleontological analysis.[12]

A team of molecular geneticists headed by S. Blair Hedges of Pennsylvania State University has also postulated this early (115–90 mya) separation of three widespread placental orders.[13] 1) The artiodactyls (camels, deer, bison, hippos, boars), heretofore thought to have appeared in the Eocene, after c. 50 mya.[14] 2) The rodents (beavers, rabbits, mice, squirrels) supposedly appeared early in the Paleocene, c. 60 mya.[15] 3) The primates, also universally thought to have shown up on the world scene as exemplified by the transitional plesiadapiforms, late Cretaceous to the Cenozoic Paleocene, c. 85–55 mya.[16]

Consider that the dinosaurs "bit the dust" c. 65 mya. The dating of the separation of the placental mammal lines, here including the primates, has now been shunted back to c. 115 mya. It is then clear that a significant mammal presence amongst the dinosaurs must be dated back deep into the Cretaceous/Jurassic, before 115 mya. Conclusion: the mammals were vigorously competing with this ancient and dominating line of reptiles long before their demise.

The growth of the placental brain by an additional four to five times to its existing average size here during the Paleocene and Eocene, c. 65–35 mya, and thence into the future, reflects the increasing internal competitive conditions attending the expansion of the placentals into all the existing ecologies on land, sea, and in the air. During the early Cenozoic, from c. 65 mya, there is only a narrow spread of brain size between ungulates and carnivores. "Both average and maximum brain size increases through time in both groups, with carnivores being generally smarter."[17]

The probability is that this increase in brain size and competitive potency of the mammals, especially the revolutionary structures and behaviors provided in placental reproductive strategies, may have had as much to do with the decline of the dinosaurs during the late Cretaceous, 75–65 mya, as did the highly vaunted and hypothetical meteorite that may have caused the iridium deposits around the world. Thence the speculated ensuing blackout of the sun, followed by a presumed photosynthetic starvation, and, finally, dinosaurian extinction.

Most authorities support this view that the Cretaceous/Cenozoic boundary (c. 65 mya) as marked by the intrusion into the planet of an extraterrestrial asteroid, caused sudden and enormous climatic alteration around the planet, affecting those animals over approximately 25 kilograms or 55 pounds, and thus extinguishing the dinosaurs as a group. Other views postulate that a combination of climatic changes, geological upheavals leading to alterations in water levels, desiccating land masses, and continental alterations of cold and warm could have had an impact on the larger ectothermic creatures. But, this boundary, c. 65 mya, also decimated many marsupial lines and wreaked havoc on many lines of plants and reefs in the seas and plankton varieties.

No question that the mammals were the beneficiaries of the complete disappearance of the dinosaurs, plesiosaurs, and pterosaurs. But the turtles, snakes, crocodiles, lizards, and other reptiles perdured. Why, as Colbert and Morales wonder, did none of the many kinds of *small* dinosaurs survive?[18]

The relatively unpopular conjecture often put forth by Simpson must still be considered: "Among the many developments within this potent reptile-mammal line, care of the young must be given high place. Eggs were no longer deposited and left at the mercy of an egg hungry world, nor even given such lesser care as external (as in birds) or internal (as in some reptiles) incubation."[19]

## Primate Timeline

a) Plesiadapidforms (sub-order)—Late Cretaceous, c. 75–70 mya—to Middle Eocene—c. 45–40mya, which equals c. 30 my tenure, before extinction.

b) Strepsirhini and Haplorhini prosimians (suborders), lemur-like adapids and tarsier-like omomyids. Flourished from early Eocene c. 50 mya to 30 mya, which equals dominance of c. 25 my. Remnant forms are still extant. Also evolving, 55–30 mya, were modern monkeys, apes, and proto-hominids.

c) Catarrhines and Platyrrhines infra-order, Old and New World Monkeys, established by c. 35 mya, originated earlier. Flourishing for c. 34 my.

d) Hominoidea: super-family. Apes and hominids, latest origination from c. 40 mya, late Eocene.
e) Evolutionary periods: Paleocene, 65–55 mya; Eocene, 55–34 mya; Oligocene, 34–23 mya; Miocene, 23–5 mya; Pliocene, 5–2 mya; Pleistocene, 2 mya-12 ka (thousand years) BP.

A gap exists in the fossil record between the discovery in Fayum (Egypt) of a rich assortment of primate fossils (c. 35–30 mya) and the definite establishment of a fossil record of apes, the super-family Hominoidea, out of which the various transitional and true apes derive. This taxonomic category includes some of the questionable Fayum fossils, as well as the related and later east African Catarrhine, *Dendropithecus*, which has hinted to some researchers of a distant relationship to the gibbon.[20]

The super-family Hominoidea includes the definitive ape and hominid fossils, including *Proconsul* and *Australopithecus*.[21] If the well-established early Oligocene coolings, c. 34 mya, and the more extreme late (c. 30 mya) Oligocene coolings did not affect the evolutionary interactions in the Fayum-Egypt/North African geographies, the final extinction of the multituberculates, possibly remnant plesiadapiforms, "Ignacius," c. 39 mya, plus many other early mammal lines, could point us to a new evolutionary boundary, and thus new evolutionary dynamics within the primate clade.[22]

The Fayum evidence is but one small sample of what was going on in the world at the end of the Eocene and early Oligocene. The assumption must be that the early radiation of Paleocene primates (65–55 mya) contained a number of covert evolving forms, which, with each environmental, ecological, or climatic lurch, extruded new specializations and potencies in some heretofore peripheral, (outsider) forms, and in turn relegated others to the historical archives. Our fossil record in general is a reflection of raw numbers where opportune paleontological excavation is possible. It does not yet illuminate the evolving character of the extant lines (hidden and evident) at any one temporal slice of evolutionary history.

Stebbins sees anatomical changes in primates being stimulated selectively by adaptation to a diurnal life requiring vision more than smell (nocturnal). Gill saw smell as critical element in the expansion of the mammal brain. Stebbins emphasized that acute vision was required for an arboreal existence. He views the mid-Oligocene (c. 32 mya) frost, and subsequent development of savannahs that replaced the heavy jungle-like tropical canopy, as conducive for the split toward human/ape divergence. Mosaic environments precipitated the mosaic evolution of many experiments. These pathways were now exploited through an adaptive brain-initiated exploratory trend rather than being driven, ecologically, from life in the trees.[23]

## Perspective

Janis considers the placentals to have been predominantly ground living, given their patterns of burial of feces.[24] The fact that numerous early prosimian primate stocks became secondarily nocturnal argues for the oncoming wave of competition from rodents, lagomorphs, insectivores, and edentates, not to speak of carnivorous creodonts. All were equipped with a good mammalian brain and the expansive reproductive and energetic food supplying adaptations that allowed them to expand over the Paleocene and Eocene landscapes, c. 65–35 mya. The return to the waters of a number of carnivorous seals, walruses, and herbivorous types, e.g., whales, further exemplifies the level of infra-class competition among the mammals.

The primate adaptive route was behavioral non-specialization, a pathway having classic mammalian antecedents—defensive, alert, omnivorous. The various routes taken by the catarrhine (monkey) branch merely exemplify the adaptive breadth provided by life in the trees as well as on the ground, adaptability to a wide range of behavioral profiles, as well as foods, a specialization of the unspecialized, in which a larger brain primed for alert defensive anonymity became the key to survival. Consider the fact that the anthropoids of Africa during the Miocene, c. 25–5 mya, the survivors of the Oligocene climatic shift, c. 30 mya, had been able to proliferate and stabilize their adaptive zone. They were now growing in size and dominance. It is a puzzle that, by the end of the Miocene, some 10–5 mya, the apes were ceding their ecology throughout the world to an oncoming wave of Old World monkeys, and then hominids, c. 6–2 mya.

Considering that chimpanzees often attack and eat ground-dwelling cercopithecine baboons plus tree living monkeys, it is doubtful that monkeys could have competed strongly with the ground-dwelling apes.[25] More probably, as with the baboon, they moved into a vacated ecological niche, now that of the open country apes. The oncoming, as yet hidden proto-hominids were probably constrained in their diet to nuts, roots, and fruit, as well as animal sustenance, as exemplified in their tooth structure. Still, they came onto the scene.

The modern African apes, two chimpanzee species and one gorilla (two races—lowland and mountain), seem to have only one possible morphological antecedent in the fossil Miocene apes, 15–10 mya.[26] Hominids, in all likelihood various Australopithecine relatives, give notice of their presence via dental evidence some 8–6 mya, at the terminal Miocene. Where did they come from, to whom are they related? What is the evolutionary significance of these late-Miocene primate transitions?

## Notes

1. Beard, C. (1996, April 9). Fossil may fill gap in early primate evolution. *New York Times*. Retrieved from http://www.nytimes.com/1996/04/09/science/fossil-may-fill-a-gap-in-early-primate-evolution.html
2. Beard, K. C., Qi, T., Dawson, M. R., Wang, B., & Li, C. (1994, April 14). A diverse new primate fauna from middle Eocene fissure-fillings in southeastern China. *Nature, 368*, 604–609; Martin, R., Soligo, C., & Tavaré, S. (2007). Primate origins: Implications of a Cretaceous ancestry. *Folia Primtologica, 78*, 277–296.
3. Yoder, A., Cartmill, M., Ruvolo, M., Smith, K., & Vilgalys, R. (1996, May 14). Ancient single origin for Malagasy primates. *PSAS, 93*, 5122–5126.
4. Hedges, S. B., Parker, P. H., Sibley, C. G., & Kumar, S. (1996, May 16). Continental breakup and the ordinal diversification of birds and mammals. *Nature, 381*, 226–229; Janke, A., Feldmaier-Fuchs, G., Thomas, W. K., von Haeseler, A., & Pääbo, S. (1994, May). The marsupial mitochondrial genome and the evolution of placental mammals. *Genetics, 137*, 243–256; Luo, Z-X, Yuan, C-X, Meng, Q-J, & Qiang, J. (2011, August 25). A Jurassic eutherian mammal and divergence of marsupials and placentals. *Nature, 476*, 442–445.
5. Wray, G. A., Levinton, J. S., & Shapiro, L. H. (1996, October 25). Molecular evidence for deep precambrian divergences among metazoan phyla. *Science, 274*, 568–573.
6. Li, W. (1997). *Molecular evolution*. Sunderland, MA: Sinauer.
7. Aboitiz F. (1993). Further comments on the evolutionary origin of the mammalian brain. *Medical Hypotheses, 41*, 409–418.
8. Kaas, J. H. (1989). The evolution of complex sensory systems in mammals. *The Journal of Experimental Biology, 146*, 170.
9. Vorobyev, M. (2006). Evolution of color vision. *Perception* (EVCB Abstract Supplement) 35; Jacobs, G. (2009, August 31). Evolution of color vision in mammals. *Philosophical Transactions of the Royal Society, 364*, 2957–2967.
10. Jerison, H. J. (1973). *The evolution of the brain and intelligence* (pp. 272–273; p. 110 #20, chapter 8). New York, NY: Academic Press; Field Museum. (2002, April 18). Scientists push back primate origins from 65 mya to 85 mya. *ScienceDaily*. Retrieved from http://www.sciencedaily.com /releases/2002/04/020418073440.htm
11. Janis, C. (1993). Victors by default. In S. J. Gould (Ed.), *The book of life* (pp. 182–184). New York, NY: Norton.

12. Janke, Feldmaier-Fuchs, Thomas, von Haeseler, & Pääbo 1994, *op. cit.*, pp. 243–256; Simpson, G. G. (1945). The principles of classification and a classification of mammals. *Bulletin of the AMNH*, 85, 1–350.
13. Hedges, Parker, Sibley, & Kumar 1996, *op. cit.*
14. Colbert, E. & Morales, M. (1991). *Evolution of the vertebrates* (p. 379). New York, NY: Wiley-Liss.
15. Colbert & Morales 1991, *op. cit.*, p. 297.
16. Jane ka, J. E., Miller, W., Pringle, T. H., Wiens, F., Zitzmann, A., Helgen, K. M., ... Murphy, W. J. (2007, November 2). Molecular and genomic data identify the closest living relative of primates. *Science*, 318, 792–794.
17. McKinney, M. (1993). *Evolution of life* (p. 274, fig. 4–32). Englewood Cliffs, NJ: Prentice Hall; see also McNamara, K. (1990). *Evolutionary trends* (p. 39). Tucson, AZ: University of Arizona Press.
18. Colbert & Morales 1991, *op. cit.*, p. 214.
19. Simpson, G. G. (1952). *The meaning of evolution* (pp. 62–63). New Haven, CT: Yale University Press; Hu, Y., Meng, J., Wang, Y., & Li, C. (2005, January 13). Large Mesozoic mammals fed on young dinosaurs. *Nature*, 433, 149–152.
20. Szalay, F. S., & Delson, E. (1979). *Evolutionary history of the primates* (pp. x–xii, 454–460). New York, NY: Academic Press; Andrews, P., & Stringer, C. (1989). *Human evolution: An illustrated guide* (pp. 14–17). Cambridge: Cambridge University Press.
21. Szalay & Delson 1979, *op. cit.*, pp. xi–xii.
22. Prothero, D. R. (1994). *The Eocene-Oligocene transition* (pp. 204–219). New York, NY: Columbia University Press; Szalay & Delson 1979, *op. cit.*, p. 36, Fig. 11.
23. Hooton, E. (1946). *Up from the ape*. New York, NY: Macmillan; Stebbins, G. (1982). *Darwin to DNA, molecules to humanity* (pp. 316–318). San Francisco, CA: W. H. Freeman; Gill, V. (2011, May 20). Mammals' large brains evolved for smell. *BBC News*. Retrieved from http://www.bbc.co.uk/nature/13448202
24. Janis 1993, *op. cit.*, p. 176.
25. Bshary, R. (2007). Interactions between red colobos monkeys and chimpanzees. In McGraw, W., Zuberbühler, K., & Noë, R. (Eds.), *Monkeys of Taï Forest* (pp. 155–170). New York, NY: Cambridge University Press.
26. Andrews, P. & Kelly, J. (2007). Middle Miocene dispersals of apes. *Folia Primatologica*, 78, 328–343.

· 4 ·

# HOMO: WHEREFROM?

## Origins: Molecular Controversies

Traditional research into the origins of *Homo* emphasized both existing and fossil primate morphology (body structure), as well as the paleontological evidence, time, and place. This ongoing debate over ape-hominid affiliations took a radically different turn in the mid-to-late 1960s. Emile Zuckerkandl and Linus Pauling, as well as Morris Goodman, began reporting on their methods of tracing both evolutionary relationships and temporal sequences in the branching of various lines of animals through an analysis of the sequences of gene coding for blood proteins and globins.[1]

At the same time, Vincent Sarich and Allan Wilson were reporting on their hybridization research with serum albumin proteins sampled from a number of primate lines. Hybridization combined the albumin of both species and compared the antiserum reactivity of the two albumin samples. This research showed that the African apes were more closely aligned with humans than were the orangutans (former favorites). In fact it showed humans as closer to chimpanzees than chimpanzees were to the gorilla. In addition, Sarich and Wilson placed the time of human and chimpanzee separation at 5 mya.[2]

Researchers Andrews and Stringer stated that changes in proteins, amino acids, and directly in DNA show that humans differ from chimpanzees at 1.2%; from orangutans at 1.8%; from gorillas at 1.4%; gorillas from orangutans, 2.4%; orangutans from chimpanzees, 1.8%; chimpanzees from gorillas, 1.2%—*equal* to humans and chimpanzees![3]

The counterintuitive evidence, that humans are thus more closely related to chimpanzees than gorillas are to chimpanzees, has inevitably raised eyebrows. Immunological differences: lysozyme showed that gorillas and humans, taxonomically very separate genera, were quite similar compared to the minimal morphological and behavioral species differences between dogs and coyotes, cats and bobcats, also, drosophila (fruit flies) species. All of these latter comparisons have quite small phylogenetic evolutionary distances as compared with these supposedly large family differences, e.g., those between apes and humans.[4]

The overall evidential serum albumin proteins difference between humans and chimpanzees, 1.2 or 1.6%, was smaller than between two gibbon species, 2.2%, or between two bird species, North American red-eyed and white-eyed vireo, which was 2.9%. Another puzzle: human blood hemoglobin is identical in all its 287 units with both chimpanzee species.[5]

Allan Wilson has concluded that in different groups of organisms, three kinds of evolutionary changes proceed at different rates relative to each other: 1) changes in protein molecular structure; 2) organization of the chromosomes; 3) anatomical structure of the body. His conclusion, because of the inherent variability of anatomical changes and even restructurings of the genetic material within the chromosome, therefore the temporal invariance of molecular change gives us a more reliable dating frame for evolutionary change.[6]

Wilson thus argued for a steady-state molecular clock in the hominoids. His game-changing claim was of the independence of change in protein structure, chromosomal organization, and thus of the consequent anatomical changes in animal lines over equal spans of evolutionary time. Early in their research, Sarich and Wilson had already stated that they "... aligned African apes more closely than the orangutan with humans not only because the albumin of the African apes reacted more strongly with human antiserum, but because they saw [this] data as [being] in qualitative agreement with anatomical relationships."[7]

However, Sarich and Wilson in their various writings on human/ape phylogenies did use one seriously questioned date: the 30 mya separation point between the Old World monkeys and the hominids, based on the now-acknowledged limited perspectives of the Fayum, Egypt, primates of the Oligocene. Recent discoveries reported by Beard, for example, that may push back the monkey/ape/prosimian divisions to the deep Eocene, c. 55–50 mya, could undermine this basic timetable of human/ape separation. There is also the postulation by Yoder of an early Paleocene date (c. 65 mya) for the African appearance of prosimian lemurs.[8]

The recent discovery of a fully formed primate, ancestral to monkeys, apes, and hominids at the surprisingly early 47 mya level, the deep Eocene, in Germany, emphasizes the problematics of the existing molecular derived time frame.[9]

## Morphological Problems

This very controversial claim that humans and chimpanzees separated from a common evolutionary line some five million years ago naturally raised up much counter-evidential controversy. Most of the objections avoided the molecular laboratory hypotheses of these scientists and addressed more traditional morphological factors.[10]

Summary:

1. Teeth: thick/thin enamel in molars; thick in *Homo* and Australopithecines, in New World monkeys, some Old World monkeys, and some Miocene African apes; thin in modern African apes (chimps, gorillas), and most modern Old World monkeys.
2. Limb structure and facial structure in African apes and Australopithecines, close; *Homo* and orangutans close; humans seem to reflect an ancestral anthropoid condition. Modern African apes are knuckle walkers, with the morphological support in the shoulders and girdle/torso. Human infants and orangutans walk on flat hands with their consequent affiliated morphological support.
3. Brow ridges: African apes, monkeys, and primitive humans have heavy brow ridges. Modern humans, gibbons, siamangs, and orangutans do not.
4. Canines: *Homo*, robust Australopithecines, ancestral line of orangutans, all similar.

5. Brain structure: humans and orangutans similar asymmetry. Not in chimpanzees and gorillas.

## Our Relatives—Hypothesis[11]

We establish a line of evolutionary descent starting in the late Oligocene-early Miocene, c. 30–25 mya. Along this hypothetical "Oklahoma Land Rush" starting line of putative apes (no monkeys), are many diverse forms, including the two that are thought to have then already disappeared: the Parapithecoideia and the Propliopithecoideia. Undoubtedly there were many others. Along this line of diverse proto-apes are the as yet unknown proto-hominid precursors. They are probably as yet unspecialized, certainly blending into an existing almost-amorphous species/genus identity of primates.

Thus, side by side with the proto-hominids are 1) future Sivapithecines along with their one surviving East Indies relic, the orangutan; 2) the varied group of apes, now mostly extinct except for the recidivistic now jungle surviving African ape, chimpanzees, and gorillas; 3) more distantly positioned but also related morphologically to the proto-hominids are the African ancestors of the gibbons, the modern survivors having long been driven into their Asian sanctuary.

We reiterate the fact that at that time, c. 30 mya, the lemur and tarsier pro-simian ancestors were then retreating in number and type, a slow process of extinction. The New World monkeys since the Oligocene have drifted with the continents far to the west of the African homeland. The precursor Old World monkeys, as with the proto-apes and proto hominids, were in this time frame still in a stage of evolving flux.

It is hypothesized that the gibbon proceeded rapidly on its own way, as the preadapted ape forms swarmed into the ecologically beckoning African Miocene. But the gibbon was able to retain certain morphological characteristics—arm structure, some remnant bipedal skills as it moved into a secure and fixed brachiating ecology, early to specialize, stabilize, and eventually migrate at a distance from the other related ape forms. The Sivapithecines, ancient Orangutan line, on the other hand, including the future *Ramapithecus*, may have shared more molecular and morphological factors with the proto-hominids (perhaps originally a greater molecular affinity than did the proto-chimpanzees and gorillas). Complicating the Sivapithecine early affinity with *Homo*, they did eventually move east, the orangutans a probable East Indies descendant.[12]

The argument is that, of the extant apes, the African survivors early on were pressed for survival into a specialized African jungle niche. Their current diverse within-species DNA profile argues for a long heritage of life in the west African jungles. The overall morphological specializations of these apes, in their knuckle-walking and hip and torso structure, testify to a long shaping for survival in a peripheral and highly specialized ecology. That the gorilla is now a grass and leaf eater, and that all three of these ape forms are thinly enameled in their molar structure, are knuckle walkers, and expert brachiators adds weight to their probable long separation from the proto-hominids.

On the other hand, as noted, the only remnant of the extensive and diverse Afro/Euro/Asiatic sivapithecine clade is the orangutan, whose preadaptations for a life in the Southeast Asian jungles could also carry with it an explanation for the great molecular distance of this group from the hominids. Still, the orangutans retained over a much longer period of evolutionary history their ancient morphological affinities with *Homo*. These ancient retentions may have been possible because this long migrating clade of apes never had to undergo the competitive pressures as did the last surviving African apes, the chimpanzees, and the gorillas.

Recent analysis has given renewed life to the contra-DNA chimpanzee/hominid alliance, i.e., the morphological and physiological similarities between the orangutan and the hominids, including *Homo*, *Australopithecus*, and *Paranthropus*. Both Schwartz, a committed minority defendant of the orangutan-hominid connection, and now Grehan are both persuasive in laying out the evidence: orangutans share forty unique anatomical features with the hominids, whereas chimpanzees share only eight.[13]

## Hominid Origins: Probabilities

> In certain characters man seems to resemble most closely the living semi-brachiating monkeys, and we have noted in particular the high index of cephalization of these primates. Man's hand and penis show close similarities to those of certain Old World monkeys. In contrast, the apes have hands that have undergone specialization for brachiation, so they have to a great extent lost their manipulative power. This situation is typical of many characters of man when they are compared with apes; we find that man is less specialized in many of his brachiating features and shares, instead, more generalized features with the Old World monkeys.[14]

Though we bear the marks of the apes in our bodies, we are profoundly different from any of them. As noted earlier, we actually share more of our locomotor morphology with *Alouatta* (New World Howler monkey) than with any living ape. This demonstrates with some force how far both we and the African apes have evolved from the condition of our ancestors.[15]

Oxnard and Stern both see the human shoulder as most functionally similar to the orangutan, noting also that the human ancestor used its forelimb as much as the orangutan, but was probably smaller in size.[16] Morton, Schultz, and Tuttle see characteristics of the brachiating structure of the gibbon as related to the human arm and shoulder, as well as the gibbon's similar, if occasional, bipedal excursions.[17]

It is evident that Campbell's reference in the above quote to a New World monkey (25 mya: they went west with the American continents) as having locomotor morphological similarities closest to humans is further support for an Oligocene (35–30 mya) distilling of the various monkey and ape lines, including the proto-hominids. We must recall the great climatic transition that occurred in the Oligocene: cooling, drying, falling sea levels, Antarctica then covered by ice, the northern latitudes composed of a mixed coniferous and deciduous temperate woodland.[18]

Primates had been honing their mix of arboreal and land surface adaptations for at least another 35–40 my before the Oligocene, since the late Cretaceous, the end of the dinosaurian hegemony. The extreme heterogeneous mosaicism implied in the mix of primate heritages as part of the human morphological composite should not surprise.

It should be possible to hypothesize that the brachiating heritage still evident in human morphology need not be one constructed in the Oligocene or afterward. What we are today as humans could reflect that more ancient tradition of anthropoid evolution before the Oligocene. In sum, at the core of any hypothesis concerning human origins, three preadaptive factors must stand as preeminent:

1. Bipedalism. Of all the anthropoid lines, one line with predominantly ape, but also bipedal, characteristics, had to have been long on the scene. A more conservative creature in structure than other apes, with a valence not sharply defined toward the platyrrhine (New World) or the catarrhine (Old World) prototype would not have been atypical of the Oligocene anthropoids. In the special case of the proto-hominids, this particular anthropoid was a bit more catarrhine, and, of course,

remaining in Africa, reflects this dimension of its heritage. Clearly it was more ape than monkey, but either it must have been forced earlier by more successful arboreal forms to specialize on the ground, or else by the time of the Oligocene proto-*Homo* was established as at least as ground oriented as was *Aegyptopithecus*, c. 32 mya, a specimen from the Egyptian Fayum.
2. Brain and intelligence. Together with bipedal preadaptations, this particular anthropoid probably had a larger-than-average defensive brain, typical of mammalian "regressives." Together with its bipedalism, its large brain enabled it to evade the real predators, probably rodents or true carnivores. It could make a diversified living on the ground and also if necessary climb up a tree, even swinging a bit. Animals, in general, especially under changing ecological conditions, make a virtue of necessity. Higher intelligence, and minimal specialization, allowed the proto-hominid to survive on the land surfaces where there were more ecological opportunities for sustenance and reproduction.
3. Size. During the Oligocene and into the early Miocene 25–20 mya, the high probability is that the proto-hominids were quite small, smaller than gibbons, in the less than 5–10 pound range. Small animals, like the early mammals, need relatively small amounts of food to survive. Small, highly intelligent semi-bipeds could maneuver through their environment relying on their efficient, large brains to fend off their expansionary anthropoid competitors, those having more specialized physical attributes. Losers at most stages of an evolutionary transition, however, tend to be on the small side.

## Discussion

Of all vertebrate adaptations, particularly in the early stages, intelligence tends to be the most environmentally malleable defense. It was originally the preeminent primate adaptation, to be gradually refined first in the omomyids (tarsier ancestors) in a more frontal binocular visual orientation, and then in a gradually expanding brain in the modern primates (anthropoids).

By the middle Miocene, when *Proconsul* and the east African apes begin to dominate in the fossil record, 22–15 mya, this hypothesis would propose the as yet unobserved presence of the proto-hominids evolving at the periphery of these still gracile and universally acknowledged monkey-like apes. The true evolving into specialization—cercopithecoids, Old World monkeys—likewise were surviving at the periphery of the African ape clade.

The Miocene seems overall to have had a drier climate. What we should bear in mind is the inevitable increase in competitive pressures by the ape clade as it carved out the parameters of its adaptive niche. The gibbons were probably evolving their specialized brachiations, perhaps as defense against the Old World monkeys. At any rate the proto-gibbon survivors left, c. 15 mya, for the Eurasian land masses within that super-continent's tropical forest zone.

One ape line seems to have led, from thick-molared *Kenyapithecus* to *Sivapithecus*, then *Ramapithecus*, *Gigantopithecus*, and finally in fragile survivorship, to the East Asian orangutan, with its suite of associated adaptations. There were other migrants, too, the so-called European Dryopithecines, *Oreopithecus*, et al. This does not mean that few apes were left in Africa, merely that the Eurasians survived into the fossil record and far longer into the present than did most of their African ape contemporary cousins, who disappear from our fossil searches at about the 10 mya level.

The Old World monkeys in general probably were not a cause of the displacement of these apes in this mixed forest-plains economy. Only the baboon has reentered the savannahs of Africa to take up a position that was widely held by the hominoids during most of the Oligocene and Miocene. Indeed, there had to be ape residuals, because there are chimpanzees and gorillas in Africa today, living side by side with Old World monkeys, and nowhere else in the fossil record. The most obvious assumption is that these latter precursors of the remnant ape contemporaries had chosen or had been driven into the west African jungles and remained long and securely ensconced, adapting to the special ecological requirements of jungle life, along with a wide assortment of monkeys.

Why no apes on the African savannahs? Was it, as Andrews and Stringer surmise, characteristic of the result of the drying up of the landscape and the inability of the apes to eat unripe fruit, an adaptation available to monkey physiology?[19] Certainly the long-existing thick enamel on the molars of *Kenyapithecus* and the various Sivapithecines was an adaptation that meshed efficiently with the requirements of temperate, seasonal, and ecological conditions. They ate nuts, roots, tubers, grittier foods, even as the thin-enameled-toothed gorillas ate silicon-rich roughage grasses and leaves. Why then the disappearance? Certainly not because of lions, leopards, hyenas, dogs. The apes and proto-hominids were much too warily intelligent. Fear and defensive avoidance allowed for the escape from the specialized prey-predator relationships that the carnivores had negotiated with the various ungulates.

Richard Klein suggestively phrases the answer to this mystery:

> In the very late-Miocene, between 10 mya and 5 mya, in response to an ever more open, non-wooded environment in eastern Africa, one of the more terrestrial forms began to alter its habitual pattern of ground locomotion to emphasize an energetically efficient form of bipedalism, and the hominid lineage emerged. More or less simultaneously, the monkeys burgeoned, probably in response to the same late-Miocene vegetational change. Under pressure from the proto-hominids and the proliferating monkeys, many thick-enameled apes became extinct in the late Miocene, but some readapted to more forested conditions. Such re-adaptation could explain the secondary dental and locomotor specializations that the chimpanzees and gorillas exhibit today.[20]

Where this writer diverges from the views of Richard Klein, is in the latter's assumption of the convenient and rapid malleability of the anthropoid gene structure ("readaptation"). It seems doubtful that such clearly specialized morphologies as exhibited severally by the hominids or the African apes could have come about through normal selective evolutionary processes in such a blink of evolutionary time, i.e., from c. 15–10 mya to recent times.

Note: in 25 my of evolution, none of the New World monkeys has descended from the trees. Why not? Most probably when they arrived in the New World, they were already well-articulated and adapted to an arboreal style of life for which there were no further genetic possibilities, morphologically.[21] Also, there were no selective pressures to return to the ground. The proto-hominids, at this period of evolutionary history (the earliest Miocene), were doubtless already well adapted into a bifurcated lifestyle of walking and climbing in the African homeland.

Further, as noted above, the singular move of a lone baboon species down into the savannahs does not argue strongly enough for a competitive surge against apes by the Old World monkey. More likely it was the relative emptying out by formerly dominating ape forms of the various ecologies, forest and savannah, that allowed the monkeys to proliferate in the forests of Africa and Asia. The monkeys were, in the late Miocene, undisturbed by the *new competitor,* who was eliminating all but several highly specialized apes, these long-departed from the mainline open country evolutionary expansion of the hominoids, *viz.* the chimpanzees and the gorillas.

The above hypothesis, which argues for a more distant point of separation between the ancestors of the modern African apes and the proto-hominid ancestors than that implied by the DNA time-clock, is given potential confirmation in a recently-reported discovery. This is a 90–110-pound animal, *Morotopithecus*, discovered in the Moroto area of Uganda in Africa. It had shoulders that would allow it to swing from tree branches as well as act as a quadruped when it was aground. Dr. Laura MacLatchy of the State University of New York, Stony Brook, a member of the research team that studied *Morotopithecus*, stated that it anticipated similar forms of apes by about 10 my. *Morotopithecus* dates from about 20 mya, and thus could have been an ancestor or a contemporary of an already evolved chimpanzee-like creature.[22] This dating would also tend to strengthen the argument for a more distant point of departure of modern apes and humans than is generally held today by the scientific consensus.[23]

## Dominating Hominids

The principle of allometry relates the growth of one morphological trait to the accompanied growth of another. This process is rooted in the linkages existing on the chromosomal and gene level. Here complexes of genes associated both within and between chromosomes and subject to the strong positive selection of one phenotype act to carry another linked feature to phenotypic expression even when the linked feature itself is not under direct positive selection. The formerly neutral feature can subsequently cross an adaptive Rubicon and become an element in the selective success or failure of the organism.[24]

The positive external element, which fitted the preadapted structure of the proto-hominids, was bipedality. The drying of the Miocene, the mixed woodland-savannah environment, put a premium on walking or running, standing above the grasses, as opposed to being fixed in a tree, else climbing down and moving quadrupedally (knuckle like) to the next tree. The ability to find more nourishment in such a setting, abetting reproductive efficiency, gradually led to growth in size. These larger, more efficient "information-processors" were now able to move efficiently over longer distances and find more food, both vegetative and animal.

Larger size pulled along with it (linkage) a larger-than-average anthropoid brain, defensive at first, but with increasingly sensory and neural energies, which gave rise to a more active and dynamic animal. At some point in the later Miocene, 15–10 mya, these proto-hominids, once timid, furtive outlanders, began to compete actively with previously well-adapted and comfortably-ensconced ape forms, the ecology now more supportive of large, formerly arboreal quadrupeds.

The proto-hominids probably did not actively kill off the various Miocene apes that had dominated this ecology for so long, and these include the ancestral Sivapithecines and gibbons. They out-reproduced them, forcing them into strange ecologies where they had to struggle to maintain their old lifestyles.[25] Such geographical shifts and the pressure to maintain the food-reproductive chain clearly cut down on adaptive viability. The apes had been generalized arborealists with some ground-dwelling abilities. Africa was becoming alien to their mixed economy. As the ground-roaming bipedal proto-hominids, still equipped with vestigial arboreal skills, pushed them out, the Old World monkeys multiplied into the now-vacant forest areas.

Only in the deep west African jungles, not penetrated as yet by ever more bipedal proto-hominids, did apes, the gorilla and the chimpanzees, continue their specialized adaptive tack. Interestingly, several million years later, the surviving orangutan and gibbon East Asian descendants must have felt such pressures from early invasions by true *Homo* (Homo erectus pithecanthropus, 2–1 mya) into the Asian continent. The orangutans also found refuge in the East Asian jungles. Their earlier morphological adjustments included an increase in the length of their arms, reduction of the legs, great wrist and shoulder flexibility, very small hallux (big toe) and thumb.[26] Yet they retained much of their ancient Sivapithecine morphology, as well as that which links them from an even earlier time period with the proto-hominids.[27]

Klein, citing Matsuda's dating of a fragmentary upper jaw, maxilla, from the Samburu hills of Kenya, notes the gorilla-like molars, yet with thick enamel (as in an orangutan or hominid), embedded in a possibly hominid maxilla that could be between 10.5 and 6.7 my old.[28]

A mandible (lower jaw) at Lothagam, southwest of Lake Turkana, Kenya, discovered in 1967 with first molar and roots of second and third molars, roots intact, is the first clearly recognizable identifiable hominid (australopithecine) structure. It dates from between 5.5 and 5 mya. See also Tobias, 1994, 1999.[29]

Hill and Ward and others have identified fragmentary hominid fossils at between 8 and 6 mya.[30] More recently, fossils, perhaps older, from East Africa have been identified as *Ardipithecus ramidus* and *Australopithecus anamensis*, also probable cousins of *Homo*.[31]

## Notes

1. Zuckerkandl, E., & Pauling, L. (1965). Evolutionary divergence and convergence in proteins. In V. Bryson & H. J. Vogel (Eds.), *Evolving genes and proteins* (p. 97). New York, NY: Academic Press; Goodman, M. (1963). Man's place in the phylogeny of the primates as reflected in serum proteins. In S. L. Washburn, (Ed.), *Classification and human evolution* (p. 204–234). Edison, NJ: Aldine.
2. Sarich, V., & Wilson, A. C. (1966, December 23). Quantitative immunochemistry and the evolution of primate albumins: Micro-complement fixation. *Science, 154,* 1563–1565; Campbell, B. (1985). Immunological distances between albumins of various Old World primates. In *Human evolution, op. cit.,* table 12.2, p. 371 (calculated from data in Sarich & Wilson 1967, *op. cit., PNAS*).
3. Andrews, P., & Stringer, C. (1993). The primates' progress. In S. J. Gould (Ed.), *The book of life* (pp. 225–226). New York, NY: Norton.
4. Stebbins, G. (1982). *Darwin to DNA, molecules to humanity* (p. 319). San Francisco, CA: W. H. Freeman.
5. Diamond, J. (1992). *The third chimpanzee* (p. 23). New York, NY: HarperCollins.
6. Wilson, A. C., Carlson, S. S., & White, T. J. (1977). Biochemical evolution. *Annual Review of Biochemistry, 46,* 573–639; Stoneking, M. (2008). Human origins: The molecular perspective. *EMBO Reports, 9,* S46–S50.
7. Sarich & Wilson 1966, *op. cit.*
8. Yoder, A. D., Cartmill, M., Ruvolo, M., Smith, K., & Vilgalys, R. (1996). Ancient single origin for Malagasy primates. *PNAS, 193,* 5122–5126.
9. Public Library of Science (2009, May 19). Common ancestor of humans, modern primates? 'Extraordinary' fossil is 47 million years old. *ScienceDaily.* Retrieved November 9, 2013, from http://www.sciencedaily.com/releases/2009/05/090519104643.htm
10. Itzkoff, S. (2000). *The inevitable domination by man: An evolutionary detective story* (pp. 149–157). Ashfield, MA: Paideia. Summary below.
11. Itzkoff 2000, *op. cit.,* pp. 172–178. The section below summarizes the research.
12. Knott, C., & Kahlenberg, S. (2007). Orangutans in perspective. In C. Campbell, A. Fuentes, K. MacKinnon, S. Bearder, & R. Stumpf (Eds.), *Primates in perspective* (p. 294ff). New York, NY: Oxford University Press.
13. Schwartz, J. (2004). Barking up the wrong ape. *Colloquium Anthropologicum, 28 Supplement 2,* 87–100; Schwartz, J. (2005). *The red ape.* Denver, CO: Westview; Grehan, J. (2006). Mona Lisa smile: The morphological enigma of great ape evolution. *Anatomical Record, 289,* 139–157.
14. Campbell, B. (1966). *Human evolution* (1st ed.) (pp. 326–327). Chicago, IL: Aldine; Straus, W. L. (1949). The riddle of man's ancestry. *The Quarterly Review of Biology, 24,* 200–223.
15. Campbell, B. (1985). *Human evolution* (3rd ed.) (p. 202). New York, NY: Aldine De Gruyter.
16. Oxnard, C. E. (1969). Evolution of the human shoulder: Some possible pathways. *American Journal of Physical Anthropology, 30,* 319–322; Stern, J. T. (1975). Before bipedality. *Yearbook of Physical Anthropology, 19,* 59–68.

17. Morton, D. J. (1924). Evolution of the human foot, 2. *American Journal of Physical Anthropology, 7*, 1–52, esp. 39; Morton, D. J. (1924, January 1). Evolution of the longitudinal arch of the human foot. *The Journal of Bone & Joint Surgery, 6*, 56–90, esp. 88; Schultz, A. H. (1927). Observations on a gorilla fetus. *Eugenical News, 12*, 37–40, esp. 40; Schultz, A. H. (1936). Characters common to higher primates and characters specific for man. *Quarterly Review of Biology, 11*, 425–455, esp. 452; Schultz, A. H. (1969). *The life of primates* (p. 251), New York, NY: Universe Books; Tuttle, R. H. (1985). Darwin's apes, dental apes, and the descent of man: Normal science in evolutionary anthropology. In R. L. Ciochon & J. G. Fleagle (Eds.), *Primate evolution and human origins* (pp. 333–342). Menlo Park, CA: Benjamin/Cummings.
18. Janis, C. (1993). Victors by default. In Gould, *op. cit.*, pp. 192–196; Prothero, D. R. (1994). *The Eocene-Oligocene transition* (pp. 167–222). New York, NY: Columbia University Press; Rylands, A., & Rittermeier, R. (2009). The diversity of new world primates, *platyrrhini*. In P. A. Garber, A. Estrada, J. C. Bicca-Marques, E. W., Heymann, & K. B. Strier (Eds.), *South American primates* (pp. 23–54). New York, NY: Springer.
19. Andrews & Stringer 1993, *op. cit.*, p. 234.
20. Klein, R. (1989). *The human career* (p. 98). Chicago, IL: University of Chicago Press.
21. Schrago, C., & Russo, C. (2003). Timing the origin of new world monkeys. *Molecular Biology and Evolution, 20*, 1620–1625.
22. Associated Press. (1997, April 18). Fossil shows apes emerged far earlier. *The New York Times*. Retrieved from http://www.nytimes.com/1997/04/18/us/fossil-shows-apes-emerged-far-earlier.html. David Pilbeam sees no great evolutionary significance in this creature. He views the missing link ancestor of man and chimpanzee at 6–5mya as a knuckle-walking, long-armed, short-legged arboreal swinger/climber. Pilbeam, D. (1989). Human fossil history and evolutionary paradigms. In M. K. Hecht (Ed.), *Evolutionary biology at the crossroads* (pp. 117–138). Flushing, NY: Queens College Press.
23. Recent interesting reports of interbreeding of related species: Macaque and Baboon (J.-J. Hublin, personal communication) and an Arabian camel with a South American llama (*The New York Times*, 1/20/98) raise questions about the seeming inability to interbreed humans and chimpanzees, considering the supposed recent 5–6 my separation of the two lines, and their close mtDNA affinities.
24. Pagel, M. D., & Harvey, P. H. (1990, February). Diversity in the brain size of newborn mammals: Allometry, energetics, or life history tactics. *BioScience, 40(2)*, 121–122.
25. Itzkoff, S. (1983). *The form of man* (p. 87). New York, NY: Lang.
26. Campbell 1985, *op. cit.*, p. 76; Tuttle 1985, *op. cit.*, pp. 333–342.
27. Schwartz, J. (1987). *The red ape*. London: Elm Tree Books; Oxnard, C. E. (1985). Hominids and hominoids, lineages and radiations. In P. V. Tobias (Ed.), *Hominid evolution: Past, present, and future* (pp. 271–278). New York, NY: Alan Liss.
28. Klein 1989, *op. cit.*, p. 93; Ishida, H., Pichford, M., Nakaya, H., & Nakano, Y. (1984). Fossil anthropoids from Nachola and Samburu Hills, Samburu District, Kenya. *African Studies Monographs (Kyoto), Supplementary Issue, 2*, 73–85; Matsuda, T., Torii, M., Koyaguchi, T., Makinouchi, T., Mitsushio, H., & Ishida, S. (1986). Geochronology of Miocene Hominids east of the Kenya Rift Valley. In J. G. Else & P. C. Lee (Eds.), *Primate evolution*. Cambridge: Cambridge University Press.

29. Tobias, P. (1999, April 13). Three mya Australopithecine skeleton at Sterkfontein. Blaine, WA: Foundation for the Future, Lecture; Tobias, P. V. (1994). The evolution of early hominids. In T. Ingold (Ed.), *Companion encyclopedia of anthropology* (pp. 33–78, esp. pp. 53–55). New York, NY: Routledge.
30. Kramer, A. (1986). Hominid-pongid distinctiveness in the miocene-pliocene fossil record: The lothagam mandible. *American Journal of Physical Anthropology, 70,* 457–473; Hill, A., & Ward, S. (1988). Origin of the hominidae: The record of African large hominoid evolution between 14my and 4my. *American Journal of Physical Anthropology, 31,* 49–83; Conroy, G. C. (1990). *Primate evolution.* New York, NY: Norton.
31. Culotta, E. (1995, August 18). New hominid crowds the field. *Science, 269,* 918; White, T. et al. (2009). Ardipithecus ramidus and the paleobiology of early hominids. *Science, 326,* 64–86.

## · 5 ·

# NATURAL SELECTION OF *HOMO*

## Hominid Evolution: Time and Structure

The hypothesis here put forth is that the proto-hominids had already separated themselves in the Miocene, c. 23 mya, no less than the modern recidivist jungle brachiators. The bodily structure of the hominids, especially *Homo*, argues for a more diffuse and variable hominid heritage than the straight lines drawn between the all-too-few fossil dots would have it.

The entire evolutionary history of the vertebrates, their land-evolving descendants, then the earliest mammal hints and all that follows, argues for much hidden evolution (see chapter 2). The clues are the often fragmentary fossil evidence and all the patching and relating, here too connecting the dots, as well as the time frame of these morphological dots. Added here is the even more tenuous evidence of the shifting of geological processes. Then we have the primary uncertainties and errors that lie in the digging of these fossils out of the ground. In the end, all we have are sets of hypothetical relationships and timelines that invite humility.

Indeed there seems to be at least a 20 my gap between the hypothetical explosion of anthropoid types at the Oligocene/Miocene boundary, 30–25 mya and the now c. 8 mya collection of fragmentary hominid remains. How they got from there to here is the mystery. But this is no less a mystery than with the evolution of the mammals an equally important set of evolutionary lacunae that calls for scientific attention.

For example, the first clear sign of intrinsic mammalian morphologies comes to us from a 215–200 mya late-Triassic time level. Scientists have identified three distinct lines of tiny proto-mammals now flourishing under an enlarging archosaur canopy.[1] Discounting the relationship of these now proto-mammal lines with the dog-sized mammal-like reptile Cynodonts of the Permian, 250–230 mya, is it really likely that these tiny Triassic creatures did not have their own points of origin at least as ancient as the Cynodonts?[2]

These three proto-mammal lines have been identified as: a) morganocodontids; b) kuehneotherids; c) haramiyids. Phylogenetic evidence is for the haramiyids to be ancestral to the multituberculates. The monotremes and the therians, marsupials and placentals evolved from the kuehneotherids. Whether the monotremes are a more primitive mammal form than the multituberculates who became extinct c. 45 mya, they, monotremes, seem to have been a very early breakaway c. 190 mya from the line that produced the marsupials and placentals. Their evolutionary status vis-à-vis the extinct multituberculates, i.e., which is the more primitive mammal, is yet a controversy. These latter infra-class mammal lines were probably well established and evolving in terms of morphology by c. 140 mya. It is probable that each line, marsupials and placentals, especially the latter were shedding (via extinctions) any morphological relationships (epipubic bones) by 100–90 mya.[3]

The fossil record for the vast changes taking place in mammal morphology and physiology during the span between c. 215–65 mya, the latter time frame for the great Paleocene breakout, parallels the above hominid hidden evolutionary adaptive fragmentation and preparation. Both the mammal breakout, the contemporary dinosaurian extinctions, as well as the ape extinctions of the middle and late Miocene, 15–10 mya, were probably a result of, first, an ever-growing defensive brain, and later, a bipedality which expanded a very tiny primate, perhaps squirrel-sized, into the two-to-three-foot range that is exemplified in the Australopithecines; these constituted the first phase of their multiplication and advance.[4]

The flourishing of the Australopithecinse and their various cousins now being continuously uncovered in the 4–2 mya range tells us of an animal coming into adaptive dominance in the mixed plains, forested domains now throughout Africa: north, south, east and west. As yet few articulated remnant fossils of *Homo* occur before c. 2 mya.

This earliest hominid genus, *Australopithecus*, was first discovered in South Africa, 1924, the Taung Australopithecine, *A. Africanus*, by Raymond Dart, now dated to c. 3 mya. In 1976 Donald Johanson uncovered the fossilized remains of an Australopithecine near Hadar, Ethiopia, *A. Afarensis*, also at about 3 mya, so far apart geographically, yet overlapping in time and morphology.[5]

Since then many other Australopithecine-type fossils have come to light in even earlier datings, others of very robust ape-like features, *P. robustus*, *P. boisei*, yet with a more *Homo*-like tooth structure than the gracile *Afarencis* and *Africanus* Australopithecines.[6]

The discovery of "Lucy," *A. Afarensis*, did set off a straight-line controversy as to the relationship with the ongoing discovery of more human-like hominids, with fewer clearly anthropoid, tree-climbing morphologies, and a much larger humanlike skull structure. These more modern morphologies were increasingly discovered within the same time and geographical range as the increasingly widespread number of ancient and now, advanced Australopithecines.[7]

The coexisting members of this new and more recent-appearing but momentarily coexisting genus were *Homo habilis*, *Homo ergaster*, and *Homo rudolfensis*, all found in east Africa (Kenya and Ethiopia), and at the 2.2–1.5 mya level. The current view is that possibly, except for the *Flores*, Indonesia remnants, the Australopithecines disappeared c. 1 mya. By that time the fossil scene had gotten quite crowded with a great number of very disparate early humans. And it is clear that the dominating selective instrument is brain size and power—not merely tool making, but the aggressive bipedal invasion of the various australopithecine life ecologies. The more distant jungle chimpanzees, bonobos, and gorillas were then largely out of range of *Homo*'s adaptive intrusions.[8]

The difference in endocranial capacity between these earliest humans and the Australopithecines is significant, the earliest *Homo ergaster*, c. 750–850 cm$^3$, at c. 1.6 mya. Compare this to c. 400–450 cm$^3$ in the Australopithecines at c. 3–2 mya. This leaves the contemporary chimpanzees at 385 cm$^3$.[9] In addition, it is quite likely that the transition to true hominid status was accompanied by a switch from the early proto-hominid hidden defensiveness, while they nurtured both their bipedal high-grass peeping, plus their higher-cognitive get-out-of-the-way protective brain, to the new aggressiveness we have earlier noted in the now distant brainy mammalian rush beyond the reptiles. Thus the various Australopithecine species and genera disappeared (genocide?) from our earth.[10]

## A Puzzling Conquest

Certainly from the period of c. 2 mya the other mammal forms accompanying the hominid advance towards the present were flourishing, this in spite of ever-larger human brains pursuing ever-larger animals in the hunt, and with increasingly effective tools. It is also true that *Homo* was repeating the same migratory patterns that had brought the Miocene apes into Europe and Asia (*Dryopithecus, Oreopithecus*). We are also aware of a period of great climatic changes in the *Pleistocene* era, from c. 1.9 mya, a series of periodic advances of the ice from the north into southern Europe and Asia succeeded again and again by interstadial warmth. This dynamic would have its ultimate selective impact on the destiny of the human race.

From this c. 2 mya time zone we see an ever-increasing allometric growth (height) and robusticity patterns in this successful clade of humans. Heavy brow ridges, thick-boned crania legs, arms, body structure heavy set, typical of an animal which is now dominant and has reached the pinnacle point of its adaptive balance with nature.

One of the most interesting examples of this trend and the mysteries and controversies that have been set off is the so-called Turkana (Kenya) boy. This *Homo erectus* exemplar is thought to be a ten-year-old boy with exceedingly long leg bones. At maturity the original hypothesis was that he would have grown into at least a six-foot-two-inch adult. More consideration of the future growth of this ancient humans has now reduced the probable adult height to between five-foot-five and five-foot-nine.[11]

The consensus view up until recently was that there is now an indubitable connection between earlier *Homo—habilis, ergaster, rudolfensis*—and the successor form *Homo erectus*, all in Africa. Subsequent migrations during the Pleistocene period began after the achievement of the taxonomic level of *Homo erectus*, considering height, robusticity, endocranial capacity. Today there is mixed opinion as to whether the advanced African line ought to be renamed *H. ergaster*, and other European and Asiatic forms retained as *H. erectus*.[12]

Lo and behold, in Georgia, the Caucasus, at Dmanisi, several *Homo erectus* skulls were found in 2004, dated to 1.85–1.75 mya.[13] In addition other fragmentary human life materials, hunting and fire, at earlier time levels were also uncovered, confirming the now assumed view that there were very early migration patterns out of Africa of early as well as advanced hominids, contemporary with still-existing earlier east African *Australopithecus* and *Homo*.

The dating, as always, gets increasingly complex and debatable. Could several species of humans in different stages of development coexisted, and as yet, also with the Australopithecines?[14]

Recently, scientists, 1993–96, have reexamined a number of Indonesian fossils, found in the 1930s, previously dated to c. 300 ka BP, Sangiran 17 and a group of Ngandong fossils of the same Homo erectus lineage. Today, through modern dating techniques, these fossils have been placed in the 53–27 ka BP level, very recent in terms of their taxonomic status, and seemingly coexistent with the Neanderthals of Europe/west Asia, as well as Homo sapiens sapiens, modern Cro-Magnons in Europe.[15]

Even more sensational has been the 2003 discovery on the island of Flores in Indonesia of a tiny and very primitive—possibly Homo erectus or earlier—type of human who seems to have lived on to c. 89–12 ka BP. A few scientists claimed that they are merely modern dwarfs because of their isolation and the dwarfed forms of life they hunted on this island. Subsequent morphological analysis now refutes the dwarfing hypothesis. In endocranial capacity the Flores people were on the chimpanzee level. They used tools, seemingly had fire. The consensus in the scientific community is that they were the remnants of migrants out of Africa at a very early stage, as with the other Indonesian types noted above, but even more primitive in morphology. Their demise, including the Ngandong and Sangiran people, was probably due to the arrival of modern humans who today live close by on these respective islands.[16]

A very recent discovery of archaic human remains, in the Altai Mountains of Siberia, Denisova Cave, c. 40 ka BP, reflects a human population that separated from Neanderthals and modern humans, their genetics showing c. 1 my separation from the ancestors of the above lines, and seemingly related to modern Melanesian and aboriginal peoples (Austronesian) of southeast Asia. It does partially confirm the independent separation at an early hominid level of the various modern races of humankind, as well as the early migrating trends of humans, a heritage of our primeval primate ancestors.[17]

Another puzzle takes us back to Africa where Louis Leakey's famous early find, Olduvai (Kenya) hominid no. 9 erectine, 1.2 mya, c. 950 cm$^3$, seems to be directly ancestral to the Kabwe (Broken Hill—Rhodesia/Zambia) erectine at c. 200 ka BP, 1100 cm$^3$ and then leading to Homo sapiens Idaltu, 1,450 cm$^3$, possibly of Khoisan–Capoid heritage, here found in Ethiopia, heavy browed but with rounded skull, a discovery announced in 2003, now also dated to

c. 150–160k BP. Carleton Coon, who reanalyzed the *Kabwe* skull and its location, hypothesized that it can now be dated to c. 62–25 ka BP.[18] This suggests that *Kabwe* was at the least a contemporary of *Homo sapiens Idaltu*.[19]

The conclusion that must be made from these many hypotheticals/facts is that a consecutive increase in brain size and power was transforming the human clade. They were now capable of fabricating tools, possibly even making fire, at the least since 2 mya, migrating, as did the ancestral apes and monkeys, to the far ranges of the interconnected continents, and creating stable adaptive social conditions.

## Modernizing the Species

The Neanderthals are probably the most intriguing of the recent ancestors of modern humans. They give tangible evidence for the spread of humans into the great Eurasian continental mass. The archeological and paleontological evidence is rich in Neanderthal evidence. However, while we can chronicle the probable circumstances and time of their final extinction as a species or race, whichever taxonomic category they will eventually fall into, their origin is more obscure. The postulation is that the Neanderthals, as yet a variable subspecies, originated probably in the Eurasian land mass, and at its northern reaches, at the latest c. 500 ka BP.

We think they were Caucasoid in racial characteristics: white of skin, light-colored hair, but in general a "blown up" erectine in their cranial and post-cranial morphology. The endocranial capacity of the Neanderthals was quite large, but the brain was primitive in structure. Their tool culture, we call Mousterian, and in certain respects seems to be an advance on the typical erectine kit. They also were cold adapted, nasal and facial bone structure, very heavy bone and physical morphology, not too unlike modern arctic living humans.[20]

There is evidence, towards the end of their European existence, of some interbreeding with the oncoming-Cro-Magnons, *Homo sapiens sapiens*, who displaced them, both in Spain and in central Europe. There is only circumstantial evidence from the fossil past as to their contacts with the Cro-Magnons in the Middle East, Palestine. The Skhul and Qafzeh skulls and fossil remains found in Israel hint at such an amalgamation.[21] And it is possible that recent populations in the Far East and the Americas represent composites of such ancient and modern peoples. It is possible that during the main line continental dominance of the Neanderthals, from c. 200 ka BP, they had pushed Eurasian relic erectine populations into extinction.[22]

The mysterious and very different, morphologically and behaviorally, Cro-Magnons coexisted with the Neanderthals until c. 40 ka BP, in Spain, the most recent dating for the Neanderthal presence as an independent cultural, racial, and evolutionary entity. Their elimination points clearly to the behavioral and thus selective consequences of a powerful new brain that the Cro-Magnons were able to put into play in their own struggles to survive, especially during the late Pleistocene periodic descent of the ice and the cold.

> One can imagine Neanderthalers watching from the edge of a cliff how the Cro-Magnons hunted in the valley. To the brutish, fear ridden Neanderthalers these almost hairless giants with jutting chin and towering forehead must have appeared to be superhuman spirits. He saw them using a miraculous technique which was utterly unfathomable and incomprehensible to him. He saw the animal herds from which he had for thousands of years picked what he wanted being ingeniously rounded and driven into traps, over precipices or through a narrow gorge into the fire, the clubs and spears of the hunters who jabbered excitedly and made strange cries while they waited for the bag. As he gazed at the elaborate preparations they made for the chase, Neanderthal Man must have felt an eerie terror and sickening weariness at the futility of his own poor efforts. He must have realized that against these—what we would call godlike beings he had not the slightest chance to compete. More and more he must have drawn away from such terrifying creatures, not because they threatened his life, but simply because their miraculous powers were too much for him to contemplate and filled him with primeval panic.[23]

## Modern Humans: Out of Africa?

In the late 1980s researchers led by Allan Wilson made a comparative analysis of the mtDNA of c. 148 individuals throughout the world. This was done by extracting and subjecting to molecular separation the comparatively small amounts of DNA to be found in the mitochondria. Mitochondria are inherited through the female line.[24]

The results of a computer analysis of the mtDNA differences in this population created a family tree that implied a modern human origin in a female living in Africa some 200 ka BP. Under criticism this figure was revised forward to c. 63–40 ka BP, as the time of origin and migration north. It was further concluded that these migrating populations into the rest of the world *would not* have interbred with other adjoining populations during this migration, nor had these out-of-Africa moderns returned to their original place of origin.

Naturally, these conclusions that truly modern humans presumably had originated in Africa and then had come north into Eurasia at about the time of the earliest Cro-Magnon tool and general cultural findings raised questions. This migration upwards in latitude paralleled the Cro-Magnon migrations east to west. Naturally there was a scientific stir. Considering that the mtDNA argument for the separation of chimpanzees and hominids at the 5–6 mya boundary was orthodoxy at that time, the 1980s, the new proposal that the out-of-Africa moderns, they at the *Homo sapiens* taxonomic grade, spread throughout the world continents, except for Antarctica and North and South America, was a very supportive piece of evidence for the political argument of a transcendent human biological uniformity, the downplaying of *Homo sapiens* racial subspecies. The "public press" created for itself a new and ongoing orthodoxy.

The scientific reception, however, was less than unanimous or glowing. Empirical evidence had argued for a much greater integration of older phylogenetic and genetic relationships into the modern form of humans than the "African Eve" hypothesis allowed. Also, the requirement for the elimination of all the resident populations prior to the earliest 65 ka BP boundary could not be supported empirically. At the very least there were the Neanderthals. As with the molecular hypothesis concerning chimpanzee and hominid separation, the laboratory evidence seemed to need supplementation with on-the-ground empirical evidence.[25]

In this case, the laboratory evidence of affinities and separateness seemed to have failed acceptance. The empirical, non-laboratory evidence has not supported this hypothesis. In the end, a supporter of the original argument of Wilson et al. wrote in 1999, the theory has "inferences that will have to be reconsidered."[26]

Still, the media, and complicit social scientists, the "orthodox" majority, accepts the argument that modern humans have recently, c. 60 ka BP, migrated out of Africa, thence eliminating existing competitor hominid forms.[27]

A sage European scientific veteran of these paleontological "wars" concluded as follows:

> In appealing to the Out of Africa model [a scholar] seems to me a victim of the fashion inspired by the gurus of the golden sixties, whose only ability was to impose 'politically correct' false truths on a credulous world. It is regrettable that members of the new generation are wasting intellectual energy trying to escape from them, since their conclusions do not favor such a model.[28]

# Notes

1. Kemp, T. S. (1982). *Mammal-like reptiles and the origin of mammals* (p. 18). New York, NY: Academic Press.
2. Benton, M. (1993). Four feet on the ground. In S. J. Gould (Ed.), *The book of life* (p. 89). New York, NY: Norton; Quiroga, J. C. (1979). The brain of two mammal-like reptiles (Cynodontia-Therapsida). *Journal für Hirnforschung, 20*, 341–350; Quiroga, J. C. (1980). The brain of the mammal-like reptile Probainognathus jenseni (Therapsida-Cynodonta): A correlative paleo-neoneurological approach to the neocortex at the reptile-mammal transition. *Journal für Hirnforschung, 21*, 299–336.
3. T. Kemp 1982, *op. cit.*, p. 316; Rowe, T. (1993). Phylogenetic systematics and the early history of the mammals. In F. S. Szalay, M. J. Novacek, M. C. McKenna (Eds.), *Mammal phylogeny* (pp. 132, 142). New York, NY: Springer; Luo, Z. (1996). Relationship and morphological evolution of early mammals. In *Carnegie Museum of Natural History Home Page*.
4. Jerison, H. J. (1983, March 11). The evolution of the mammalian brain as an information-processing system. In J. F. Eisenberg & D. G. Kleiman (Eds.), *Advances in the study of mammalian behavior, special publication no. 7* (p. 131). Shippensburg, PA: The American Society of Mammalogists.
5. Oxnard, C. E. (1985). Hominids and hominoids, lineages and radiations. In P. V. Tobias (Ed.), *Hominid evolution: Past, present, and future* (pp. 271–278). New York, NY: Alan Liss.
6. Rak, Y. (1983). *The australopithecine face* (pp. 120, 215–219). New York, NY: Academic Press; Zihlman, A. L. (1990). Knuckling under: Controversy over hominid origins. In G. Sperber (Ed.), *From apes to angels: Essays in anthropology in honor of Philip V. Tobias* (pp. 185–196, 191). New York, NY: Wiley-Liss; see also: Bromage, T. G. (1985). Taung facial remodeling. In Tobias 1985, *op. cit.*, pp. 239–245; Bromage, T. G., & Dean, M. C. (1985). Re-evaluation of the age at death of immature fossil hominids. *Nature, 317*, 525–527; Conroy, G. C., & Vannier, M. W. (1987, October 21). Dental development of the taung skull from computerized tomography. *Nature, 329*, 625–627; Beynon, A. D., & Wood, B. A. (1987). Patterns and rates of enamel growth in the molar teeth of early hominids. *Nature, 326*, 493–496.
7. Suwa, G., Asfaw, B., Beyene, Y., White, T. D., Katoh, S., Nagaoka, S., … WoldeGabriel, G. (1997, October 2). The first skull of *Australopithecus boisei*. *Nature, 389*, 489–492; Wilford, J. N. (1997, October 7). African skull suggests diversity of early human relatives. *The New York Times*, p. C9. Wilford quotes E. Delson in same *Nature* issue: Delson, E. (1997, October 2). The robust australopithecine skull of Konso, Ethiopia. *Nature, 389*(6650). Delson, of the American Museum of Natural History, comments on the diversity of the australopithecine clade and includes himself in the category of a taxonomic lumper, rather than a splitter; Malapa cave South Africa, c. 2mya. *Science*, September, 2011.
8. Wills, C. (1993). *The runaway brain* (pp. 137–138). New York, NY: Basic; Skelton, R., & McHenry, H. (1992). Evolutionary relationships among early hominids. *Journal of Human Evolution, 23*, 309–349; Andrews, P., & Stringer, C. (1989). *Human evolution: An illustrated guide* (pp. 36–37). Cambridge: Cambridge University Press; Wood, B., & Collard, M. (1999, April 2). The human genus. *Science, 284*, 65–71.

9. Tobias, P. (1994). The evolution of early hominids. In T. Ingold (Ed.), *Companion Encyclopedia of Anthropology* (p. 61). New York, NY: Routledge.
10. Philip Tobias places the extinction of the Australopithecines at 1.2 mya, contemporary with the first evidence of the use of fire by H. erectus (P. V. Tobias, personal communication, April 12, 1995); Stanley, S. (1998). *Children of the ice age* (pp. 112–123). New York, NY: W. H. Freeman.
11. Walker, A., & Shipman P. (1996). *The wisdom of the bones* (pp. 123–134). New York, NY: Knopf.
12. Boas, N. (1995). Calibration and extension of the record of Pliocene–mid Pleistocene hominidae. In N. Boas & D. Wolfe (Eds.), *Biological anthropology* (p. 32). Central Oregon University Center; Rightmire, C. (1985). The tempo of change in the evolution of mid-Pleistocene homo. In E. Delson (Ed.), *Ancestors: The hard evidence*. New York, NY: Wiley-Liss.
13. Walker & Shipman 1996, *op. cit.*, p. 259; smaller H *habilis* types 1470,1509; Wood & Collard 1999, *op. cit.*; Strait et al. (1997). *Journal of Human Evolution, 32*, 17.
14. Gabunia, I., & Vekua, A., (1995). A plio-pleistocene hominid from Dmanisi, East Georgia, Caucasus. *Nature, 373*, 509–512.
15. Swisher, C., & Anton, S. (1996, December 13). Ngandong, Solo River, H. Erectus sites redated. *Science, 274*, 1870; Gibbons, A. (1996, December 13). Homo erectus in Java: A 250,000 year anachronism. *Science, 274*, 1841–1842; Ward, P. (1994). *The end of evolution* (pp. 242–243). New York, NY: Bantam; Wilford, J. (1996, December 13). Three human species coexisted on Earth, new data suggest. *The New York Times*. Retrieved from http://www.nytimes.com/1996/12/13/us/3-human-species-coexisted-eons-ago-new-data-suggest.html
16. Brown, P., Sutikna, T., Morwood, M. J., Soejono, R. P., Jatmiko, Wayhu Saptomo, E., & Due, R. A. (2004). A new small-bodied hominim from the late Pleistocene of Flores, Indonesia. *Nature, 431*, 1055–1061; Morwood, M. & Oosterzee, P. (2007). *A New Human*. Washington, D.C.: Smithsonian Books.
17. Reich, D., Green, R. E., Kircher, M., Krause, J., Patterson, N., Durand, E. Y., ... Pääbo, S. (2010, December 23). Genetic history of an archaic hominen group from Denisova Cave, Siberia. *Nature, 468*, 1053–1060.
18. Walker, A. (1993). In A. Walker & R. Leakey (Eds.), *The Nariokotome homo erectus skeleton* (pp. 415–416). Cambridge, MA: Harvard University Press; Coon, C. (1962). *The origin of races* (p. 616). New York, NY: Knopf; Pilbeam, D. (1972). *The ascent of man* (p. 183). New York, NY: Macmillan.
19. White, T. D., Asfaw, B., DeGusta, D., Filbert, H., Richards, G. D., Suwa, G., & Howell, F. C. (2003). Pleistocene *Homo sapiens* [sic] from Middle Awash, Ethiopia. *Nature, 423*, 742–747. [the above "sic" is from the author]
20. Pääbo, S. (1997, July 11). *Cell*; Trinkaus, E., & Zilhao, J. (2000). *PNAS*; Tattersall, I. (1995). *The last Neanderthal* (illustration #103, p. 149). New York, NY: Macmillan.
21. Quintyn, C. (2006). *The Morphometric Affinities of the Qafzeh and Skhul Hominans*. Available from http://www.amazon.com/Morphometric-Affinities-Qafzeh-Skhul-Hominans/dp/1425958494

22. Tattersall, I. 1995, *op. cit.*, illustration #115, pp.168–169; Herrera, J., Somarelli, J. A., Lowery, R. K., & Herrera, R. J. (2009). To what extent did Neanderthals and modern humans interact? *Biological Reviews, 84,* 245–257; Viegas, J. (2010, May 6). Neanderthals, humans interbred, DNA proves. *Discovery News.* Retrieved from http://news.discovery.com/human/evolution/neanderthal-human-interbreed-dna.htm
23. Simeons, A. (1962). *Man's presumptuous brain* (p. 276). New York, NY: Dutton.
24. Cann, R., Stoneking, M., & Wilson, A. (1987, January 1). Mitochondrial DNA and human evolution. *Nature, 325,* 31–36.
25. Dawkins, R. (1995). *River out of Eden* (pp. 48–49). New York, NY: Basic; de Duve, C. (1995). *Vital dust* (pp. 232–234). New York, NY: Basic; Templeton, A. (1992, February 7). Technical comments: Human origins and analysis of mitochondrial DNA sequence. *Science, 255,* 737. (P. 240–241 Dawkins, de Duve, Templeton)
26. Awadalla, P., Eyre-Walker, A., & Smith, J. M. (1999, December 24). Linkage disequilibrium and recombination in hominid mitochondrial DNA. *Science, 286,* 2524–2525.
27. Mellars, P. (2006). Why did modern humans disperse from Africa sixty thousand years ago? *PNAS, 103,* 9381–9386.
28. Otte, M. (1998). *Current Anthropology, June Supplement, 39.*

## · 6 ·

# CRO-MAGNON—*HOMO SAPIENS SAPIENS*

### Primeval Humanity

Had the Cro-Magnons not arrived in west Asia/Europe c. 45 ka BP, we probably would not have seen the subsequent development of the literary civilizations of the world. Indeed, throughout the three continents Africa, Europe, and Asia, we see a continued precursor process of cranial enlargement and some cultural advancements in the period 150–50 ka BP.

In north Africa, c. 100 ka BP, we have the Jebel Irhoud series of fossils, which show an endocranial capacity of 1,500cm$^3$, not inconsiderable yet with a still primitive morphological structure, brow ridges, etc.[1] These fossils seem closer to subsequent Capoid (Boskopoid-Bushman) ethnics, also *H. ergaster*, 1.6 mya, still close to the *H. habilis* stage of human evolution. But J. Irhoud was also found in the context of Mousterian tools (Neanderthals, Eurasian Caucasoids).[2]

The Neanderthals were already well ensconced, adapted both physically and culturally, hunting, gathering, tool making. Here, as well into east Asia, there seems to be a well-adapted human form that could have gone on for eons in balance with the economics of life, as well as the periodic changes in climate and ecology. The one possible exception is the Boskopoids of Africa, and their subsequent venture into Spain.

This racial group dominated in Africa for many hundreds of thousands of years. There is some evidence of a relationship starting with KNMR 3733 *H. ergaster*, noted above, also of a relationship between subsequent Mongoloid types and the Capoids—epicanthic fold, skin color, but not hair, Mongoloids with straight hair. The Boskopoids seem to be a late Pleistocene development of the ancient Capoid heritage in Africa but yet apart from other lines of *H. habilis* evolutionary levels, c. 2–1 mya.[3] The Boskopoids had a very enlarged cranial capacity, more modern than the Neanderthals. They dominated in Africa, created art. We have wall paintings from c. 15 ka BP to recent times; also an advanced Howieson's Poort, Wilton and Aterian tool kit close to the Cro-Magnon forms. It is now thought that they spread throughout all of Africa in this time period, 100 ka BP to c. 15 ka BP, during which the first Negroid fossils seem to appear.[4] The Boskopoids migrated into Spain during this period, but were clearly driven out, and forcefully, given the tangible evidence of Cro-Magnon artistic and artifactual disdain (a bowl cut from a Capoid-like skull cap in a Cro-Magnon settlement, plus drawings of an encaged Capoid, the cage held by a rope on the side of a hill encampment).

These interesting premodern peoples were at first driven south, out of Spain, thence out of North Africa by oncoming migrations of Cro-Magnon descendants, the Berbers of North Africa, thence further south into the Kalahari Desert by the oncoming and vigorous Negroids out of the west African tropics. The Bushman thence went through a dwarfing process by which they ingeniously survived a very challenging ecology until their recent transport into new zoo-like sequestration. Today there are also remnant, hybridized Hottentots and, along with the Bushman, they are on the verge of extinction.[5]

## "New Guy on the Block"

From c. 45 ka BP the Cro-Magnons drifted into Europe from the east. As with the Neanderthals they were Caucasoid in racial characteristics but highly modernized, taller, a skull that soars above the nose line, rounded and tucked into the neck at the rear. At the most, brow ridges are remnants, a distinct chin, high vertical forehead. The thickness of Neanderthal and earlier erectine skulls are in the 10–13 mm range. Cro-Magnon and their modern descendants are in the 4–5 mm range, relatively delicate as with other post-cranial bone structures. Clearly these and many other differences from their Neanderthal neighbors, and all the other still extant human forms at this period throughout the world, have led the anthropologist Richard Klein to assert that there is here "substantial variability in the expression of many features ... but never sufficient to incorporate earlier forms of people."[6]

Along with the fossils of the Cro-Magnon types we see a new technology in formation: delicate blades, knives or spear points, arrowheads, scrapers, harpoons, burins. Along with the practical—these all delicately shaped and reshaped for subsequent uses—were the artistically purposed: decorated and incised shells, beads, bracelets also made from shells, mammoth ivory, bone, stone-flints, teeth of animals. Simultaneous with these tool and fossil finds: wherever there were cave shelters we find the paintings, the paints ingeniously manufactured out of plant and mineral components. Also carved stone lamps with wicks, to light the dark. The artists used crevices and undulations of the cave walls to paint in three dimensions the living and dynamic images of the natural world around them, that by which they survived, all the time in wonder and admiration.

Because the tools and the fossils of this people begin to show up, first in Russia and in Eastern Europe, c. 45 ka BP doesn't mean that this is the sudden "creationist" origin of the Cro-Magnons, as Goldschmidt once described. Sudden appearances as these were described as "hopeful monster."[7] As with the mammals, the sudden appearance in the fossil record of the Cro-Magnons probably signifies more of a selective and adaptive tipping point in their demographic expansion. We do not know the origin of the Boskopoids' as yet unexplained balloon-like cranial expansion, which seemingly reshaped their lifestyle. Before their appearance, the Capoid fossil types from c. 100–70 ka BP, as with the Caucasoid Neanderthals, reveal expanding erectine morphologies. It is not impossible that prototype Cro-Magnon wanderers penetrated into Africa. We find unexplained Cro-Magnon-type tools deep in the jungles of west Africa, dated hypothetically to c. 90 ka BP.

More concretely we do find a number of fossil skulls that both puzzle and suggest. They are the Skhul 5 and Qafzeh 6 exemplars from today's Israel, both dated to the 90–75 ka BP time frame. This dating is well before the dating of the Amud fossil, c. 40 ka BP, from the same general area, a six-foot Neanderthal giant. Skhul and Qafzeh don't fit because they have expanded Cro-Magnon-like skulls with many Neanderthal characteristics and thicknesses. Further, the tools found with Skhul and Qafzeh are Mousterian, i.e., Neanderthal.[8]

Over 50 ka later in Central Europe, we have the discovered Mladek and Predmost skulls from Bohemia, c. 30 ka BP, very similar to Qafzeh and Skhul in morphology. But now these humans were surrounded by an Aurignacian tool kit, orthodox Cro-Magnon. A few scientists hypothesize a Neanderthal transition into *Homo sapiens sapiens*.[9] Hybridized exemplars have been found in Spain and Portugal at the c. 24 ka BP level. DNA of the Neanderthals has been analyzed to argue that there is no linear connection between the two races/species, i.e., Cro-Magnon and Neanderthal. Rather, both the Skhul/Qafzeh exemplars hint that the Cro-Magnons may here too have been wandering about and spreading their genes in small amounts before their breakout, c. 45 ka BP.[10]

The Mladek/Predmost exemplars could reveal that functional hybridized Neanderthal/Cro-Magnons could have existed within the Cro-Magnon cultural environment.[11] After all, in a line of animals in which brain size and complexity had been dominant for tens of millions of years, this orthoselective (selection in a straight line) trend would make the genes of the more advanced forms of *Homo* highly dominant in the offspring, even given the morphological retention of other ancient physical structures. These retentions have existed into modern times.

What then would be the best estimate for the origins of *Homo sapiens sapiens*, i.e., Cro-Magnon? Further, under what circumstances can we understand the coming into being of this unique human type? Clearly this was an outlander type, not arising in Africa, given both its racial coloration, plus its exhibition of some Neanderthal-like racial characteristics different from humans then living in other geographies. Note that the Mongoloids, even in their seeming northern Beijing origins and geographical concentration, still have a darker coloration than their European brethren.[12] And they moved from Africa at least 1.5 mya. Also the modern Capoids, having roamed throughout Africa, retain a coloration not too different from their Mongoloid cousins. Hair differences between these two groups could be climate adaptive, but why not sharper skin-color differences after all this time? In sum, it is extremely doubtful that the hair and skin colorations of the Europeans could have been formed within the time frame of the "out-of-Africa–modern humans" claimants.

An estimate in the 300–200 ka BP range sounds reasonable enough for the various adaptive skills of these people to have become operative alongside the clearly radical physical/structural changes taking place within the clade. It took time to put into play the subsequent tangible adaptive and selective dynamics. So too, we must hypothesize a period of great selective stress (the Ice Ages of the Pleistocene, from 1.9 mya), during which the formation of highly corticalized deviants in the ancestral Eurasian stock, resident from at least 800 ka BP, would have utilized these features for reproductive advantage. Indeed, their gracilized profiles argue for a climate not long-term frigid so as to put these delicate-boned humans under selective stress.

The guess is that the Caucasus might have been an advantageous environment for a bleached but not cold-adapting group of human beings to survive, and then prosper in their search for ever more beneficent environments. Recall that erectine humans are dated back to 1.8 mya in Dmanisi, Georgia. Earlier humans are also hinted at in this area.[13] We must consider that over the c. 35 ka in which Cro-Magnon prospered in Europe, there were many periods of extreme chill, the Magdalenian (Würm) glaciation climax 16–12 ka BP, especially. But by then they had perfected their hunting practices, knew they had to survive defensively in the cold, and were already in the process of domesticating horses, cattle, and reindeer.[14]

## Genetic Bottleneck

The research of Allan Wilson as to the origin of modern humans, that small set of humans he hypothesizes to have participated in the "genetic bottleneck," who comprised the innovative out-of-Africa moderns, has now been incorporated and is in general use by scientists as part of the new information provided in mtDNA research. The empirical paleontological difficulties of Wilson's theory, however, have produced a number of counter models more in tune with the factual physical evidence.

The current estimates of the originating population that spread its genes around the world vary in a time frame of origin from 400 ka BP to 70 ka BP.[15] A concurring view of the bottleneck problem is given by Tishkoff.[16] These scholars view the separation of the races (subspecies of humanity) as taking place at least 100 ka ago, with a surge in population taking place from this original breeding population that varied from 1,000 to 10,000 breeding individuals, some 30 ka later.[17]

Clearly, the attempt to use current mtDNA data to construct a hypothetical scenario for the origin of these modern populations throughout the world is a task that often stretches empirical credulity. The interesting point that Rogers and Jorde make is that, given that the mtDNA *diversity* evidence holds up, a point of current contention, as compared to all the other populations of the world taken together, "it would not follow that Africa is the point of origin."[18]

In another critique of the "African Eve" scenario of A. Wilson (University of California, Berkeley) et al., especially their sampling of only 147 individuals, University of Geneva researchers L. Excoffier and A. Langaney offered a human mitochondrial analysis of 1,064 individuals. They viewed the Berkeley group as having made serious "topological errors," undermining their "out-of-Africa Eve" thesis. Instead the Swiss researchers offer a perspective of a molecular diversity in modern humans that has to go back at least 400 ka. Most important, their genetic tree model of origination is that the Caucasoids "could be closest to an ancestral population from which all other continental groups would have diverged." Harris and Hey's recent DNA research puts the African/non-African separation to at least 220 ka BP, " ... suggesting the transformation to modern humans occurred in a subdivided population."[19]

A. Torroni and his group concurred with this view of the origination of the mtDNA sequences in present-day Caucasoids. Their date for the Caucasoid origins lies in the 100 ka–80 ka BP range, but they propose that the mtDNA profile is unique in its origins, pointing only to this one particular human subspecies.[20]

> Klein:
> Early modern peoples everywhere tend to be most like the historic inhabitants of the same region. This is clear above all for Europe, where the variability in early modern (Upper Paleolithic) cranial form is completely encompassed by the variability in living Europeans and where early modern people are set off only by a tendency toward greater robusticity.[21]

Martin Richards and his international group based at Oxford University see a complete continuity in the Caucasoid populations of Europe from the Upper Paleolithic to the Neolithic agricultural period from at least 35 ka BP to the Holocene, c. 8 ka BP and beyond. From this it is clear that a genetic bottleneck based somewhere in Eurasia from which the modern genes of *Homo sapiens sapiens* have spread throughout the world along with population expansion is well within probability.[22]

The archaeological evidence in this case seems to buttress the genetic data. The Upper Paleolithic Cro-Magnon peoples were the modernists of the late Pleistocene. There were no other contemporary "competitors" for this appellation anywhere else in the world, including Africa. In terms of morphology, their behavioral profile, the culture that seemed to flow biologically from this morphology, these are the peoples whose very unique origins in the still-hypothetical bottleneck of origin constitute the long-sought-after human source for an incubating "Garden of Eden."[23]

Adding to this surge of evidence for a genetic bottleneck of originating Caucasoid-Cro-Magnons from c. 400 ka BP to 100 ka BP, is the work on linguistic affinities contributed by L. L. Cavalli-Sforza and his group.[24] Their genetic-linguistic tree confirms the closeness of origins of the European and central Asian languages and that African and southeast Asian languages are outliers.[25]

## Understanding the Human Revolution

How can we explain the revolutionary morphology that produced a creature with a brain and behavior so different from its contemporaries? This brain/behavioral revolution has led to deadly evolutionary consequences.

The most important hint as to the circumstances surrounding the origin of modern humans, the Cro-Magnons, and their ultimate widely dispersed genetic progeny, as hinted at by the presumed genetic bottleneck thought to have existed some 200 ka–100 ka BP, lies in their unique morphology. The neighboring Neanderthals clearly reflect a not-too-revolutionary expansion on the prototypical *Homo erectus* pattern. Their special northerly hunting robusticity is added to a large endocranial capacity, along with highly specialized skull and facial structures.[26]

Cro-Magnon, by contrast, is a revolutionary "sport," unprecedented in human evolutionary history. The vertically oriented skull, on which a towering cortical mass is delicately balanced, points to a radical evolutionary restructuring. Today the term "heterochrony" is used to signify alterations in the developmental processes of a line of creatures during the ontogenetic development of the individual. The great debate now taking place is not whether or not truly modern human beings have been subject to radical heterochronic genetic processes, but the actual nature of these processes.[27]

Paedomorphosis defines the slowing down of developmental timetables so as to retain the juvenile characteristics of earlier forms (primates), thus the retention in the sexually mature creature of the infantile characteristics of the ancestral type, "neoteny."[28] The other view involves "sequential organizational hypermorphosis," late cessation of development leading to peramorphosis, the extension of development, as in a brain continuing to grow beyond the parameters of the ancestral type.

The classic work of Gavin de Beer in elaborating on the previous work of researchers, Bolk, Portmann, Griffiths, Gregory, etc., to create a synthetic evolutionary description of modern humans in comparison both with their ape as well as earlier human progenitors, first resulted in the acceptance of the view that *Homo sapiens sapiens* has been subject to radical heterochronic or "rate gene" alterations in development, productive of its radical cranial and post-cranial morphology.[29] It is this radical "rate gene" (heterochronic) reconstruction that is now postulated to be the biological source of the explosive corticalization of human behavior.

Paedomorphic elements in the creation of modern humans are: hairlessness, light-colored skin, slow developmental closing of the sutures of the skull over the brain, epicanthic fold over the Mongoloid and Capoid eye.[30] Most significant in humans is the adult retention of the embryonic mammal flexion curve in the spinal cord, in its connecting of the cranium and post-cranial morphology. In this new evolutionary arrangement the human skull sits directly, at a 90-degree angle, on the spinal cord. In dogs and other mammals, including the chimpanzee, it is positioned toward the rear.[31]

Modern humans are born after roughly the same length of gestation, consonant with the comparative adult size of other primates. They are born in a state that Gould calls, after Adolf Portmann, secondary altricality. At birth, humans are relatively undeveloped and helpless, but with a real average weight of 3,300 grams as compared to their expected relative gestational primate weight of 2,200 grams. On the other hand, humans achieve the at-birth developmental state of modern apes much later in ontogeny, and only at age 21 months.[32] Schultz has noted that only in humans are the long limb bones and digits entirely cartilaginous at birth, unlike all other primates.[33]

McKinney and McNamara, in a comprehensive examination of the evolutionary phenomenon of heterochrony, have argued that previous writings on the impact of paedomorphosis and neoteny on the unique evolution of modern humans are largely in error. Instead they propose that the dominant feature in modern humans that distinguishes them from early hominids and primate ancestors in general, is the process called hypermorphosis.

Instead of the slowing down of developmental processes in humans, it is rather the steady elongation or delay in the time spent during ontogeny in each stage of development that is critical. What they call "peramorphosis," the extension of development beyond the adult stages of the ancestral form, is considered to be the dominant factor that explains the unique position of *Homo* within the primate clade.[34]

Supporting this perspective from the standpoint of developmental genetics is the writing of Raff and Deacon. They argue for the postnatal development of the human brain as being crucial. Not mere increase in size here, but significant structural realignment from the traditional primate plan. This extension in time for the development of ever-larger brain size is naturally the key element that allows for the unique behavioral restructuring of the hominid clade as represented in *Homo sapiens sapiens*.

> Humans show faster brain growth but delayed mental development ... this does not mean that we have not gone through the same general stages of the ancestral or ape pattern. We have only delayed them, ... not permanently "arrested" [them] as would be the case in paedomorphosis ... Human behavior shows *sequential organizational hypermorphosis*.[35]

One explanatory hurdle that the theory of human hypermorphosis has to face in explaining the unique morphology of *Homo sapiens sapiens* is the fact that the elongation of the developmental stages of maturity would ordinarily be thought to produce the great bony super-orbital tori, brow ridges, and other robust exemplifications of late-stage elongation and emphasis. McKinney and McNamara, for example, use the Irish elk as "a classic example of hypermorphosis," in which allometric growth, extended ontogenetically, produced those great if ultimately weakening antler protuberances.[36]

In contrast to the Neanderthals and other borderline *sapiens*, especially exemplified in the late, very large and "bony" *Paranthropus*, Australopithecines, modern humans are very gracile and childlike in morphology—notably the delicacy of bone structure, almost as if, in certain important physical dimensions, their growth period was truncated.

## Out of the Darkness

Covert evolution is the term often used to describe the sudden appearance of creatures seemingly successfully preadapted to a new set of ecological and environmental circumstances. These forms often bring with them tangible evidence of the workings of the heterochronic process. In an earlier time frame they probably were maladapted "hangers on" at the edge, while more successful members of their clade prospered and multiplied.

The explanation must be directed to the "outlier" effect, in which one particular variant in a line of animals that contains a measure of structural and behavioral variability is subject to strong selective pressures.[37] Those particular members (outliers) that carry with them a genetic heritage of rate gene variability, and a tradition of survival on the periphery of the line, can, with the subsequent and happenstance alteration and mitigation of preexisting and sharp external negative selective pressures, suddenly escape into the bright light of success. The heterochronic results of this earlier covert, unseen evolutionary trend are usually affected by small populations of the variant. This would make it easier for the variant to fit into the new adaptive and selective niche that has opened up for them.

As A. C. Hardy noted, this process of being a marginalized variant, often on the edge of extinction, can concomitantly carry with it a lack of the specialized adaptive grooving characteristic of opportunistic, dominant, and successful forms of the clade in question. Escape from specialization, covert or hidden evolution, necessitates that certain negative external conditions be lifted from the pressured variants, in order for there to be a second chance for adaptive dominance. How the human evolutionary scene factually fits into this model has yet to be determined. Yet it is clear that the great climatic variation of the Pleistocene had to have had a variety of adaptive impacts on existing human lines.[38]

When one considers that human culture, and behind it human behavior, does not reveal clear-cut primate adaptive and selective specializations, the conclusions of McKinney and McNamara are important.[39] They view evolution as being shaped, to a great extent, by two "non-Darwinian" processes, i.e., not sharply influenced by external or internal selective conditions. One is the random "internal-developmental" genetic trajectory of early-established metazoan body plans—*orthoselection*. The second is random, catastrophic external selection, which has in the long extensions of evolutionary time eliminated so many earlier phyla and cleared the way for more successful, often hidden, but "luckier" lines.

"Luck" throughout the evolutionary process is what the sociobiologist Edward Wilson assigns as the major factor behind the evolutionary extrapolation of the hominids and *Homo sapiens sapiens*.[40] But of course, "luck" has no explanatory scientific meaning. Science looks for causes and determinative and concrete structures and events that can explain and further the ongoing search for specific causal factors that will clarify the *why* of things that happen in the way they do.

## Notes

1. Hublin, J. (1993). Recent human evolution in northwestern Africa. In C. B. Stringer, M. Aitken, P. A. Mellard, & P. Mellars (Eds.), *The origin of modern humans and the impact of chronometric dating* (pp. 118–131). Princeton, NJ: Princeton University Press.
2. Smith, F. (1993). Models and realities in modern human origins. In Stringer, Aitkin, Mellard & Methers, *op. cit.*
3. The existence of the Capoid epicanthic fold that shields the inside corner of the eye, presumably in the Mongoloids from the cold because of the layer of fat that this fold contains, or the glare of the sun for the Capoids, is another morphological element that relates the two-widely separated peoples. See Stringer, C. B., & Gamble, C. (1993). *In search of the neanderthals: Solving the puzzle of human origins* (pp. 138–139). London: Thames & Hudson.
4. Lynch, G., & Granger, R. (2008). *Big brain*. New York, NY: Palgrave Macmillan.
5. Tishkoff, S., Gonder, M. K., Henn, B. M., Mortensen, H., Knight, A., Gignoux, C., ... Mountain, J. L. (2007). History of click speaking populations of Africa inferred from mtDNA and Y chromosome genetic variation. *Molecular Biology and Evolution*, 24(10), 2180–2195.
6. Klein, R. (1989). *The human career* (p. 349). Chicago, IL: University of Chicago Press; Fagan, B. (2010). *Cro-Magnon*. New York, NY: Bloomsbury.
7. Goldschmidt, R. (1940). *The material basis of evolution*. New Haven, CT: Yale University Press.
8. Tattersall, I. (1995). *The last neanderthal* (p. 116). New York, NY: Macmillan; Quintyn, C. (2006). *The morphometric affinities of the Qafzeh and Skhul hominans* [Kindle edition].
9. Gambier, D. (1989). Fossil hominids from the early upper Paleolithic (Aurignacian) of France. In P. Mellars & C. Stringer (Eds.), *The human revolution* (pp. 194–211). Princeton, NJ: Princeton University Press.
10. see: Trinkaus, E., & Zilhao, J. (2000). *PNAS*; Quintyn 2006, *op. cit.*
11. Svoboda, A. (2008). The upper Pleistocene burial area of Predmost. *Journal of Human Evolution*, 54, 15–33.
12. Norton, H. et al. (2007). Gametic evidence of the convergent evolution of the very light skin of northern Eur-Asians and some east Asians. *Molecular Biological Evolution*, 24, 710–722.
13. Gabunia, L., Vekua, A., Lordkipanidze, D., Swisher C. C. III, Ferring, R., Justus, A., ... Mouskhelishvili, A. (2000, May 12). Earliest Pleistocene hominid cranial remains from Dmanisi. *Science*, 288, 1019–1025; Conner, S. (2009, September 9). A skull that rewrites the history of man. *The Independent*. Retrieved from http://www.independent.co.uk/news/science/a-skull-that-rewrites-the-history-of-man-1783861.html
14. Rogers, A. R., & Jorde, L. B. (1995, February). Genetic evidence on modern human origins. *Human Biology*, 67(1), 1–36; Torroni, A., Lott, M. T., Cabell, M. F., Chen, Y. S., Lavergne, L., & Wallace, D. C. (1994). mtDNA and the origin of the Caucasians: Identification of ancient Caucasian-specific haplogroups, one of which is prone to a recurrent

somatic duplication in the D-loop region. *The American Journal of Human Genetics, 55,* 760–766.
15. Mountain, J. L., & Cavalli-Sforza, L. L. (1993). Evolution of modern humans: Evidence from nuclear DNA polymorphosis. In Aitken, Stringer, & Mellars, *op. cit.*, pp. 60–83; Kaiser, M., & Shevoroshkin, V. (1988). Nostratic. *Annual Review of Anthropology, 17,* 309–329.
16. Tishkoff, S. et al. (1996, March 8). *Science*, and as reported in *The New York Times*, 3/8/96; Takahata, N., Satta, Y., & Klein, J. (1995). Divergence time and population size in the lineage leading to modern humans. *Theoretical and Population Biology, 48,* 198–221, quoted in Gibbons, A. (1995, January 6). The mystery of humanity's missing mutations. *Science, 267,* 35–36; Smith, J. M., et al. (1993, October 1). *Science*, 27; see Ch. 23, "Modern Humans: African Origins."
17. Masatoshi, N. (2005, May 1). Bottlenecks, genetic polymorphism and speciation. *Genetics, 170,* 1–4.
18. Rogers & Jorde 1995, *op. cit.*, p. 23.
19. Excoffier, L., & Langaney, A. (1989). Origin and differentiation of human mitochondrial DNA. *American Journal of Human Genetics, 4,* 73–85, cited in Brown, M. (1990). *The search for Eve* (pp. 278–279). New York, NY: Harper & Row; Harris, E. E., & Hey, J. (1999, March 6). X Chromosome evidence for ancient human histories. *PNAS, 96*(6), 3320–3324.
20. Torroni, Lott, Cabell, Chen, Lavergne, & Wallace 1994, *op. cit.*
21. Klein 1989, *op. cit.*, p. 351; see also Howells, W. W. (1973). Cranial variation in man: A study by multivariate analysis. *Paper of the Peabody Museum of Archaeology and Enthnology, 67,* 1–259; Howells, W. W. (1973). *The evolution of the genus "Homo."* Reading, MA: Addison-Wesley.
22. Torroni, Lott, Cabell, Chen, Lavergne, & Wallace 1994, *op. cit.*
23. Roach, J. (2002, July 4). Skull fossil challenges out-of-Africa theory. *National Geographic News.* Retrieved http://news.nationalgeographic.com/news/2002/07/0703_020704_georgianskull.html
24. Cavalli-Sforza, L. L., Piazza, A., Menozzi, P., & Mountain, J. L. (1988, August). Reconstruction of human evolution. *PNAS, 85,* 6002–6006, esp. 6002; Cavalli-Sforza, L. L., Minch, E., & Mountain, J. L. (1992). Coevolution of genes and language revisited. *PNAS, 89,* 5620–5624; Kaiser & Sheveroshkin 1988, *op. cit.*
25. Cavalli-Sforza, Piazza, Menozzi, & Mountain 1988, *op. cit.*; Cavalli-Sforza, L. L., Menozzi, P., & Piazza, A. (1994). *History and geography of human genes.* Princeton, NJ: Princeton University Press; Mountain & Cavalli-Sforza 1993, *op. cit.*; Kaiser & Sheveroshkin 1988, *op. cit.*
26. Hawks, J., Hunley, K., Lee, S-H, & Wolpoff, M. (2000). Population bottlenecks and Pleistocene human evolution. *Molecular Biology and Evolution, 17,* 2–22.
27. Oppenheimer, S. (2003). *The real Eve.* New York, NY: Carroll & Graf.
28. Abzhanov, A., Bhullar, B. A., & Norell, M. (2012, May 29). *Nature.* These researchers note the paedomorphic elements in the transition from dinosaur to birds in that the skull shape of adult birds is similar to that of young dinosaurs.

29. de Beer, G. (1958). *Embryos and ancestors* (3rd ed.). Oxford: Clarendon; Bolk, L. (1926). *Das Problem der Menschenwerdung*. Jena: Fischer; Stringer & Gamble 1993, *op. cit.*; Brues, A. (1977). *People and races* (pp. 115–117). New York, NY: Macmillan.
30. Itzkoff, S. W. (1983). *The form of man* (pp. 16, 57, 119, 129–131); New York, NY: Lang; Itzkoff 1983, *op. cit.*, diagram, p. 130, from Bolk 1926, *op. cit.*; Portmann, A. (1941). Die Tragzeiten der Primaten und die Dauer der Schwangerschaft beim Menschen: Ein Problem der Vergleichen Biologie. *Revue suisse de zoologie*, 48, 511–518, 516; Gould, S. J. (1977). *Ontogeny and phylogeny* (p. 369). Cambridge, MA: Harvard University Press.
31. Schultz, A. H. (1926). Fetal growth of man and other primates. *Quarterly Review of Biology*, 1(4), 465–521.
32. Portmann 1941, *op. cit.*, p. 312.
33. Schultz 1926, *op. cit.*
34. McKinney, M., & McNamara, K. J. (1991). *Heterochrony: The evolution of ontogeny* (esp. pp. 291–326). New York, NY: Plenum; also, Purves, D. (1988). *Body and brain*. Cambridge, MA: Harvard University Press; Shea, B. T. (1988). Heterochrony in Primates. In M. McKinney (Ed.), *Heterochrony in evolution: A multidisciplinary approach* (pp. 237–266). New York, NY: Plenum; Raff, R. A. (1996). *The shape of life: Genes, development, and the evolution of animal form*. Chicago, IL: University of Chicago Press; Deacon, T. W. (1997). What makes the human brain different? *Annual Review of Anthropology*, 26, 337–357.
35. Raff 1996, *op. cit.*; Deacon 1997, *op. cit.*
36. McKinney & McNamara 1991, *op. cit.*, p. 227.
37. Mayr, E. (1991). *One long argument: Charles Darwin and the genesis of modern evolutionary thought* (pp. 141–164). Cambridge, MA: Harvard University Press.
38. Hardy, A. C. (1954). Escape from specialization. In J. Huxley, A. C. Hardy, & E. B. Ford (Eds.), *Evolution as a process* (p. 122). London: Allen and Unwin.
39. McKinney & McNamara 1991, *op. cit.*, pp. 338–339; see also Waddington, C. H. (1957). *The strategy of the genes*. London: Allen & Unwin; Itzkoff 1989, *op. cit.*, Ch. 5, "Selection and Survival."
40. Wilson, E. (2012). *The social conquest of Earth* (pp. 22, 45). New York, NY: Liveright.

# PART II—EVOLUTIONARY OUTCOMES

# · 7 ·

# *HOMO SAPIENS SAPIENS:* A UNIQUE ANIMAL INTELLIGENCE

… [T]wo subspecies of the same species do not occur in the same geographic area. … To imagine one species of man living together on equal terms for long with another subspecies is but wishful thinking and leads only to disaster and oblivion for one or the other.[1]

## Orthoselection

For over a billion years nature's impersonal principles have given selective advantage to a creature equipped with the neurology to rapidly adapt to a changed environment. The vertebrate brain and its capacity to receive and react to external sensory stimuli, thence to organize these stimuli and respond behaviorally, has been a great success. Natural selection also built into the body plan of the vertebrates a genetic restraint to slow down responses, allow for life rhythms in fairly placid environments, and structure the survival responses to a fairly restricted range of spontaneous commands—instinct.

At the same time, nature selectively gave the okay for a variety of animal types more or less equipped with the same genetically rooted instinctual patterns, i.e., species/races to exist as potential dissidents at the periphery. Thus, what is taxonomically a species or even a genus was found to maintain itself in the adaptive and selective play over hundreds of millions of years. This taxonomically recorded flexibility, genetic and thus structural and behavioral variability, did not inhibit interbreeding and thence successful rearing of the young. It did allow for both genetic and behavioral adaptations, positive phenotypic selection, in the course of the inevitable changes in the environment with which nature constantly provokes.

Thus in the mammals we find long-distance migratory patterns to be supported genetically in the successful interbreeding of mammal wanderers at the edges of the clade. They may happen to meet after many, many generations of apartness, and yet be able to interbreed, form new races, potentially species and genera. In human evolution the ever-greater viability of a larger brain, and its alerting sensory receptors in a head held high, was helped by the erectness given by bipedality. The ability to adapt to a changing environment was here genetically supported. The world was in ever-dynamic alteration—climate, geology, animal rivals, food source changes, etc.—so that a brainy behavioral generalist could learn to function in a variety of environments even within one generation. Here again, we note the ancient power of the vertebrate brain to allow for changes in behavior within the generation, not needing the occasional and often "too late" mutation that might have gotten a line of animals out of their selective hole.

The brain was growing orthoselectively; mutations that had been successful adaptively and selectively earlier in time were reoccurring with regularity, our primate biochemistry here having its own inner time clock, and allowing for a great variety of human forms to coexist. Finally under conditions of significant Pleistocene duress a true outlier form, having unique, probably earlier-suppressed genetic potential, appeared and survived. What once was a sport at the edge of the human clade now became an exemplar of a new set of dynamic genetic alterations.

The words are: paedomorphosis, neoteny, heterochronic development, all relevant to the creation of *Homo sapiens sapiens*, Cro-Magnon.

*In retrospect, Homo sapiens sapiens represents a major taxonomic revolution in the history of life on earth.*

The process by which Cro-Magnon solidified its social/behavioral interactions on the fields of Eurasia probably took many thousands of generations, first to filter out of its breeding pool the less cerebral members. Eventually, assortative mating solidified their ethnic perceptions of life and they wandered forth in search of sustenance. It was the beginning of a whole new biological game on planet earth.

## A Brain for Survival?

In truth this competitive sport of life-survival on earth is concentrated on the roulette wheel of reproduction and the bringing of the young to their own reproductive maturity. Plants are casual about this act, animals increasingly involved and caring. Yet, it is the genetics of instinct that has always carved out the pathways of this universal obligation. And it is usually clear, at least to the observant human mind, what the mechanics and specificities are of the specified genetically controlled behaviors.

We must ask of modern humans: first the Cro-Magnons, what are the critical elements of our behavior that can be seen as key to the survival rhythms of human society in the upbringing of the young to sexual maturity?

Is it the weapons of the hunt, the spear, the bow and arrow, the blade knives to cut? But what about the art, the overly delicate blades made out of stone, bone, ivory, some hardly instrumental for survival? Then we note the chronometric notations, the search *to know* on the various material artifacts, the hand-held carved Venuses denoting luxuriant love and sex, the cave paintings revealing an awe for animal life, the experiments in their search for and manufacture of vegetative and mineral colors to paint, the imaginative mind seeing in every undulating cave wall, the reflection of an animal form and livingness?

What adaptive survival instincts were being put into play by such behaviors? A number of years ago the geneticist Theodosius Dobzhansky attempted to explain this conundrum. His solution was to posit a biologically selective advantage for those individuals with artistic and musical talents, perhaps taking his inspiration from J. S. Bach's two wives and twenty children.[2]

This human behavioral dilemma has puzzled countless sociobiologists, most of them forced to concoct fantastic selectionist scenarios to create supposed reproductive advantages out of the complex fabric of human cultural expression, what Richard Lewontin and Ernst Mayr have called the adaptationist fallacy.[3] Countless generations of behaviorist psychologists and semanticists well before the sociobiologists have attempted to reconcile what has been the perverse delight of metaphysical philosophers—glorying in the ideational character of human thought—with the reality that we are biological creatures, subject to the same laws and principles that explain the evolution and behavior of other life forms. What gives?

Always, only a tentative and hypothetical reply. The explosive reconstruction of the brain in *Homo sapiens sapiens* completed the gradual severing of human behavior with that ancient and supremely successful sign/signal system that had defined animal life over vast spans of time. Successful that is, until *Homo sapiens sapiens* appeared on the scene.

Now, as twentieth-century philosopher Ernst Cassirer emphasized in his writings, a new system, the sign/symbol system of thought has neutralized the traditional biological imperatives of vertebrate behavior.[4]

It is probably incorrect to assume that the symbol/cultural system by which humans now organize their behavior was uniquely created in *Homo sapiens sapiens*. No doubt the Neanderthals operated on the basis of an effective cultural web of meaning/behavior, if not the pulsating cognitive dynamics of the Cro-Magnids. There were probably no predefined iconic/instinctual behavioral sureties rigidly determined by the Neanderthal genes, but rather, a vague sense of tradition and necessity by which an inchoately aware mind coped with the here-and-now realities that must be faced. They made tools. They may even have had a form of language use.

Yes, the Neanderthals may have had (this is controversial today) only a rudimentary language morphology, Broca's, Wernicke's areas, and the articulatory (larynx/pharynx) for the vowel/consonant mix that undergirds speech in most contemporary humans. In *Homo sapiens sapiens*, human language has become the great specialization function underlying our mental ability to bring together vast experiential sensory material into a structure of meaning out of which we act to ensure the future. But we do use language for love, poetry, drama, and song merely to understand and express without the automatic desire to act instrumentally on the basis of our verbal proclivities.

Consider the classical "primitive" mind's response to nature's vagaries—magic. The ritual dance around fire; fearful totems and taboos of superstition. Deep within such emotional resonances there lies an implicit substrate of instrumental action. Here are symbolized fixed cultural traditions hardly changed by external events over the centuries and millennia. As long as the externalities of life support the symbolics, magic, totemism, etc., the culture and the participants may survive. Then, consider the modern scientific and inquiring mind's approach to these same phenomena—hypothetical, experimental, always in search of the flaws in the assumed structures of meaning.

The former symbolic system leads to embeddedness and social stagnancy over time. The latter inexorably lurches toward instrumental attempts to understand and control nature's and humanity's power. Both human symbolic traditions reflect the breadth of possibilities in the sign/symbol system of human intelligence. The fundamental question, even beyond this separation in the human use of symbols that create cultural systems, is: How far back in human evolution did those first inchoate symbolic behaviors, most probably built out of our linguistic utterances, slip the noose of instinctual directiveness?

## Sociobiological Controversy

As far as we can judge, the human symbol system of behavior operates relatively autochthonously, far beyond any clearly practical selective envisionments, as comparatively rooted in traditional animal genetics. As noted earlier, sociobiologists, especially those whose model uses the theme of "inclusive fitness," have pointed to many mammalian and primate reminiscences in much of human behavior, from the protection and favoritism of the male for his own blood children, to a wide variety of other social/kin affinities that seem to derive from deeper levels of genetic consanguinity, "the selfish gene."

There can be no doubt that the work of evolution operates on the gene level, and indeed at the level of the individual carrier, and not the so-called "eusocial" group as Edward O. Wilson had recently written of in an apparent attempt to further reconcile his views with orthodox liberal sociological thinking.[5] We must agree with Richard Dawkins's critique of Edward Wilson, representing the major group of theoreticians who have lined up against Wilson's evolving views seen in his most recent book, *The Conquest of Earth*.[6] Dawkins:

> Inclusive fitness was coined as a mathematical device to allow us to keep treating the individual organism ("vehicle") as the level of agency, when we could equivalently have switched to the gene ("replicator"). You can say that natural selection maximizes individual inclusive fitness, or that it maximizes gene survival. The two are equivalent by definition. ... Gene survival is what ultimately counts in natural selection, and the world becomes full of genes that are good at surviving. But they do it vicariously, by embryologically programming "phenotypes": programming the development of individual bodies, their brains, limbs and sense organs, in such a way as to maximize their own survival. Genes program the embryonic development of their vehicles, then ride inside them to share their fate and, if successful, get passed onto future generations.[7]

And while natural selection must be seen in the operational dynamics of the singular gene or complex undergoing natural selection, something unique has happened in hominid evolution. The growth of the human cortex and its production of cultural symbols now operates selectively, as a complex of genes underlying the psychometric g factor in abstract intelligence, but still inside a cultural web of existing meanings, and thus in a very indirect manner, selectively.

Unlike other mammals, "free will" now allowed for by the sapient brain gives individuals and societies much room to violate these blood allegiances, often with terrible and tragic consequences. In contrast, no animal can step back from the regulations imposed by the genes. As the psychologist Edward Thorndike once noted, in contrast to *Homo sapiens sapiens*, all animals must say "yes" to their instinctual mandates.

## A Mind Divided

The brain that dissolved the ancient instinctual directivity of behavior, in mammals a unity of emotional affect and practical intentionalities, was precipitated by our now vast cortical mantle soaring above our gracile brows. And though the nature and extent of this vast swelling of silent brain tissue is clearly definitive of what we humans now are, a residue of the past has accompanied this great expansion. The allo-cortex, and the so-called limbic system, the emotional, sensory, and integrative aspects of thinking and feeling, here including the creation of our language capacities, have surged in size and power over our person.

For example, the hippocampus, critical for sensory integration and memory, is four times what it would be in the average primate of current human size. But the growth of the cerebral cortex has expanded beyond comparison with the primate tradition, when considerations of body size and bulk are included.

Out of this brain spewed the multiplicities of symbolic expression in the richness and diversities of meaning that we call "culture." Try to explain the differences in language between peoples, even the ever-changing dynamics of the natural spoken version. Through the symbolic bonds that create unique languages and their cultures, individuals are bound together in social units, ever larger in number and complexity. The seeming necessity for group life to ensure the reproductive success of the minimal band in early humans, as it protected the immature and vulnerable neonate, took on a dynamic living power as greater cortical instrumentalities of objectification and predictive behavior (science/philosophy) brought under the umbrella of ethnicity/language ever-larger numbers of humans into tribes, nations, and civilizations.

This richness of symbolic expression—in religion, the arts, sport, technology, science, philosophy, history, ritual festivity—represents a primal puzzlement about the nature and meaning of culture. The cause lies in our tychistic, unpredictable brain functioning, in terms of the direction and nature of the symbols of meaning that will be produced within any one culture, let alone the full range of human groups across the spectrum of history. Clearly, the resolution to this conundrum of meaning lies in our long-term understanding of the morphological/psychological complexity of the human brain, both intellectually and emotionally. On the macro level we can only observe this public enunciation of our "buzzing-blooming" psycho-morphological intellectual complexity.

The so-called "universals" of culture, examples of which were noted above, testify to a similarity in brain and psychological structures across the palette of human ethnicities and races. These hint at the probability that at a relatively ancient locus in the evolution of the genus *Homo*, basic psychologically expressed sign vectors were already fixed in human brain morphology, and were selectively passed on in the diversity of races and ethnicities that constitutes current *Homo sapiens* forms. The inevitable next question is, what content or grade of symbolic expression is represented in the particular cultural entity that we are involved with? More clearly expressed, what is the measure of cortical and/or limbic activity in a particular social group?

## Thinking Begins

Consider the increasing level of sophisticated symbolic objectivization exhibited by the Cro-Magnids, both in conception and external realization. Take into account the as yet undeveloped technological instrumentalities of these Ice Age peoples, their then-naïve and dawning awareness of their own unsuspected powers. This fact must be acknowledged even in hindsight, considering the relative undeveloped condition of all the other peripheral human groups then extant. These Eurasian Caucasoid ancestors and their descendants are to be the predicted, subsequent, indeed, recent, political and economic dominators.

Alexander Marshack has noted that the many Cro-Magnon-incised bone, flint, and ivory plaques found throughout their Eurasian domains contained more than mere decorative designs.[8] They seemed to denote mnemonic memory markings, attempts to symbolize the chronometric regularities of external events, just as a hunter often makes slashes on the wood of his rifle, the warrior on his spear, to note the number of shots or kills he has made with the weapon. It could be any materials set aside to attempt to understand, place in memory, or significate what is happening "out there," and over time.

> Even when the notational artifacts were engraved in the same style and came from the same site and level, the specific intentional differences between them turned out to be as important in establishing the fact of notation as the similarities due to the common cultural tradition. These data are part of the evidence that what we have is not design patterns or geometric motifs but an open and variable system of notation. The open and variable aspect of the system is found upon every notational slate I have examined, from the Aurignacian to the terminal Magdalenian and into the Mesolithic.
>
> We have evidence of an open, variable system of notation. In general cognitive terms we can say that the "purpose" of these notations was the sequential accumulation of sets, subsets and superordinate sums. They were differentiated by a complex series of visual-kinesthetic and spatio-temporal inputs, recognition and feedbacks ... together these uses imply a sense of recurrence and periodicity as well as a sense of constancy within the open, variable system.[9]

The waxing and waning of the moon, the yearly trajectory of the sun over the hills, the migration of animals, the fish in the river, the regularity of the seasons, the course of the stars and the planets, the pulsation of human and animal life, birth, maturity, death. All of these events now outside the body and subject to analysis, time binding, gave rise to a system of thought within which one's ethnicity, language, psychological consanguity, cousins all, could come together in a survival/belief system, in which hunting, lovemaking, artistic endeavors, craft skills, dance, song, and the patriotisms of battle all created a culture, the symbols being external embodiments of what often lay latent in the new human mind.[10]

## Humans Are Not Materialists

It will not surprise the reader to hear once again that most animals in their current adaptation to the external challenges of survival spend most of their time searching for food and/or physical survival. The adaptationist view of humans, of sociobiologists also, is Darwinian: "the survival of the fittest." The model that they use has to involve for every species, *Homo sapiens* included, a practical materialistic sense that what we do all day, in spite of the cultural *falderal* that appears to obliterate the raw struggle, fits the Darwinian selectionist model and a larger Newtonian conceptual universality.[11]

However, even on the surface of things it does appear that little that mankind is involved with comes close to the traditional vertebrate model. Humans, as *animal symbolicum*, are a game changer in evolutionary history. We are a new kind of vertebrate/mammal/primate, deserving of a special taxonomic mounting. Yet we are animals. Darwinism still applies. Our dominance may only be temporary. Temporary, because we have only been an observable subspecies, *Homo sapiens sapiens*, for some forty-five thousand years. We could turn out to be a nova that will have wreaked unimaginable devastation on the physical as well as the biological world around us, thence to disappear in a conflagration of our own making. We may have already fouled our nest in an irretrievable manner. This subspecies that has come and may be gone over a hundred-thousand-year span of time will yet not have made an impression on the insects and bacteria who will probably inherit the earth after we have flamed out.

Indeed, the absurdity of a materialistic, simplistic Darwinian explanation, let alone the bizarre ideological delusions of the theologians and the sociological creationists, only reinforces the message of the complexity of the problem of the significance of *Homo sapiens sapiens*, stay on earth. Non-survivalistic altruistic behavior, unrelated to reproductive potencies, has been underlined by the reality of humans voluntarily giving up their lives in hunger strikes, monks and other Saint Francis- and Buddha-like ascetics throwing away their wealth and privilege for a life of struggle, labor, self-privation, and complete sexual asceticism. This writer sees no genetic individual advantage in this form of altruism. Think hard to find a clear-cut and universally applicable advantage to the "groups" that support these ascetics. The basic needs of humans for food, shelter, clothing, take on a wide ranging set of "howevers" when one tries to ascertain the general nature of human bio/physical survival requirements and wants.

How far humans could go in sacrificing the emoluments of civilizational comforts and wealth and yet keep activating those creative juices in the arts and communal/ethnic life cannot be reckoned. All the great creative civilizations in our own historical calculus have been built on surplus wealth. Even those working men who paid their few pence for a chance to be intellectually shaken and emotionally moved in a play by Shakespeare at the Globe in late sixteenth-century England lived in a time of surplus wealth. They had the brainpower and a few extra coins taken from their daily food rations that made it necessary for them to feel and appreciate the language and dramatic possibilities of one of the greatest minds in human history.

The revolutionary anger that we hear today, 2016: the formerly well-off, seeing their standards of material life reduced, are angry not because of the absolute reduction in material emoluments, but rather because of the symbolic diminishment of their societal standing. There are also larger factors of social class, political competition, and religious and ethnic issues. The rationales are infinite.

How far down human material existence could fall without wiping out the traditional cultural enhancements that the *Homo sapiens sapiens* mind needs is hard to assess. A society at the verge of starvation due to sudden and cataclysmic circumstances is certainly beyond any need for the symbolics of the arts. But let us take a people living on the thin side of the edge of poverty, hard-scrabble collecting, scavenging. They might yet have want to sing a song of love, to converse, to create verbal images and metaphors, poetry, objectivizing in emotion and mind, their social existence.

Meagerness alone will not deny our cultural humanity. Given even a shadow of the ancient *Homo sapiens sapiens* intelligence, a people might yet retain the brain juices, mustered if only to recall the ancient times of plenty. The art of the Upper Paleolithic had to have been created amidst the constant material struggles that the Cro-Magnons engaged in at the edge of the ice packs.

In general, the place of *Homo sapiens sapiens* in the firmament of evolutionary novelty has to primarily involve this huge cortical excrescence. It can absorb vast amounts of sensory experience, time bind this sensory stimulation (as Alfred Korzybski put it) to be ordered into a structure of predictions, always prelude to instrumental action, but action at a time or place of one's cognitive choosing.[12] Now, how one thinks about this sensory bombardment becomes the key to physical or material survival. But this *how* one thinks about a set of circumstances is also, and at once, enfiladed with a wide input of diverse cognitive and limbic-system urges and passions.

Thinking about the means for physical survival of humans today involves far more than raw physical objects, food, water, shelter, clothing. Now the words are "cuisine," "bottled," "condo," "Saks." A new world of survival closes in on us, the world of thought, intelligence, emotional/conceptual structures.

No longer front and center do we struggle with raw fang and claw. Our survival takes on a new evolutionary character: symbolic dynamics, here involving the creation of the Parthenon and the H-bomb.

## Notes

1. Hall, E., R. & Kelsen, K. (1959). *The mammals of North America*. New York, NY: Ronald Press.
2. Dobzhansky, T. (1962). *Mankind evolving*. New Haven, CT: Yale University Press.
3. Lewontin, R. (1979). Sociobiology as an adaptationist program. *Behavioral Science, 24*, 5–14; Mayr, E. (1983). How to carry out the adaptationist program? *The American Naturalist, 121*, 324–334; Pinker, S. (1997). *How the mind works* (pp. 163–164). New York, NY: Norton.
4. Cassirer, E. (1944). *An essay on man*. New Haven, CT: Yale University Press.
5. Wilson, E. (2012). *The social conquest of Earth*. New York, NY: Liveright.
6. Wilson, E., Nowak, M., & Tarnita, C. (2010). "The evolution of eusociality." *Nature, 466*, 1057–1062; Wilson 2012, *op. cit.* Dawkins, R. (2012, May 12). The descent of Edward Wilson. *Prospect Magazine*. Retrieved from http://www.prospectmagazine.co.uk/magazine/edward-wilson-social-conquest-earth-evolutionary-errors-origin-species/#.Uojp TeL9W-0
7. Dawkins 2012, *op. cit.*
8. Marshack, A. (1972). Cognitive aspects of upper Paleolithic engraving. *Current Anthropology, 13*, 3–4, 445–477, esp. 449; Marshack, A. (1972). *The roots of civilization*. London: Weidenfeld & Nicolson.
9. Marshack 1972, *op cit.*, 457.
10. Robinson, J. (1992). Not counting on Marshack: A reassessment. *Journal of Mediterranean Studies, 2*, 1–16, (a critique); Bahn, P. (Ed.). (2009). *An enquiring mind: Studies in honor of Alexander Marshack*. Oxford: Oxbow Books.
11. See these modest reframings of the sociobiological model: Segerstrale, U. (2000). *Defenders of the truth*. New York, NY: Oxford University Press; Pinker, S. (2002). *The blank slate*. New York, NY: Viking.
12. Korzybski, A. (1941). *Science and sanity*. Lancaster, PA: The Science Press Printing Company.

# · 8 ·

# CIVILIZATION: SYMBOLIC DYNAMICS

## Cultural Relativism?

Why civilization, not culture, as the generic term? Neanderthals seem to have had distinct cultural traditions, tool styles and living structures, probably not too different than the most simple and naïve patterns of undeveloped peoples discovered from the seventeenth to the nineteenth centuries. There is no question that the Cro-Magnons had a geographically wide-ranging nonliterate civilizational tradition—their technology, variety of art forms, the plan of their material existence, living styles, clothing manufactures, jewelry, burial traditions and techniques. Their civilizational reach went from today's Russia to Spain, quite a transnational civilizational tradition, and in slow dynamic evolution: the arts, hunting techniques, lifestyles.

Humans can live in an almost infinite number of cultural configurations, and seemingly with contentment, as long as the external challenges beyond the boundaries of the unit, tribe, band, or nation are steady. That is why cultural anthropologists have trumpeted the glories of "cultural relativism" thumbing their noses at the pretensions, claims, and paeans of the Eurocentric elitists. Ostensibly, there is no intrinsically superior pattern of cultural life.

However, such an analysis disregards the actual realities of the cultural dynamics since the descendants of Cro-Magnon moved into more temperate and inviting climes. One could then argue that a calculus of survivability was now added as the simple tribal structures morphed into civilizational structures. Since the beginning of literate history, these complex national units have been flexing their expanding symbolic muscle. This dynamic clearly reveals the factual erosion of simple nonliterate cultural entities.

The succession of sophisticated complex civilizations has over time revealed in their growing power a contestation over their respective instrumental intellectual powers as symbolized in their control over nature through science and technology. This cultural progression finally overwhelmed the simple folk either by the use of new weaponry or demographic expansion—in the end, colonialism, and for many cultural losers, even slavery.

It may very well be that the ultimate destiny of our current international model of civilization is to be chaos and dissolution, the breakup of mankind into simpler, less complex sets of political, economic, and ethnic units, a long step back from the implicit projections of the past five thousand years. But can we really hypothesize that such surviving political/economic/ethnic units in the centuries beyond our own will be less materialistically effulgent, even as they become even more literate and technologically sophisticated? Here we must again propose the selective and historical heritage of Cro-Magnon brainpower. Further, we argue that the progress of humans, culturally in the widest sense, is determined cognitively as an ongoing civilizational effort to understand and control the physical and moral environment of humans.

The direction of the human clade for the past several million years has been characterized by an ongoing adaptation to the demands of the evolving hominid brain: thinking, planning, organizing, problem solving, testing today's actions by their consequences, and adjusting future behavior accordingly. In the end this brain created a literate platform from which material and intellectual progress can be maintained. So, in an important sense culture is not relative. It is dynamic and, in terms of the message of human evolution, it is unidirectional, ever towards the cognitive, intellectual ordering of human life. But it is not necessarily smooth and without antithetical friction, conflict, or dissolutions. Humans are still finding their way in the understanding of human nature, the human cognitive and emotional brain, and the symbolic products that pour out of this brain.

## Platform for Human Nature

It is a pity that we do not know more about the cultural life of the Cro-Magnons from a now-distant perspective of twelve to fifteen thousand years. Life in Europe became even more puzzling as the ice receded and a continental climate of very cold winters and warm summers set in, the forests returned, and the explosive civilizational exuberance of the Cro-Magnons disappeared into the Mesolithic period, many groups migrating south into the Mediterranean littoral, where new civilizational opportunities were opening up.

The Sumerians in Mesopotamia invented written language in the period 3500–3000 BCE. They were a black-haired Caucasoid people coming south probably from the Iranian plateau and other geographies to the north. Extraordinarily enterprising, they had by 4000 BCE created agricultural communities of mixed farming and herding, draining the swamps and perfecting great irrigation systems at the edge of the Persian Gulf where the two great rivers emptied. They gradually became urban, with craft manufacture and trade, evidently giving an initial push to the distant and evolving Egyptian civilization by the early Pharaonic employment of skilled Sumerian builders and tradesmen.

Early on we find these Sumerians building, decorating, playing games and musical instruments, and creating beautiful things, their architecture imbued with the spirit of the artist as well as the architect. It took time, several thousands of years, for these newcomers down south to learn to perfect the survival institutions of life. But as soon as we sense a modicum of surplus wealth in the build of their towns, the irrigation and religious laws, the regulation of the surpluses of their industries, the sense of their semi-democratic, post Cro-Magnon tribal councils of "big men" (wise elders), there flowed outward the full panoply of human cognitive culture. The limbic system was pouring more and more of its energies through the cortex in achieving this most powerful civilizational impact on the human psyche.

Here and always, in the procession of civilized life there is a recurring theme. Our world of universal symbolic meanings is infused with all the psychological valences of our minds. These valences flow out in sports, religion-myth, philosophy, poetry/drama, song, playing a musical instrument, dance, aggression/war/violence, painting-drawing, sculpting, building-architecture, sexuality (not mere biological reproduction but monogamous love/pornography/prostitution), the politics of power, scientific curiosity-investigation, technology, clothing/style, personal beautification, and trading—capitalist speculation/

gambling. These are only some of the "universals" of culture. In the context of the historic literary civilizations, the thrust is toward the cognitive, the intellectual. Life is transformed into a game; no longer do we observe the inchoate, emotional outpourings of mammalian instinctual survival.

In the earliest civilizations, once the basic economic institutional structures built up beyond subsistence and hard-scrabble survival, the creation of surplus wealth, and the raising up of resources for defense to help ensure the integrity of the ethnic/political entity, the human mind is released to pursue understanding. The building of ziggurats and pyramids, the growth of a teaching class of priests and their writings to rationalize belief and understanding, exemplifies this power that comes of wonder.

Civilizations represent a composite of these psychological valences inherent in the human mind, now raised up into tangible institutional realities. To understand the modal character of a civilization is to observe the center of dynamic involvement. What moves the Egyptian mind or Assyrian creative passions? A civilization exists only as long as it has an inner dynamic of change that reflects the human need for ever-new sets of symbolic commitments to act creatively, to pursue the "new." It can be the excitement of the seasonal flow of the Nile, the passion to build a testament to the hoped-for reality of an afterlife, the pyramids, the temples. It can be the Assyrian passion for war and conquest, along with the building of great libraries to preserve the tablets of their Mesopotamian heritage. The sense humans have of the opportunity to innovate, to explore the as yet unknown, this we call freedom.

Almost any coming together of such cultural universals can become part of the essential brickwork of a viable culture-civilization. The key lies in the existence of institutional symbolic cores of activity that release the creative new, the excitement that comes from putting ourselves on the line. If at all points in the symbolic valences of civilizational life there are created institutional or mental blockades for innovation, short circuits of the freedom to try out the new, a civilization will stagnate and slowly die. If it weakens significantly after a long run, as in Rome, external (barbarian tribes) or internal forces (Christianity) will crack open the hollow shell of institutional decadence and the civilization will shrivel and break up. Historically, it will be the past.

Looking back at five thousand years of literate civilizational life, we observe this perennial push. Highly creative, cognitive cultures/civilizations try to quickly put aside the purely physical disciplines of providing the basic necessities. We just can't be work drudges. We have got to turn life into a symbolic game. The social historian Jan Huizinga termed this drama "man the play animal." From the earliest cultural emanations of the Cro-Magnons, we see the mental creative efforts of these people trying to go beyond the mundane acts of hunting, gathering, and clothing themselves, even while yet embedded in their caves. They distanced their garbage dumps far from their living headquarters, searched into the deepest dark of caves high above the "hometown" to express through flickering wicks of light and paint the artistic visions their minds perceived in the daylight. The ordinary dross of life had to be distanced through these Masonic refuges and Sistine Chapels. When one considers the steady increase in the skill levels of these artists and craftsmen, the mental efforts that went into the act of creation, we have to be persuaded that the esthetic sensibility is in reality a crucial form of our cortical functioning.

Civilizations, however we define them, therefore, are in the larger scheme of things platforms for the cognitive self-actualization of a people sharing the basic cultural unities, language, ethnic heritage, religion, or philosophy. Certainly the uniqueness of the art and literature of a nationality or ethnicity reflects a genetic consanguinity that allows the communal mind and heart to come together. That is why when we begin to analyze the culture/civilization within which we now live, the existence or not of art and communication that rises above the "belly button" tells us much about the nature and character of a nation, a people.

## Civilizational Progress

The locus of dynamic symbolic energy that is deemed civilizational progress can change from time to time. It need not necessarily be technological/scientific change. For many centuries the dynamic of church/Christian guidance became the great overriding theme of European culture. It withered when it ran up against an even more dynamic set of symbolic meanings: science, mercantilism, trade, exploration, secular philosophical thinking/the scientific revolution. To buttress this trend, a new middle class arose, a new economic locus of power and meaning. To finish off the decrepit old (the feudal, agricultural hierarchy, churchly supernaturalism), secular democracy now energized the West.

Similarly, a new philosophical/social dynamic arose with socialist/communist Marxism. For generations it motivated political activity and shaped literature and the arts, all in the name of altering the supposed capitalist free-market culture. Eventually it died, becoming ossified by top-down bureaucratic statist control of every aspect of life. Finally, it committed the genocide of its most talented.

To be realistic about the enormous surge of energy that poured out of Europe starting in the fifteenth and sixteenth centuries, one must speak about high culture, the arts, music, painting, literature, philosophy, and crafts, then technology and industrialism, a demographic avalanche that was precipitated to a great extant by scientific medicine, hygienic practice, sanitation, and potable water. For over two hundred years the Europeans tolerated the dying medieval political structure while they embarked on their passionate modernization in the other symbolic realms of thought and action. Even the Italian popes, their theocracy only at the surface, made Renaissance art glow in anticipation of the new.

Long before the modern era, the Greeks had created the most complete assemblage of dynamic symbolic cores, freeing the human mind to create. From the momentary release of democratic self-governance in a complex urban setting to the creation of the forms of philosophical and scientific thought, these Hellenes taught us what a dynamic civilization can create when its citizens are universally capacitated to express symbolically this overriding panoply of human psychological valences.

We have an exemplar today in 2016 China. The paradox: how to explain the passionate surge for modernity in every area of life, even in the arts, all while the Chinese people, increasingly restive, remain under the ungiving thumb of an authoritarian and corrupt political machine.

Going back in time, for a few decades the Russian/Soviet people created a modern state, a modern war machine, and high technology, all the while knowing that millions of their own were being murdered in Stalinist genocides. Eventually the antithetical symbolics of totalitarian barbarism versus a modest rise in the standards of living of the people in both the Soviet Union and Maoist China required the end of political and cultural totalitarianism, but not yet the elimination of authoritarian controls in both nations.

In both of the above cases, as well as in the post–World War II West, the inner contradictions of institutional structural commitments slowed up the progress of society and caused the eventual collapse of the overriding socialist philosophical modeling of life. What had long existed in their historic cultural traditions in Russia and China, as a living memory of the symbolic valences of life, had now been suppressed under the supposed halcyonic visions of forced redistribution of wealth. Wealth exists as a symbolic/psychological value. Its power lies in its ability to seduce creative energies in individuals and corporations. When the creation of "wealth" is supervised from above, it eventually loses its creative dynamic energy. The spontaneous creation of individual and social meaning is stifled; the generative cognitive juices of living, thinking human beings dry up. Then, disaffection, the renewed withering of a dying cultural/civilizational tradition.

## Failing Models

Lesson to the political leadership: you are leaders because you have gained power by exercising a symbolic model of civilizational life that has brought you peacefully to the fore. In order to maintain the privilege of leadership you ought to very carefully examine the premises, the laws under which you can lead. They should allow for the release of the cognitive powers of the people.

These cognitive powers constitute the mysterious dynamics and needs of the human psyche. Use history; use the experience of the failed societies of our time. Indeed, some recent models that have worked did create peace, at the least a semi-democratic consent of the governed. Even political autocracies can allow for a moment the free flow of imagination and thought in all the various hard and soft institutions of cultural/civilizational life. Political and economic autocracy itself has to eventually shut down the free flow of the imagination elsewhere in the cultural pantheon. Allow for this flow of freedom, even at the risk of sweeping you out of office. At the least, you may not have to flee for your life.

To create a highly cognitive, creative model of civilized life, one needs to score a run. Safe on first is de rigueur. First base in this metaphor requires a culture of highly educable people. Brilliant but naïve types as with the Cro-Magnons will not now make it. The Sumerians changed everything with literacy. The upriver Semitic hicks, epitomized by Sargon, went south to show the world that the smart/naïve can learn and quickly. So too the Hyksos, c. 1600 BCE, came out of the west Asiatic mists to conquer then-sophisticated but already slow-moving and decadent Egypt. This shift in ethnic power gave the north African isolate a moment of creative energy—new innovative genes as well as explorative ideas.

## Failed Civilizations/Nations

Why do civilizations and nations fail? The symbol system of society constitutes the dynamo for evoking the creative new out of our neuronic reservoir. Innovative success can come into being spontaneously. A benevolent accident gifted into the seemingly unfriendly ecology of rock and clay in the Hellenic archipelago. These Indo-European immigrants from the east were descending south only for the warmth. Out of that rock and clay would one day come a critical turning point in the civilizational perspective of the human species.

The surge of the new can also arise as a conscious and historically unprecedented turn in the leadership mentality from a previously reactionary restrictive sense of power. Here we examine the political/economic setting that brought to the papacy control by the aristocratic mercantile families of north Italy. Out of this transformation in the mentality of religious power came a momentary nova of glorious corruption, but elemental creativity, all within a slowly dying institution.

In the earliest civilizational settings it was the new and luxurious river valley ecologies of Sumer and Egypt that gave a great spurt to economic, technological, esthetic, and sociopolitical development. It exploded these peoples onto history. But ideological stagnancy, control by priests or a Pharaonic bureaucracy, suppressed innovation. There was no longer opportunity for the Egyptian mind to recreate their symbolic structure. A people deadened by wars, and religious autocracy, the world bypassed Egypt.

The riches of Mesopotamia, constantly in the eye of ever-new northern wanderers, gave this culture periodic renewals, linguistically and ethnically. Eventually they were undone by the constant bloodletting. The curve downward in creativity could not stand up against Indo-European Persians, nor the Greeks and Romans. Interestingly and eventually, the Romans lost their elemental touch and the reinvigorated Parthians/Sassanians could eventually hold them off. These indigenous powers were able to retake first base, but again war and the killing of elites created ever-new cultural stagnancies. The talent was there, if hidden. Eventually a more vigorous set of symbolic motivators, this time Islam from the desert of Arabia, but only for a short time, reinvented mid-Eastern civilization.

Some would argue that the transfer of civilizational progress from one region to another—one dying, stagnating in religious or ideological rigidification, then obsolescence—is inevitable and salubrious. The "new" arrives vigorous with an innovative symbolic meaning structure. And we can point to such examples from recent human history.

But one wonders. Were this civilizational rigor mortis of belief and idea not accompanied by the suppressive thumb of those gaining material advantage—the purveyors of the ideology, priests, rabbis, mullahs or commissars—would inherent pluralistic symbolic trends naturally percolating within the populace by itself right the listing cultural entity?

Usually the leading intellectuals of the society—in many cases the above mentioned theological purveyors—enlist the sword to help them retain their perks and national security. But there is also a lurking suffocation of innovation in all political forms: kings, queens, dictators, and even modern governmental bureaucracies bribing through redistributionary propaganda to stifle change and maintain their power.

Political power groups will always try to have absorbed within their system of social and legal controls the rituals, regulations, and always the educational system—in sum, the totality of the natural symbolic glue within the society. Modern control of communication also can allow the power elites to maintain a structure of values and privilege that leaves little breathing room symbolically for individual and small community groups. These latter are our modest modern incarnation of the primeval community, the band, the tribe, crucial for creating the social breathing room for a free people, necessary to innovate and renew.

Expanding civilizations, even those with central controls, can work as long as there is an *élan vital* in the symbolic structure of the civilization—such as in ancient Rome, the communist world of the twentieth century. This energy and innovation is usually the precursor condition for the centralization of the dynamic, to give it more national or international potency. Eventually, the centralization of power itself creates the braking element stifling the natural innovative momentum of the free human mind.

The nation/society can no longer move in plural waves of creativity, as did our exemplar civilizations of the small city-states in ancient Sumer, Greece, the Renaissance, and the early/modern European towns. Creativity in the ethnic or national settings of humans can be maintained only in the context of pluralistic institutions that allow for breathing room to initiate new ideas and ways of thinking and living. Human innovation can percolate outward to enfilade the values and actions of adjacent groups. In this way civilizations can grow and renew themselves, create the future.

As in biological evolution, the existence of outlier groups within a biological or civilizational clade—associated groupings—can provide the opportunity for renewal, such that history need not always involve the theme of precipitous risings and bloody declines.

# · 9 ·
# CIVILIZATIONAL DYNAMICS: EXEMPLARS

## Perspective

We cannot understand our own civilizational dilemmas unless we obtain perspective from the past. After all, these were humans with the same basic intelligence that we have today, perhaps even more so. What we need to know is how they succeeded. Then we must take an even greater hypothetical flyer, why they failed. The case of course has to be made that they did fail. Did the incarnation of new values, new ways of thinking about experience, perhaps even more fundamentally, new languages, new religious values, a new modal system of thinking about the world of nature and the world of man, make the case for failure? Perhaps it was an even deeper force connoting simple natural succession.

Here we will suggest in a schematic setting-forth of issues, those that will need to be taken up by others in a more systematic research effort. The argument to be presented here is derived from the preceding chapter analyses of evolutionary dynamics, especially the creation and transformation into civilization of the highly cognitive primate, *Homo sapiens sapiens*.

## Ancient Greece

The Hellenes, who come under historical scrutiny before the Romans, came west and south into their rocky archipelago. In language they were Indo-Europeans, of the eastern branch (Hindi and Persian) as compared to the Roman version of Indo-European, this closer to the Slavs and Germans. There had to be something about the unique genetic quality of these Hellenes. They probably were no more brilliant than the Sumerians and Semites of Mesopotamia from whom they learned much, especially after they took to ship building. Thence they sailed to the ports east of Troy along the eastern edge of the Mediterranean, and the coastal towns, these in what is now Turkey down through Israel, Gaza and Egypt. These early Hellenes, c. 1200 BCE, become the Sea Peoples and Philistines. Eventually, under the press of success and overpopulation the Greek cities c. 800–700 BCE sent out large emigrant groups from the ancient homeland both east to Ionia (Turkey) and west to Italy, Sicily, and south to what is now Libya (Cyrenaica).

They learned much from the indigenous easterners, especially of their religions, alphabetic writing, and trade. There had always existed a mysterious spark of Hellenic creativity in the arts, possibly a Cro-Magnon inheritance, but also an extraordinary communal individualism. This latter element in their cultural ethos has been thought by historians to have been their undoing. Yet, it was a tribe of northern-country Greeks, Macedonians, c. 350 BCE, who did bring them all together politically and militarily to conquer the civilized western world: Philip and Alexander. They made Greek an international language of culture and intellect.

The receptivity to a now matured Greek culture, promoted and imposed at the tip of the long speared phalanx, did puncture the dying institutions of Eastern, religiously undergirded tyranny. This was a striking historical alteration. The Jews, ever a culturally resistant *ethné*, could not help but be entranced, at the least, by Hellenic intellectualism. But the monotheistic ethicism of the Jews was a mutually attractive vision of human life to the Hellenistic world. The Greek thinkers called the Jews "a nation of philosophers." Greeks and later, Romans, flocked to the *synagogue*, a Greek stimulated institution (Alexandria/Egypt) for the study of the treasured Israelite texts.

We cannot argue that it was the bare-bones Achaean soil, nor a diet of onions and garlic, that contributed to their aspiration for *Paideia*, high culture, and education. We must note that some of the greatest intellectual and artistic achievements of the Greeks took place at one time or another, in Ionia, now the Turkish coast, Sicily, Italy, Alexandria Egypt, Cyrene, and just about anywhere the Greek mentality set its foot. Greek was the intellectual and esthetic language of the world, Hebrew perhaps a brief exception, for 1,200 to 1,300 years—from before Homer, c. 1000 BCE, to the hegemony of Christianity in the time of Constantine, Saint Jerome, and John Chrysostom, then Byzantium and Greek Orthodox Christianity.

The Greeks and their civilization were a spectacular nova of innovation and depth of symbolic creativity. They literally fabricated the mind of modern humans. Transmutated from independent city-states into a great international military machine, the various pulsations of artistic, poetic, and philosophical creativity were gradually transformed, as with the Sumerians, into educational rituals, overlain by a new and universal Roman polity.

Here came the first dilution of Greek ethnicity, ultimately to absorb Christian theology. How many reincarnations could this civilizational tradition transform before these interconnected symbolic structures became frayed and incoherent? Hellenic civilization finally became history, under the thumb of Ottoman Islam. Today, the name Greece evokes pity and disdain.

## Rome

It is fair to say that the residents of the Italic peninsula matured as different Indo-Europeans compared with the Greeks. Their first conquering foreigners, the Etruscans from Ionia and beyond, semi-Hellenized interlopers dominated the Italic tribes for many centuries in north central Italy. Then came the *echt* Greeks to *Neapolis*, *Crotone*, and *Tarentum* in the south, and of course Hellenic Sicily. Certainly the Latin tribes thus learned to fight, trade, fabricate craft items, and engage in large-scale agricultural development. In the days of the elder Socrates, c. 390 BCE, the transalpine Gauls descended from haughty Milan and whipped them badly. Can one but fairly say that the basic character of these indigenous Italic peoples remained relatively untouched even while fighting these intruders, learning from them, finally both absorbing and expelling them from the mainland?

Finally these tribes battled each other for supremacy, were united under sober Rome, and made their way into human history. The history of early Greece is not too different from the time of Homer, the internecine battles for national/*polis* dominance. The great difference was that the Greek homeland was for long untouched by foreign sandals until Rome, late in the day of Hellenic civilization.

Another interpretation of the unique sober and down-to-earth character of the Roman people would have it that it was a combination of the implicit natural wealth of Italy and the need to fight for domination over its potential that shaped their national character. This inertial set of symbolic dynamics eventually led to them going ever further abroad in defense of the political and economic integrity of Rome, first to absorb the Greek immigrants, then against the ethnic-Greek-led (Hasdrubal, Hannibal) Carthaginians of North Africa. The military learning curve was a slow one. Eventually perfected, they followed the exhilaration of the sword into creating an international culture—political, economic, linguistic, and above all militaristic—for five hundred years.

For the most part, the civilized world accepted Rome's domination. It meant peace, an efficient bureaucracy to uphold a universal set of laws, eventually citizenship by the Edict of Caracalla, c. 212 CE, under the law. At the least, Rome learned to respect Greek genius in the arts, philosophy, and literature, and to an extent attempted to mimic its ideals. Thus, in every sense of the word, Rome was a modern universal civilization, allowing its various internal ethnic, national, and religious groups great freedom to speak their own languages, worship their own gods. What it did not allow was the push for political as well as religious independence, which the Jews aspired to in the first and second centuries. The Jews took up the sword, were vanquished three times, and became once more, a people alone, often tolerated but largely marginalized. At the borders of Rome were the unconquered Celts of Scotland, the Germans in Central Europe, and Indo-European Parthians and Sassanians at the eastern borders of Mesopotamia. Eventually, a weakened Rome would be bled to death from each of these directions.

Why did Rome first decline and then dissolve into two states, east and west, eventually only Byzantium emerging as viable unit, until the advent of Islam, a final fifteenth-century death at the cusp of modernity? It is doubtful that it was the lead water pipes fed by the Roman aquifer.

*Hypotheses*: 1. Rome was at war for all of its half a millennium of civilizational dominance. The transition from republic to imperium changed little in the militaristic solutions that the leadership groups conjured up. The dominance of the military preoccupation of the leadership, even beyond the period of defense after Hadrian (117–138 CE), began to pull back from the previous expansions of Trajan. Yet Hadrian hated the Jews and their pretense for freedom. The Jews reciprocated this hatred in their rejection of Greco-Roman dominance. Wars throughout the Roman Empire continued unabated until the barbarian elimination of the Roman succession c. 430

CE. It must be remembered that as early as Marcus Aurelius, c. 160–180 CE, emperor soldiers spent most of their careers defending the frontiers and their own pretensions.

2. The basic symbolic structure of beliefs and values, the structuring of Roman society, was tired after this long travail of conquest and killings, even within the cultured *latifundia* whose aristocratic and educated leadership preserved this Greco-Roman Hellenistic tradition. Little re-creative energies emerged from the various leadership groups. The schools were sclerotic, the games were barbaric, and the moral degeneration in the context of the wealth of the leading social classes reflected a deadening of disciplined cultural aspiration. The baths were a rare example of a populist gift by the leadership to the urban masses.

3. Amidst this deadening of internal symbolic energies for the re-creation of an aging civilizational lifestyle, Christianity was establishing itself amongst the downtrodden and the working middle classes. It represented an antidote to the corruptions of power. It spoke to the inner disciplines of personal asceticism, the integrity of the family, a vision of immortality that was rich in the heritage of the Pharisees of the Jews, from whom Jesus himself had emerged. Christianity was building a new literature of belief, a theology that had deep moral resonances. Following the efficient political structure of Roman bureaucracy, secular Christian juices would, under the noses of Roman authority, seep into the petrifying cells of the system. Soon the bishops would have the emperors (Theodosius supplicating to Ambrose) on their knees, bowing down to the representatives on earth of this higher power. And thus a new civilizational model would arise out of the lawful and systematic skeletal remains of the Roman mind.

# China

A historical overview of Chinese civilization complicates the Western perspective of rise and decline, and then the substitution of new claimants to civilizational dominance. Chinese civilization, since it became a recipient of literacy, c. 2000–1600 BCE, has not only maintained its integrity, linguistically, culturally, and politically, but it has arisen in the late twentieth century and early twenty-first to a position as a world contender to lead a universal Western technological secular/scientific civilization to the borders of the twenty-second century CE.

A recent statistic may present an augur for the future of this oncoming world civilization, perhaps to be led by China, but also including Japan and

Korea, inevitable satellite powerhouses of this northeastern Asiatic wave of the future. In the United States, late 2011, a "super elite public high school in New York City, Stuyvesant High School" reported on the successful examination results for their entering first-year class. Qualifying were 569 Asian Americans/Mongoloids, 179 Caucasoids/whites, 13 Hispanics/mixed race, and 12 African Americans/mixed-race/statistical "blacks."[1]

An ancient civilization which has seen its economic and political ups and downs but its cultural and social integrity maintained seems to have arrived on the cusp of a new century with great educational and intellectual potential. We think of China as an insular civilization, the "inner kingdom." The reality is different, and twofold. First, China has been a migratory way station, as well as an immigrant way station, for many thousands of years. We see the Chinese as racially Mongoloid. But in truth they, like most of the other races, are a late evolutionary and historical re-creation through interbreeding with outlander groups.

Cro-Magnon technology has been found in eastern China dating back at least 15–20 ka years BP. The Amero-Indians, from c. 40–12 ka years BP, traveled east through China and Siberia and across the Bering land bridge in a variety of hybrid racial profiles. In the state of Washington, Caucasoid skeletal remains dating back to this migratory era have been found near Kennewick. This evidence partially explains the very European visage of many of the Indian tribes of the United States in the nineteenth century. In the Tarim Basin of western China, Xinjiang Province, there have been recent finds of Caucasoid peoples dating from 2000–1200 BCE, with Germanic textile techniques and styles possibly related to the historical Tokharians, who spoke a Celtic-Germanic West Indo-European dialect. These Indo-Europeans survived into c. 900 CE before being absorbed by Han Chinese and Central Asian (Turkic) immigrants.

Historic China begins with the coming of the Hsia, Shang, and Chu dynasties, c. 2000–1500 BCE. These horse riders settled in the upper Yellow River valley near the present city of Xi'an. Chinese historians have described them as a red-haired, green-eyed people. It is now thought that they may have been Persian-derived wanderers. They gave the indigenous peoples literacy. There have been suggestions that the unique orthography of Chinese writing has similar characteristics to Norwegian Runes. The exploratory nature of humans should not peremptorily rule out such an "outrageous hypothesis."[2]

In Xi'an today there is a great museum dedicated to the thousands of terra-cotta soldiers, buried there by a Qin-dynasty emperor, c. 300–200 BCE, rather than sacrificing "the real thing." We have here a reflection of the racial and ethnic make-up of this region some 1,500 years after the original invasions from the west. Contemporary Chinese anthropologists do not consider the visage and height, five-foot-ten-inches, of these soldiers to be Han in race-ethnicity. More like contemporary hybrid (Caucasoid-Mongoloid) Kazakh-like people. Certainly in more recent times this ancient blend has been further enfiladed with more typical Han Chinese genes.

The "invaders" from the west have been added to by "invaders" from the north, hence the building of the "Great Wall." Here, over the centuries, Tatars, Huns, Tungus, Luao, Mongols, Hakkas, and Manchus have poured over the borders, in spite of walls and indigenous Han Chinese warriors, to make their way south into the expanding Chinese heartland. The interesting part of this story is the cultural absorbability of the foreign ethnic and racial elements by the now maturing Chinese civilization, its commitment to higher learning, and high art, poetry, beautiful ceramics, and ethical philosophy.

One is reminded of the northern Germanic barbarians and their intent to breach the borders of the Roman Empire. They wanted this cultural and lawful stability. But Rome was by then too corrupt and decadent in its ways to be able to make a smooth transition. Byzantium, anchored in the ancient East, made a good attempt of reinventing itself. In both west and east, the tidal wave of religious mysticism effaced these ancient secular visions. But, not in China!

Each of the invading untutored ones grabbed onto Chinese civilizational values with a passion, adding new blood and a needed push along the horizontal perspective of calm intransigence to outside events. The Hakka, for example, migrated deeply into south China. Deng Xiaoping, an ethnic Hakka, was born in the area around Kwangtung Province, near Hong Kong. In the nineteenth century "opium wars," the Hakka were at the modernizing center of the revolt against the emperor and the Western colonialist forces.

China has itself expanded north, west, and south. North into Manchuria and Inner Mongolia, west into Xingjiang Province and Tibet, south into the Austronesian language areas bordering Laos, and Cambodia, also contested Vietnam border areas. One travels south and west from Hong Kong to Guilin in Guangxi Province, the home of the indigenous Miao, a non-Han people and one will see as much building and modernization as in the ancient Xi'an homeland of the Shang. Also, there is intermarriage, a recognition by the oncoming Han that there are no essential intellectual or cultural anomalies in these borderline Chinese.

And thus the pattern is clear.: Absorb the feisty newcomers, genetically and culturally. Expand the borders of Han to absorb as yet undeveloped peoples, expecting that the 90% demographic dominance of the Han, today, will dilute ethnic friction, that which still resonates in the western desert areas of Xinjiang where the indigenous Turkic majority of Islamic religious traditions fight the oncoming masses of secular and enterprising Han migrants from the east.

In Tibet, that vast frontier land that the communist Chinese government has absorbed, as with the southern provinces, there are enormous geopolitical advantages at stake, i.e., the control of the southern rivers of Asia, from the Indus to the Mekong. The Tibetans have little Mongoloid blood and just as deep a hatred of the Han as the Turkic peoples of Xinjiang. But there are vast mineral deposits in the Himalayas, enormous water resources that Pakistan, India, Burma, Vietnam, and Thailand need, that Han-built dams can potentially block.

And of course, this secular-authoritarian regime wielding the powers of a modern scientific-secular nation, the Chinese, on a dime, are turning away from that heritage of fifteenth-century Manchu leadership's refusal to "play" with modernity. Under that policy China virtually became, if not in name, a colony of the Western powers in the nineteenth and early twentieth centuries. The intellectual talent of the Han has over time been preserved by a continuing devotion to the bureaucratic rule of the scholar, along with his selective Han Chinese polygamous and concubinage practices.

The tremendous centrifugal ethnic pride of all of these northeast Asiatic peoples, their pride in their high culture and intellectual potential, has allowed them to refute the basic orthodoxy that the symbolics of civilization cannot possibly be infused with the new over a period of several thousands of years. It needs studying: the reality of one slowly evolving culture and its people retaining its intellectual potential for both accommodating itself to an aggressive externally powerful modernity and being able to quickly turn and master the symbolics of that very same external and modern scientific culture.

## Notes

1. Brooks, D. (2011, December 20). The Sydney Awards, Part I. *The New York Times*, p. A33.
2. Wu, X. (1998). The relationship between Upper Paleolithic fossils from China and Japan. *Acta Anthropologica Sinica*, 7, 235–238; Brown, P. (1993). Recent human evolution in East Asia and Australia. In C. B. Stringer, M. Aitken, P. A. Mellard, & P. Mellars (Eds.), *The origin of modern humans and the impact of chronometric dating* (pp. 217–233). Princeton, NJ: Princeton University Press; Itzkoff, S. (2003). *Intellectual capital in twenty-first-century politics* (pp. 97–98). Ashfield, MA: Paideia. Itzkoff, S. 2000 *The Inevitable Domination by Man, An Evolutionary Detective Story* New York: Peter Lang. P. 303–306; pp. 80–94.

ized cells of the dog. To be extracted according to the method of I.

# · 1 0 ·

# SYMBOLIC THOUGHT:
# THE UNIVERSAL, THE PLURAL

## Symbolic Vectors

Here we discuss the two modalities of human symbolism that enter into the shaping of cultures and civilizations. These modalities, discursive and non-discursive symbolic forms, arise out of the depths of human nature. This duality issues from the interaction of humans with the outside world, whence our sensory information presumably arises. The human mind is not passive in the interaction between sensory information, the dynamic outside world from where this stimulative information arises, and this human form which attempts to regulate, order, and interact with the blooming, buzzing world that is impacting on us.

It is as if the mind is bouncing questions off of the incoming sensory information. The hard immovability of the physical world, even in its changing, recurring patterns, tends to lead our minds towards the causal mode of thought: why are there regularities, and why the occasional alterations in these seemingly regular inputs of information? There is a sky: sometimes with clouds, sometimes with sunshine, sometimes with thunder and lightning and rain. We presume to create a structured vision of this external world of sensory inputs. Here is the external stimulus for all discursive thought, the existence of regularities in our experience and then the mind's need and ability to create inner predictions, rules, ultimately universal principles to guide us in dealing not merely with the stable but the breaks from stability—the variations. What the discursive attitude of our inner vertebrate cognition asks, as with all instinctively regulated animal behavior, is the universal implication, a rule that regulates: everywhere, all the time. Here is the impetus for human action.[1]

If we can bring together enough secular cortical discursive brainpower to resist the emotions of the lower brain, then we can hope to order and assimilate for our social minds a system of local lawful sensory regularities. These will lead the mind to ever broader abstract principles. Eventually, with the help of a written symbolic system, the mind will be so buttressed to deal with levels of information that demand more than visceral memory capacities can provide. Otherwise we will remain behind, mired in a world where sensory information is attached only to our emotional nature, the need to translate a world of possibly secular material/sensory inputs into totems, gods, holy and/or corrupt powers, inchoate fears and joys. In such cultural context, secular analysis of cause and effect, yes or no, remain a "foreign language."

We have to recognize that the symbolic inputs that derive from our lower brain system and analyzed by weak cortical function, in all stages of culture/civilization constitute the roots of the later creative cognitive systems. These symbolic energies, as they course upward through the cortex, create the psycho-biological sources of the creative arts, religion, etc. This is why in all human cultures we find the universals of art, sculpture, music, dance. But, not to be cerebralized/corticalized, these mental evocations remain "primitive." In modern societies with complex human layers of cognitive potential, in what is called music or art, even in the technological arts, photography, cinema, etc.—much of the non-discursive symbolic emotion remains at a primitive level as compared with the great civilized epochs. Aristotle himself saw this in his distinction between the arts and "entertainment."

The dominance of cortical analysis of causes and their effects—the evolving relationship between sets of causal information in our forms of knowledge and the timeline behavioral consequences of our use of this knowledge, these structures of symbolic information—finds its origin in the capacities of the Cro-Magnon brain. Here, in cortical discursive thought, the world begins to build on a terra firma of relationships—in time, ever expanding in causal values. The discursive intellectual mind attempts to consecutively expand beyond the domains of sensory experience.

Once the human mind begins to note discrete causal keys to sensory events, the mind then focuses powerful energies, an unending thrust outward to relate, to subsume under ever-wider symbolic structures, concepts, a sense of universal causality. The end point of this vector is, of course, the scientific integration into large-scale functional theoretical instrumentalities for discovering, ever more, how singular events and objects, seemingly diverse and unrelated, really do fit causally into the scheme of things—*a unified field theory, a Darwinian envisionment of bio-cultural evolution.*

High civilization is impossible to create without the capacity of major portions of the populace being able to think in the literate, lawful, universal mode. Inside our minds is the assumption that how we act individually and with our cohorts—whether it be in the arts, religion, ritual, sports, sexual patterns, cuisine—a principle exists, the organizing words being: *everywhere, always.* We have noted the similarities in the art and culture of the Cro-Magnids from c. 45 ka BP to c. 12,000 ka BP, extended from deep in Russia to southern Spain. This universality of outlook, taking into consideration that this culture did evolve and did have local variations over time, had to have had its roots in a genetic consanguinity originating in that ancient and mysterious "genetic bottleneck" that created *Homo sapiens sapiens.*

## Cause, Law, Universality

To search for cause is to search for law. Animals are mostly programmed by their genes to react similarly, species-wide, to external stimuli: the shadow of the eagle triggers the escape pattern of the mouse. As we go higher up the phylogenetic scale of mammals there is more leeway given to the brain to react to unique sensory, life-challenging situations, yet always within a circumscribed domain of genetically stored behaviors, an animal, usually species-wide version of the universality principle. In humans this pre-programmed behavior is virtually eliminated, this in spite of sociobiological attempts to see universal selective values in ordinary human social relationships and responses. The difficulty is that all of these seemingly logical reactions of humans—the physical protection of a child by its biological parents, one example—can be violated under special unpredicted social circumstances. There is almost nothing in the historical cultural repertoire of human behaviors that is fixed in genetic cement.

Thus humans have to rely on cortical expectations of recurring stimuli to create a fabric of meaning, a structure of the relationships between self and external sensory-related physical experiences, as well as the often softer symbolic world of family, tribe, and nation. To search for recurring relationships in order to predict the future, a law-like set of presumptions enters the human brain and is constantly tested by experience; thus many lawful assumptions must be constantly revised. Humans search for the conceptual, *always, everywhere*, all things considered. This leads the mind to the universal mode of thinking, what philosophers Ernst Cassirer and Susanne Langer called discursive thinking: the ongoing search to create conceptual constancies and universalities out of our physical and social experience.

The most recent case was the Einsteinian search for a unified field theory in physics, today called "supersymmetry," joining the macro- and microworlds in a unity of causal regularities. It didn't play out for Einstein; quantum mechanics and the indeterminacy factor in the world of microparticles fouled up our ability to be the objective observer. Niels Bohr and Werner Heisenberg, amongst others, presented us with new intellectual challenges, yet ongoing. Isaac Newton had started us on the way towards bringing together celestial and earthly physical motions; Charles Darwin revealed the unity between human and animal life in his evolutionary theory; Karl Marx attempted to show us how economic dynamics and class structure, over time, were the real unifying causal factors in shaping the political character of society, and not the superficial dynamics of the rule of kings and queens.

So too in social evolution, this force in our mental apparatus attempts to bring the seeming chaos of sensory experience under a causal, law-like order. It eventuates in producing ever more universal assumptions about the world. Thus Greek culture, the Roman Imperium, Christianity, Islam, Chinese civilization, and finally Western scientific, technological civilization have had their expansive moments in history. The universal mode of thinking, whether initiated at the point of a spear or the mushroom clouds of an atomic explosion has an impact in shaping human thought and action, telling us that something all-powerful and all-encompassing is taking place. This modality of thought in our brain structure unleashes enormous symbolic enthusiasm, the glue of participation, the energy for the realization of the new, the powerful idea.

## Pluralism, Non-Discursive Symbolism

The inevitable slowing down of the creative dynamic of a universal trend, whether in physics or sciences in general, including the social sciences, political innovations and enforcements, creates a countertrend. When the universal energy-inducing romance wanes, those inevitable inner contradictions in mysterious reality slowing things up, new brain dynamics will take over. Transitions such as in late Roman political/military chaos, the decline of the Renaissance papacy, the industrial importation of slave labor from Africa into the Muslim world, or the unfruitful theoretical promises of an old conceptual model in the sciences (Newtonianism) prompt the mind to shift focus.

Here we come face-to-face with the so-called non-discursive symbolic modalities. In the basic human symbolic pantheon of thought, there already exist psychological valences that direct minds and hearts closer to home: the human persona, local or cultural affiliations. One does not look for the same logical categories of scientific thought in the arts, in ethnic cultural patterns of thought and behavior, or even, to a certain extent, in family and community patterns of life. It gets interesting when the non-discursive world of more pluralistic and emotional valences begins to impinge or interact with universal economic and materialistic symbolic values.

Complicated are the practical interactions of these two modalities of thought. Given the enormous forward unifying thrust of Western civilization since the beginning of the fifteenth century, we still observe—in the concretia of the various art forms, the retention of preexisting pluralistic national symbolic patterns in the visual and musical arts, in religion, in language use—the persistence of the non-discursive symbols gluing together our various ethnic heritages. Rome may have succumbed to and imitated many Greek cultural patterns, as well as philosophic traditions. But they built upon these discursive and universal systems of thought and action with new and formidable engineering skills, a new architectural vocabulary, and of course a new tactical and strategic military thrust.

In the arts of painting and music, the nations of modern Europe cultivated differences using similar painting and sculpting techniques. We differentiate between the German and Italian mentality in classical music, derived in part from their disparate linguistic, political, and geographical heritage. Yet, the musicians and composers came together with similar instruments and universal musical forms: the sonata, symphony, opera, comedic and tragic. But where the various languages persisted, the styles remained essentially nationalistic. In religion too, the push of centralization and universalism ran out of steam. The Reformation created a multiplicity of Protestant sects. Even in the universal Catholic system, there is a real difference in the day-to-day observances and styles of worship—Irish as compared to Latin American. In Islam, Shia and Sunni divisions seem most explicit internationally. But on closer examination, these ways of worshipping and thinking about their theological visions vary from nation to nation, not even considering the many peripheral sects. Think Persian and Iraqi Shia, Syrian Alawites.

We can thus understand why in physics or chemistry, in neurobiology and genetics, the tendency will always be towards the universal theoretical vision. In physics, chemistry, engineering—all the hard, discursive sciences—the differences in thought and experimental practice will be minimal. Here we all live in a universal world. The criteria for what will work in practice, scientific experimental confirmation or disconfirmation does not differ between Japan and South Africa. In the biological sciences, where we study *Homo sapiens*, we will have to take into account the relatively minor human differences that still exist in this super species. But, as the modern expansive world of the West begins to slow down in its inertial motion forward, the surfacing of too many reactive negatives, the mind of modern humans, will inevitably search out for a new and more dynamic universal fulcrum of thought. Simultaneously, non-discursive pluralist symbolism and cultural dynamics will help break up waning universal pretensions.

First there will be a centrifugal turning inward to the non-discursive symbolic structures, elements of human thought and actions focused on the locality, wherever it is not blockaded by the heavy weight of dying political, economic, and social institutions. The end of Rome in the West saw the universal Latin dissolve into innumerable derivative Romance dialects, then to be transformed into formal if colloquial languages. Language used in philosophy or the sciences, in historical or economic research, can maintain its connectivity with the ideal of universality. But in interpersonal speech, in the marketplace, in the home and community, in poetry and song, such expression will ally itself closer to the heart than the cortex. Even technological instruments of the mass universal culture—television, the Internet, radio, and now Twitter, Facebook, e-mail, and YouTube—will not be exempt from a massive reversion, the pluralization of cultural and local nuances.

The example of the Chinese language is instructive. Before the recent modernizing trends impacted China, before the communist revolution—followed by the limited capitalist and technological expansions of private initiative, here writ on a continental scale—Mandarin was the written language of the scholar and the central government. But because of the inability of any of the various dynastic traditions of China to bureaucratically control this vast geographical entity, given limited communication and transportation universals over the many thousands of years, regional dialects had been maintained throughout China. At the same time, the ruling classes saw the necessity of recruiting from a wide set of provinces for obvious political and military reasons, and so there occurred a feedback use of Mandarin as the official language.

Mandarin thus found its way back into the provinces as the language to be used in literature, the writ of government, and communication between the intellectual classes, always highly regarded in this Confucian, Taoist, ethical non-supernatural religious tradition. What happened was that Mandarin was translated orally into the dialects of the Chinese regions. One could now universally read and understand the non-phonetic logographs of Mandarin Chinese orthography. But when asked to read out loud with meaning, what would emerge was the provincial dialect, mutually unintelligible to citizens from an adjacent province, possibly even down the road, within the province itself. Here is a simple exemplification of the plural vector in human symbolic thought at work.

Now we must ask ourselves what the future will be of all of these local spoken versions of Chinese. People now travel by plane, high-speed trains, and auto, hear the propaganda of Beijing on TV and radio, visit many more provinces and locales than ever before. The assumption must be that the official spoken version of Mandarin will prevail, with local languages and dialects withering away—that is, until the central universalizing powers begin to lose their efficacy and input and the center begins to stagnate.

At the moment English is the universal language of the West. The dominance of Britain in the eighteenth and nineteenth centuries, and the wealth and power of the United States, Canada, Australia—the old English colonial outposts—in the twentieth, have catapulted this language into the lingua franca of the world, the vehicle for the communication of modernity. Note that China, the inner kingdom, while moving outward north, south, and west, was also unleashing a constant flow of Chinese migrants throughout the world, to the Philippines, Singapore, Malaysia, Vietnam, and now in North and South America, perhaps even in Africa. It is possible that power and wealth will bring Chinese forth as the international language. The primacy of English itself could succumb to old age, weakness.

## Religion

Here is an interesting, pervasive, and puzzling symbolic form. The United States Constitution attempted to write into law the shearing of institutional religions from their power base in traditional monarchical, papal, feudal, military, and political rooting in Europe. In a sense the U.S. was saying to the churches, synagogues, and potentially the mosques: "Go back to your non-discursive functions to succor the inner needs of individuals and local communities. Don't get messed up with politics or economic power plays. You are to be a private cultural attribute of the citizenry, hopefully a plural exemplification of those deeper human concerns that religious communion represents to human nature."

There is no question that religious concerns, which go beyond the secular curiosity of humans about the universe, have an important place in the pantheon of human culture, the great transitions in family and community life, birth, marriage, reproduction, and death. Ruling cliques have been quick to latch onto the religious allegiances of a people as a means for grasping power, self-enunciating their union with deity. So too, are the priests, ministers, rabbis, and mullahs eager to rake in a bit more wealth, as well as authority and power, by allying themselves with the ruling political potentates, or are themselves lurching for supernatural as well mundane political and economic power.

In this way, religious concerns find a way of intruding into the discursive domain of human thought, aligning themselves through their institutional allegiance with political forces. In the case of medieval Europe, Rome as well as Geneva, the papacy and the Protestant elite became powers within their own right. Today Saudi Arabia and Iran are exemplifications of this trend. Terrorist Islam, unable to master the intellectual and educational modalities of modern scientific thought, has enveloped itself with an ancient vision of religious jihad. Certainly the communist ideology of the first half of the twentieth century, while ostensibly against old-time religion, appropriated the cultural paraphernalia, mausoleums, and ritual abasement of the masses to the leadership, holy writings, and the all-powerful church/party with successions of all powerful "holy" leaders. They mandated orthodox forms of music, poetry, and literary works and outfitted the commissars with the paraphernalia of priesthood, establishing a whole new order of religious themes to grab the eyes, ears, and hearts of the opiated masses.

Also, as with the modern Catholic church, a gross violation of its internal moral precepts has taken place amongst the bishops and the priesthood, the historic non-discursive emotional glue that holds the communicants to their religious heritage was put into jeopardy. The circle of commitment was broken down. Again, when one looks at the United States in 2016 and sees the growth of a religious move into the political arena, here amongst conservative Republicans, it reminds us that there is a weakening of trust in the traditional discursive domains of political leadership, military and economic security, moral and social values.

Ultimately the legal underpinnings of a commitment to rational decision-making by the citizenry can be undermined and dissolved. The need for surety, a rock of belief in a fast evaporating discursive understanding of social reality, leads to a search for the evanescent if powerful emotional truths of religious commitment. Into the softer social domains of human life religious beliefs—either secular ideologies or the old-time church, synagogue, or mosque—reenter the fray in the attempt to dominate the minds of the polity.

## Yin and Yang

The perdurance of religion has to inform us of the fragility of our assumptions about the predictability of historic trends. All we can identify with surety is that there are movements in history that are inexplicable. Just ask why the *tsunami* of genocidal totalitarian ideologies took over the advanced Western mentality in a century—the twentieth—pregnant with human enlightenment and prosperity given the explosion of scientific knowledge. Call it too rapid social changes or the explosion of urban demographics. Here, with religious authoritarianism "on the run" we had a tidal wave of horrific "true belief" that few religious epochs have experienced, here in the most advanced societies of the world. We have much to learn about the successive transitions, sometimes peacefully, sometimes with much blood, between the discursive and non-discursive modalities of human thought and belief.

Immanuel Kant and his twentieth-century followers, Ernst Cassirer and Susanne Langer, saw these diverse human modalities of thought to be permanently reified into public institutional ways of thinking and creating. They elicit energies and, as such, will be with us always, whether or not as part of a universal expansive mode in the discursive or non-discursive areas of symbolic thought. But it should alert political and intellectual leaders of nations and worldwide institutions that the basic function of a leadership group is to keep the society, world or national, glued together by balancing those modalities of symbolic thought, which are on the cusp of the new and have the capability for expanding and exploiting the cognitive and emotional energy potential of the citizenry.

The world of humanity will gyrate back and forth from an expansive, mostly discursive opening for innovation and progress to the cultivation of the local and individual, the deeper less material motifs of thought and life. The greatest civilizations will, however, simultaneously unite and expand all dimensions of our symbolic creativity. Exemplars go back in ancient times to the Upper Paleolithic nonliterate Cro-Magnon civilization, as reflected in what we have discovered about their technology and art. Certainly the Hellenic Greeks stand out, as does the Renaissance surge into modernity at all foci of the human creative intellect. Or consider the ancient Sumerian nova that created written language as well as a highly developed literature, technology, visual art, and performance culture. In all these unique moments in human history, cultures have opened the floodgates of high intelligence, exploring both worlds, the discursive and non-discursive valences of the human mind.

These pulses of creativity lasted for many centuries. We miss the mark if we see civilizational progress only in terms of the high-tech breakthroughs of today when we compare today with the ancient inner-city "perfumery" of downtown Uruk, Athens, or Rome. What we should look for is the intellectual depth of each symbolic form as it compares with its own past and present. Movement of the total compass of the mind should be the key to understanding civilizational progress. The criterion is not where you are in reference to the material conditions of earlier civilizations. Rather, the criterion of measurement has to lie in the given symbolic structure of any nation or people; how it compares intellectually in its dynamic movement beyond its immediate past.

Here, we may have missed the quiet inner dynamics of community and esthetic life in China during all those centuries (fifteenth to nineteenth) in which that civilization was seen as moribund when one compares it with the simultaneous dynamics of the West. With all these external conquerors coming down from the north, as well as Han Chinese moving south and outward in migration, the foreigners to be absorbed, the migrants to retain their heritage even from afar, there must have been something unique in the rhythms of that great culture/civilization. The Chinese still kept themselves together as an *ethné*. Now, they are finally moving outward towards the universality of the modern under the aegis of a wholly different ruling, but yet an internal political clique. They have a passionate commitment to be both Chinese and Western, hopefully at some point to be liberated politically and universally as a free people.

## Conclusion

Our human destiny is determined by our given structure of symbolic meanings, always self-created. Behind this reality is an even greater mystery and problem. We are yet an "unresolved super-species." We don't as yet live under one discursive, species-wide set of behavioral rules in terms of our sociopolitical-economic goals of life. Science is universal as a method of testing the above belief, but for an as yet limited portion of the world's human population.

In sum, we have not as yet integrated the species into *Homo sapiens sapiens*. The various tendrils of our evolutionary past have not as yet caught up to our scientific timeframe. This issue is not necessarily an issue of race or ethnic diversity. We will have to unify our thinking, at the least on the discursive level of symbolic action. Here is where the bloody focus of disagreement, the ideological-religious fantasies, take up their armaments, swords, guns, poison gas, and atomic bombs.

In the long run the cortex must always intervene to cut through the lower brain's symbolic passions of the moment. In the end we humans will always be thrown back to that ultimate evolutionary gift for our species' survival, the discursive potentiality of our brain capacity for critical cognitive analysis; its ability to fathom the structure of the present so as to predict and behave competently into the future. We can't depend upon our disappearing biological mammal/primate instincts any longer. This is because we are now the personification of one of evolution's great shifts, *animal symbolicum*.

## Note

1. Cassirer, E. (1965). *Philosophy of symbolic forms* (Vols. 1–3) (R. Manheim, Trans.). New Haven, CT: Yale University Press; Cassirer, E. (1944). *An essay on man*. New Haven, CT: Yale University Press. (Original work published 1923–1929); Langer, S. (1942). *Philosophy in a new key*. New York, NY: New American Library; Langer. S. (1967–1982). *Mind: An essay on human feeling*. Baltimore, MD: The Johns Hopkins University Press.

# · 1 1 ·

# CRO-MAGNON'S PROGENY: THE MODERN MIND

## Humans: A Counter-Entropic Process

We are part of a trend of living things on our planet, counter-entropy. Entropy is a concept developed from our observation of the process of energy transfer. Put two water-carrying containers close by, and the temperature of the heated container will give off heat energy to the surrounding, cooler environment. The sun gives off its heat into our universe. Someday it will darken, take its place in the cold of the universe, and of course, life on earth will probably end. The earth itself receives much of its energy from the sun. There is still a molten core deep within the earth that reflects much energy into the surrounding environment.

Life has made its way into our planetary reality by the fact that it is a counter-entropic element in the system: not enough energy accumulation to violate the entropic rule in the larger planetary system, but enough to have gobbled up available energy from the surrounding environment to make its momentary counter-entropic energic play into sidereal history. We humans are for now a culminating element in this drive for energy accumulation from our surrounding environment, to a great extent dependent on the light and heat from the sun so that we can meet the omnivorous requirements of life and reproduction.

The human brain is a unique instrument in the mobilization of energy. It is a within-the-generations processing machine for information about how, where, and when we can meet our dynamic needs. Once we figure out the structure of things external to our bodies, and can conjure up the necessary life energy resources, the mind spontaneously regurgitates other symbolic desires, first, to know, e.g., the chronometric cuts on bone to register regularities in this puzzling world, then to express our wonder, feelings of order and symmetry in the art that we render related to our social and economic experiences. It is a powerful mental symphony of needs, the limbic system and cortex ready to break out into song and dance, an inner bow to that powerful internal concept we call beauty.

This search for structural mental relationships, the need to cognitively and instrumentally organize the world around us, Cro-Magnon revealed to humankind many tens of thousands of years ago. And this is what *Homo sapiens* has engaged in, off and on, since then. Ultimately the energy that is evoked in our symbolic interactions with physical and human reality is catalyzed for the purpose of living, for those moments in which we surmount the inevitability of entropic degradation. The key to our physical survival lies in providing our mental urges with the knowledge that will work, counter-entropically, leading us forward into the ever unknown that is the future.

## The Road toward Secular Modernity

The mind of Cro-Magnon, in essence the modern mentality of all *Homo sapiens sapiens*, turned those five sensory inputs into a series of questions about symbolic meaning, understanding, not the automaticity, the reactive signal inducing instincts of reproductive behavior. There is an artistic rendering in one of the caves, created perhaps twenty thousand years ago, of a human seemingly dancing, decorated with animal headdress and tail, perhaps a religious shaman, as with the Australian aboriginal people.

We have no sure evidence about Cro-Magnon's religious reifications of what to them must have been a very complex, puzzling world. After the first questions that our senses introduce to our mind comes the attempt to create relationships and meanings between this and other sensory experience, then to place them into a structure of relationships, how all these "things" work together. Then comes the larger vision to find causes and effects, the conceptual laws that can illuminate the inner workings of these seemingly related impressions, symbols, ideas. Finally it must be applied to the desire to live, function.

Eventually we arrive at a system of laws, rules which consist of words like *always, everywhere*. Our world gradually becomes truly meaningful and instrumental for our physical and mental symbolic operations. In the process, humans, to accommodate interaction with this cognitive mix of ideas and emotions, strive to create not merely a family or band, but soon an ethnicity and tribe. In time, as we discover ever-wider relationships of laws of cause and effect, we become practically successful in dealing (surviving) with the physicality of things. We can create an economy that leads us away from a subsistence equilibrium to the plenty of an economy of surplus. Surplus relaxes and broadens our mentation, and inevitably our social and political horizons, such that we tend to create larger national units, cities, or expansive nations.

The laws we create to regulate our interactions with the material world, economic surpluses, are then applied to regulate the *sturm und drang* of human sociality. We first apply primeval psychological laws regulating human sociality to protect ourselves against our own kind and its mysterious, often violent behavior. We then turn to ensure long-term economic and political sustainability, ultimately and most importantly, our ethnicity, culture, or civilization. Underneath the connoted violence of survival is the energy that lures the human towards art.

Religion early on enters into this search for meaning, the causes of things, the larger search for an intellectual vision of human experience. In the beginning the gods and goddesses serve to symbolize our instinctless insecurity, the need for humans to attain power both intellectual and physical. Ultimately we humans, as the modern-day existentialists tell us, are alone in the world. Oh, for the surety of vertebrate automaticity!

The underlying challenge for the human cortex is to substitute for the instrumental actions rooted in myth and religion, the always fickle reassurances of the gods, a conceptual symbolic structure that is a bit more predictive. Too often the gods have as their surrogates upon earth venal and self-serving human delegates, priests, mullahs, rabbis, and ministers. Twenty five hundred years ago the Hellenes almost accomplished this goal. From Athens to Alexandria we had a succession of thinkers who freed themselves from the ethnic and esthetic religious traditions of the early Hellenes and their Mesopotamian anticipators, to open themselves up to an inquiry into the secular, naturalistic view of what caused what. Here too came a substation of theological imperatives with an ethical, moral rationalism, this search being in tune with the desire for more predictive scientific relationships.

But the time was not ripe to translate this search for geometrical and mathematical envisionments of planetary motions, animal and human relations, into a concomitant search for practical societal realizations. Such an advance could have reinforced the Hellenic infatuation with *theoria* into a practical social system for searching out in physico/mathematical terms how the down-to-earth world works. The writings and experiments of an Aristotle, Eratosthenes, Aristarchus, Hipparchus, or Ptolemy were passed down in history as mostly intellectual visions, the world, however, continuing on its military-autocratic pursuits of secular or theological power and dominance.

This successor Hellenistic world, from c. 300 BCE, was richly innovative in the practical sense, eventually, however, to be eroded by the deeper needs of the moral mind for causes, laws, and human discipline. Buddhism, Judaism, Christianity, Islam, for an eon contributed to an ongoing human underground of supernaturalism, gods, goddesses, saviors, prophets, fundamentalist symbolics, rules, and regulations, the laws of the body to be ruled from on high, given our belief in an immortal soul.

Historically it was probably a fortuitous stepping back from the earlier paralyzing social/military dynastic structures and systems of the ancient historical world. This was the trade-off even at the debit of abandoning a rich universal civilizational tradition, here the Greco-Roman, Hellenic/Hellenistic way of life and thought. Out of the new medieval diversities of power/economic structures into which Europe disintegrated, after c. 400 CE, the ancient knowledge and know-how was not lost, merely put on the back burner by functional institutional disuse. Gradually the necessities of economic and social survival teased the human mind back again to attend to those perennial discursive economic lures of the new and the possible.

Out of the burgeoning textile industry of Florence, the Mediterranean commerce of Venice, the general political and social turbulence of the north Italian cities, did come the Renaissance. The great Gothic-cathedral-building tradition had preceded this surge of innovation in economics and art. But also, the universities were humming not merely with theological debates but with nascent motion scientists: Roger Bacon, Nicholas of Cusa, Buridan, and many others. The weakness of power in Europe, even of the papacy, lured the mental curiosity of Cro-Magnon's descendants towards a reconstruction and amplification of the Hellenic intellectual tradition. The ferment came from every point in a very politically pluralistic setting of peoples, ethnicities, and religions. In the north it was the Hanseatic League. In the south the papacy itself was, in the fifteenth and sixteenth centuries, in the hands of the wealthy mercantile families (Medici) of north Italy.

The ships built for Mediterranean trade were soon redirected to the exploration of long-hinted-at destinations for economic exploitation. Exploration coincided with a surge in map making, and the inventions of telescope, astrolabe, printing press, and compass, some of these ideas transmitted from the now insular Far East. The hoped-for wealth and power only hinted in the earlier medieval centuries now saw the new scientific inquiries and resultant technologies riding over the established theocratic institutionalism, whether of the Catholic Church or the new Reformation Calvinism.

Copernicus and Kepler went beyond Ptolemy and the Greek astronomical tradition. Brahe and Galileo added observational and experimental concretia. A combination of the intellectual search for lawful order and predictable understandings of the laws of the skies and the solid earth, plus the oncoming search for secular laws of the human condition, gave these modern successors of the Cro-Magnids, those who first carved chronometric incisions on antler bone, a new pathway for humankind.

The subsequent wealth coming into Europe—first from Italy, Spain and Portugal, then post-Reformation France (Huguenots), Holland, and England—was an enormous spur to the developing middle classes increasingly divesting themselves of monarchical and theocratic commitments. The demand was for the new, a sense of unlimited horizons of wealth, control, and understanding. The discovered Western Hemisphere figured dominantly into this mix of exploration and exploitation, even slavery from Africa. The transformation of the intellectual and scientific revolution into the political, economic, and societal revolution of the seventeenth and eighteenth century gave an enormous boost to these burgeoning independent middle classes and their ambition to attain control over nature.

## Search for the Rational

The loss of instinct in the exchange for understanding has been a fragile calculus for humans. Instinct is geared to respond to the status quo. But, the world does change. Our unique cognitive openness to adapt to change does not always lead us into the most functional solutions for survival, for the species as well as its discrete cultural components. Thus the discovery of the scientific method, a means of joining the mind's search for theoretical unifications with the further command to test out in practice the implications of these theoretical injunctions, marked a great divide in the progress of humankind. It has been a crucial step in ensuring our distancing from mysticism, self-deception, and thus possible annihilation.

The practical power of the mathematical and experimental study of planetary and terrestrial physical experiences inevitably opened the eyes of the early European moderns to their social and political conditions. The heritage of Greco-Roman and Judeo-Christian thinking of these ethical and social matters, now linked to the rationality of scientific investigation, brought forth an explosion of thought and writing about the established institutions of power.

Individuals such as Thomas Hobbes (1588–1679) and Baruch Spinoza (1632–1677) represent singular thinkers in the post-Renaissance hunger to explore the roots of power and belief. The former critiqued the claims for divine right monarchy, linking political power to the atomistic vision of physical reality, but only to maintain order in our chaotic universe. The latter searched for an ethical paradigm that would replace the theocratic underpinnings of moral behavior, here a pantheistic invocation of the unity of man and nature implied in the then current scientific vision. It is not surprising, considering the time frame, that they both were ostracized and on the run.

In this great intellectual revolution first came the search for a secular understanding of the bio-physical world. Then there followed a similar search for an understanding of humanity in his sociopolitical contexts. By the eighteenth century, the underpinnings of theocratic power and its undergirding of monarchical privilege had been undercut intellectually, if not completely dissolved in terms of power and privilege.

The United States was the paradigm of this new age. A political entity ensconced on an untouched continent, without the detritus of an oppressive aristocratic and theocratic elite: an ecology and geography of enormous economic potential; a political class of highly intelligent progressive secular minds; a unified Anglo-Saxon ethnicity, yet open to enterprising immigrants from around the world. Still, they were burdened by a commitment to African slavery, the implicit assumptions of European/Cro-Magnon superiority.

The result of the political emancipation of this American people can be seen in the Declaration of Independence, the Constitution, the Bill of Rights. The Federalist Papers, which amplified on the Constitutional vision. Here was echoed the ancient Hellenic theme of the value of individual creativity, a democracy of the people, the attempt to hold economic differences at the periphery of social life. There was also, as noted above, the heritage of the Judeo-Christian moral system, and the vision of justice dispensed without social prejudice.

The many French Enlightenment thinkers paralleled and were buttressed by the writings of John Locke, Adam Smith, and David Hume for the English-speaking world, all influential in providing the ground for the American Declaration of Independence and Constitution, a political and ecological tabula rasa for a vision of the individual, created in freedom from coercive and tyrannical ideological power. This was to be a "diminished state." All but essential powers were to be decentralized to the states and the people.

In retrospect what happened in the United States was preceded to an extent in England, and then followed in bloody revolution in France. It was the political and social culmination of events that had been evolving for two hundred fifty years towards this human acme. This belief system, this fulcrum of philosophical assumptions about the individual, the need to diminish the powers of centralized coercion to free the talents of high intelligence for productive progress, economic enterprise, and freedom, was to last, as with the Hellenes, at most, for another one hundred years.

In the nineteenth century a conflict of assumptions would soon see the light. This new intellectual foundation for thinking about man and society would attempt to turn the whole Enlightenment framework upside down. Part of this fundamental change in outlook would be caused by the demographic and resource consequences of the great scientific, medical, and technological innovations that the secular, scientific system had by then accumulated.

## Explosive Social Change

The savage French Revolution of 1789 heralded a new age. Demography, however tells us much about the macro changes in perception of ever-expanding opportunity and wealth, and the need to change political trains.

People tend to have fewer children in hard times. They are often aborted, intentionally and unintentionally, or they die at birth or shortly after. Life expectancy is low; people die at earlier ages. This is all reversed when opportunity takes over the human psyche. Indeed, the development of manufacture and mining, the expanding food supply, scientific medicine, and sanitation, plus scientific agriculture, invited the expansion of the world population.

In 1400, at the very beginning of our universal European surge for prosperity, there were fewer than c. 500 million humans on board our planet. Five hundred years later, shortly after the beginning of the nineteenth century, as industrialism and the lure of the cities set in, world population, mainly Europe, had doubled to one billion. A century later, 1900, c. 750 million more humans had come on board.

In this interval the mineral resources of the world began to be exploited, a critical factor in the expansion of both industry and population. Coal, and the application of coking processes to make steel from iron, was one element. The search for sources of energy for light, heat, and power went beyond coal to other coal products, coal gas, kerosene (coal plus bituminous tar), and camphene (turpentine plus alcohol); also whale oil, lard oil. But it was the drilling of the first oil wells in Pennsylvania and Ontario in 1859 that created the greatest push forward in the search for ever-growing standards of living, and the industrialization and urbanization that made it possible.

There is no question that the growth of science and the advances in scientific medicine, immunization, sanitation, and hygiene lowered death rates throughout the world. This diminishing of the sequence of great plagues that have afflicted humankind over the millennia allowed for the further explosion of our population in the twentieth century. By 1930 the population of the world had reached two billion. Not even the butchering of hundreds of millions of our most intellectually and educationally advanced cohorts in the twentieth-century wars and genocides succeeded in dampening down these successive waves of new humans coming onto our planet. This population surge exploded to 6.2 billion by 2000, over three times as many people as lived upon the earth seventy years earlier. By late 2012 the world population had crossed the seven billion mark and is slated to grow to at least nine billion by 2050, if no great natural or human catastrophe bursts the bubble.

It is not difficult to explain the quandary that has beset philosophers and intellectuals in trying to understand this ever-new set of social, political, and economic circumstances under which this expanding tidal wave of humans was living. The ideas came fast and furious. And behind the ideas were chaotic political slogans and movements that attempted to rationalize and indeed improve the state of this motley mass that now inhabited our earth.

The Enlightenment argued for laissez-faire, the freedom of individuals to take on the challenges of an ever-new world. It argued that we are free humans able to care for ourselves and live in harmony with our fellows by dint of our ability to associate freely under the law. This point of view worked adequately in a world still relatively empty of humans. By mid-nineteenth century Europe, the contrasts in those new institutions of productivity (the urban factory system/the agricultural feudal and slave system), between freely-obtained wealth and "freely"-obtained poverty, was stark.

Thus began an intellectual and social war ostensibly against capitalist wealth, but also against those individuals that had accumulated this wealth. No longer were the visionary intellectuals, the Marxists and socialists, those at the forefront of a new ideological crusade, fighting the old aristocratic and theocratic elites. The world was turning in confusion attempting to rationally see through the scientifically induced industrial and technological surge of change.

Not only did this new rationalization of our societal structure lead to the bloody conflicts of the twentieth century, but already in the nineteenth century, in the United States, in Britain, and Germany, there were attempts to limit the power of now-institutionalized corporate power, wealth, and exploitation, this wealth now to be redistributed within national borders. By the twentieth century, especially after World War II, when the contrasts between the various peoples of the world came sharply into focus, national guilt over colonialism, slavery, segregation, and the poverty of the so-called "third world" as contrasted with the Caucasoid/Cro-Magnid West, an international rescue mission was generated, centered in the United Nations and a host of international organizations, plus private and nation-to-nation outreach.

This attempt to right the stark and seemingly rigidified social inequalities either through revolutionary blood or peaceful redistribution now included infrastructure, food aid, and massive medical and sanitation intervention to stem high death rates. The conceptual vision (ideology), which placed exploitative guilt on the shoulders of the haves of the world as contrasted with the newly expanding masses left behind, was itself a factor in stimulating the bloated increases of humans on a now highly stressed planet.

Here in a nutshell was illustrated the problem presented by *Homo sapiens sapiens*, Cro-Magnon's release from the vertebrate servitude to instinctual regulation. The choice given by Mother Nature, now allowing this new species the option of resolving the challenges of both external change with the rapid-firing events created by *Homo sapiens sapiens*' own actions, argued for deep thinking and intellectual analysis of the meaning of what was happening, for the future of the species.

The wars and genocides of the twentieth century at the least constitute the evidence for this fragility of the mental compass and the consequent decision making analysis of the species. It tells us that to be free of instinct is to live and die dangerously.

· 1 2 ·

# DREAM OF A UNIVERSAL HUMANITY

## Science and the Universal

The human mind searches for relational meanings. It wants to know how things work, how these understandings will affect the future. In times of a breakthrough in understandings, one that leads to material prosperity, the search is for universal principles that undergird this newfound material prosperity. Here again we need to organize how perceptions of physical, biological, and social experiences flow into a web of symbolic relationships.

By the beginning of the seventeenth century, the scientific web of relationships and the technological tools that were being created to further such theories had produced a new vision of physical reality inevitably to be extended to social and political institutions. The Enlightenment was born in an attempt to universalize the physical, biological, and social world. Monarchy and theism were seriously questioned in their limitless claims for belief, obedience, and social organization. It took time and revolutions to dethrone them from these claims.

The Renaissance had symbolized the union of art and craft, with the papacy even at the forefront of this initiative. The rediscovery of the corpus of Greek science stimulated the exploration of the heavens, then the earth. The

Reformation set loose the northern integration of capitalist legality and productivity with the scientific search for technological innovation, the conquest of the physical and economic world by the human mind, certainly a godly task.

The astounding powers of the secular mind led inevitably to the conclusion that the individual was more than a mere product of a higher being, no longer servile in a hierarchy of established privilege. No, the individual had natural rights that went beyond the reach of the church and the synagogue. The European individual now had a unique position in the dynamic flow of the new in an expanding world of secular power and knowledge, knowledge that could be obtained independently of the old hierarchies.

The American Revolution and its Constitution heralded this new universal in thought, the free individual and his unconditioned right to exercise his intelligence in the name of scientific reason and unencumbered enterprise, ever in search of new symbolic structures of meaning.

## Equality of Condition

At the very time that the vision of individual freedom to think and act—equality of opportunity, laissez-faire, freedom from the heavy controls of the "center," those early revolutions in Britain, America, and France—arose, ever more powerful economic and technological dynamics were changing the face of the mercantile world. People from the servile farms were flowing into the coal mines, steel mills were burgeoning along with textile factories. People were pouring into the towns and cities, populations were expanding in Europe and America. Out from serfdom into a new vassalage the poor came in numbers.

We must first note that by the beginning of the eighteenth century, a new middle-class life was being shaped. In the medieval age, the paucity of physical emoluments for the rich and powerful, not to say the serf, was in contrast to the earlier life of the ordinary Roman citizen. Here we think of sanitation, the comforts of heated homes, transport, even the physical safety of the person. By the eighteenth century the fruits of science and technology were being once more felt down to the ordinary farmer, merchant, and craftsman. There was, most importantly, a growing awareness of the tangible lifestyle fruits of money, wealth, even power.

Jean-Jacques Rousseau (1712–1778) foresaw the consequences of this new economic and demographic reality that was coming into being. Especially in his *Social Contract* (1762), he predicted that the individualism to be glorified by Adam Smith in England (*The Wealth of Nations*, 1776), and then established in the ninth and tenth amendments to the U.S. Constitution (c. 1789), would eventually be subject to the will of the burgeoning masses. And indeed, as the population of the world crossed the one-billion mark in the early nineteenth century, as new inventions stimulated by steam power were dynamically changing the nature of economic and social life, the advanced societies saw a surge in social protests against the economic and social inequalities that were now being thrown off by this new economic and social system.

Marxism was the beacon, the exemplar of a new search for universal principles that would encompass this rapidly transitioning, industrializing world. The writings of Karl Marx (1818–1883) brought this movement to a head by the late nineteenth century. But the rapidly changing profile of Western society—political, military, and social—was the instrumentality for changing a way of thinking about the relation of human to human, and individual man to human history and destiny. The assumption that all humans were and should be equal, both in terms of law and opportunity, but also social outcomes, took hold. This was certainly made possible by dint of the ongoing technological dissolution of the barriers of space, time, and national condition. The world was getting smaller and more crowded. It had to become more equal.

Marxist socialism/communism added an element of demonization to this egalitarian ideal. The enormous wealth that capitalist entrepreneurs had accumulated, supposedly a new class of exploiters, constituted, to the followers, an obstacle to a new universal social utopia. The antithesis was the building of a new universalistic fulcrum from which our conceptualization of man's place in the world would be built. To be fair to Karl Marx, his vision of human equality would have had an essentially libertarian outcome: the goal was the victorious revolution by the industrial proletariat, encompassing all the social classes of the world. The consequent synthesis would be for the withering away of the state, and its all-consuming powers, now held by a capitalist hegemony.

This utopian, universal goal was to be the eventual realization by each individual of their value to their fellow humans in terms of their productive work contributions. No longer would there be the debasing exploitation of the working classes by capital's extortion of surplus value from the productive labor of this industrial proletariat. You invest, fine. But you only can derive from such an association your fair share, and not through the exercise of this new economic power to control.

During the progress of the nineteenth century, the ferment of scientific and technological change, industrial and population growth, the latter primarily from the most humble social classes, the nation-state became ever more powerful. Social order demanded an alliance of industry and political power. During this ferment there was, in all the advanced nations, an effort to ameliorate the growing distance, socially, between the proletarian classes and the new wealth of the capitalist plutocrats. Both in Britain and in Germany, social welfare, educational, and health programs spoke to the needs and demands of the masses, given the ever-growing intellectual socialist agitation to spread this enormous wealth around. The United States, a special historical case, was in the advance of the democratic political dispensing of local and national wealth (taxation) for the benefit of ordinary citizens.

When one examines the enormous changes in the character of urban life, in the surge of creativity in the arts and literature, the vastly expanding and deepening secular research in the universities, it is understandable that much of the social agitation for change, often inchoate, blended into a thousand shades of cultural/symbolic change. Yet the wars went on, often as cover for the maintenance of the social and economic status quo. The American Civil War was an exemplar of the bloody industrialized conflicts to come. Underneath all the agitation, the message became clearer decade by decade throughout the West. The redistribution of wealth through political means and the promise of at least a semi-egalitarian life style was becoming the universal philosophical theme in this vision of the future state of humanity.

## Perversion of Utopia

The millions poured forth upon the planet. Scientific medicine and its sanitary offshoots—scientific agriculture, the fertilizers and pesticides that technology and industry now produced in quantity—all had their demographic impact, now in the twentieth and twenty-first centuries and throughout the world. It cannot be denied that the new inventions in communication and transportation, the power of the scientific secular to envision new political and societal relationships, had created a wholly new human lifestyle: imagine! A pill that would prevent the sexual act from causing a pregnancy. The growing energy resources that poured out of the earth gave further impetus to the words economic growth, concomitant with the disappearance of famine and disease in the secular, scientific West.

One could call the twentieth century a century of epochal change. Rules by which humans lived, seemingly established for eternity, were broken, dissolved with impunity. The First World War brought vast casualties in the trenches only hinted at by the earlier nineteenth-century bloodletting, the American Civil War—but now with poison gas. Consider again the more recent burning of the civilian populations in the cities during World War II. Here we note in ironic passing the ideological infection of educated Germans and Europeans with the universal and "just" ideal of gassing, then burning up six million noncombatant Jews. This ultimate elevation in human barbarism concluded, whether justified or not, in the crowning incinerations of barbaric, if Westernizing, Japan, Hiroshima and Nagasaki.

Before and after these events we had genocides: the Armenians in early twentieth-century Ottoman Turkey, 1.5 million; the Soviet Union, 1935–1953, at least 20 million. After the Second World War, the universalist utopian communist ideology of Mao in China. To purify the whole he needed to rid the land of 30–40 million Chinese "landlords" and others, by starvation, here helped, as earlier in the Soviet Union, by governmental control of transport and communication. After this, genocides galore throughout Africa, Asia, even post-war Europe—in Islamic Bosnia by Christians. Something had changed in our modern, supposedly scientifically advanced world.

The nineteenth and twentieth centuries had produced two hundred years of epochal social change. There were about 800 million people on our planet earth in 1800. Industrialism setting in, new resources, and new scientific, hygienic, and technological innovations created our great industrial transformation, first in Europe and North America. By 1900 this population had more than doubled to c. 1.75 billion people. And then the twentieth century: modern medicine, plus two horrific world wars, sequential genocides in the hundreds of millions, and lo and behold we still arrived into the twenty-first century with a massive increase in humans on board planet earth, a total of 6.2 billion.

On the surface, the horrors of this new post-Rousseauian era could be seen as an intellectual and social war against capitalist wealth, predicated in part on the need to be rid of the vestiges of monarchism and theocracy. But it also led to two world wars: first the destruction of the youth of Europe in those terrible trenches. Then, the genocides and the *Holocaust*. In essence the West had created an evolutionary retrogressive ideological war against the intelligence of their own Cro-Magnids, the cream of Eurasia. In retrospect, humanity may look back on all these events of this awful century as an endemic insanity, the human mind going off the tracks in its attempt to understand the enormous changes which they themselves had caused to be created. A *fine* sociobiological resolution of the selective power of hominid genetics.

This ideological *idée fixe* continued on after the mass murders of World War II, transmuted now into international guilt and attempted acts of altruism. The newly interconnected Caucasoid/Cro-Magnid world in grievous remorse for the mid-twentieth century horrors set out to do penance for this guilt, colonialism, slavery, and exploitation of the now "third-world" billions of people of "color." These humans they had helped to usher into bio-social reality during this century by means of Western science. Here, centered in the United Nations and a host of international organizations, plus private and nation-to-nation outreach, this deeply embedded intellectual envisionment of universal legality again reached out to encompass factual reality.

These visions of mammalian altruistic moral remorse constituted a real challenge to reason. Here came a dawning secular scientific awareness in the advanced segments of the human clade that history linked to traditional evolutionary dynamics now required species-wide social unification.

This trillions of dollars in redistribution not only included infrastructure and food aid, but also massive medical and sanitation intervention to stem high death rates. The moral explanation for this attempt to "right the wrongs" of the past placed exploitative guilt on the shoulders of the haves of the world as contrasted with the newly expanding masses left behind. As the twentieth century came to an end, it was clear that most of the wealth redistribution had resulted in great population surges, which "surprisingly" were leaving the recipients in even direr straits than when under the colonial thumb. The new indigenous power brokers of colonial independence themselves were securely ensconced by this contributed wealth, Swiss bank accounts engorged.

## The Why of Secular Insanity

The need to understand the dynamics of social change was clearly at the forefront of the new secular ideology of the nineteenth century and then the revolutionary actions of the twentieth. Whereas the earlier periods of human history had brought to the forefront power brokers of social-class domination, the warriors and theists, Marx and his followers saw the new capitalist entrepreneurs and their followers, even the scientists, technologists, artists, and musicians of the new class structure as complicit exploiters.

Of course, soon ensconced into power, even the revolutionary advocates of a universal proletariat had need to provide themselves with the appurtenances of the new power structures of revolution, especially now enrobed as they were in the warrior mentality. The underlying *why* of the new social structure was only inchoately analyzed, but the level of social change, chaos trailing along with enormous dynamic economic growth, necessitated explanation. Totalitarianism for the moment seemed to persuade.

What was occurring in the developing scientific/industrial complex of the West, the capitalist world, could not be easily turned aside. This was especially true of those nations where a democratic political ethos had developed. To mobilize for the revolution the leadership groups, fascistic and communist, had dredged up a variety of ancient demonological modalities of thought. World War I was to be an exemplification of the old order's attempt to maintain itself by raising those ancient national and ethnic antipathies in a context of industrial and technological competition for dominance. The old order lost and the revolutionaries cheered: no longer Hapsburg, Romanoff, Hohenzollern. What was left of the monarchical tradition, as in the Hanover monarchy in Britain, was now in a ceremonial holding pattern of non-discursive symbolism, tradition, history, ethnicity, and religion. This first great war did bring fascism and communism into a real-world universalist struggle for ideological and politico/military legitimacy.

To maintain their own political controls, the leadership of the modern democratic/capitalist societies of the West had to rationalize the growing contrast between the exploding demographics from the bottom in the "third world" and those individuals and groups who had leaped to the modern forefront of wealth and power in the "first" world. The contrast also extended itself to a growing middle class of Europeans and North American Caucasoid/Cro-Magnids. Redistribution and retribution became the dominant themes of the twentieth century. Billions of humans were now enveloped in poverty.

The universalist mentality could not now live with this stain. This was an especially poignant theme in the West after the destruction of fascism in the Second World War. The great colonial empires were seen as a political, economic, and historical remnant and cause of an unjust era and the impoverishment of this "third world." Such human inequality of condition had to be relegated to the dust bin of history. The vast growth of wealth and the unification of information around the human world could no longer tolerate "apartheid" in the human species.

But had not the demand for universal social and economic equality of condition "necessitated" the elimination of dominant social classes through genocide? Note that the genocides extended to innocent ethnic groups—Christians in Turkey, Jews in the Nazi-occupied lands of Europe. Most of Europe in this wartime period participated in this "holy endeavor" of the "cleansing" of supposed exploiters of the downtrodden. In the post-war period, after 1945, this continued in Europe with the genocide of the Muslim Bosnians, in Asia with the Cambodian and Chinese middle- and upper-classes, in Africa with the Christian Igbo and the racially mixed Tutsi of Rwanda and Burundi. It continues to this time in the Muslim world. What had happened to the Cro-Magnid search for reasoned prediction for the survival of the most intelligent?

There was a basic assumption underlying Western intellectual support of even the more benign redistributive efforts of the West, both domestically within their own nations and through the new international agencies. The advanced nations could lift up the impoverished masses of the "third world." Those clear and existing distinctions in education and social opportunity, which had left so many behind in a world modernizing into a hopefully classless middle class scientific-secular planet, were merely historical anomalies. Worldwide social inequalities could be rectified, now through more humane efforts by the developed world. Simply, transfer the existing productive wealth of the haves to the have-nots, and voilà, equality of condition.

## Denouement

It is probably true that in the early post–World War II decades, the union in Europe and North America between government and the private sector, the institution of a number of social welfare programs, and, in the United States, the attempt to remove government from the race issue were progressive efforts that improved the lives of ordinary citizens now living within the just constitutionalism of democracies.

But little by little, as each crisis, war, recession, and natural disaster had to be faced, the role of government, taxes and subsidies, and regulations waxed. The independent sectors of society gradually became secondary in the dynamic of the ongoing social ethos. Government taxes, debt, and then expenditures meant government control. The ever-glowing promises for utopian equality and unification of the mass became as insistent as the growth of the governmental bureaucracies.

With the entrance of new hybrid post-Cro-Magnid economic players—Japan, Korea, India, China—the vaunted productivity and dominance of Western economies began to be undermined. Productivity fell, but the rules and regulations, the spending of governmental bureaucracies, continued unabated. A Western middle class, however, had been created upon this bulging mountain of governmental controls and spending. Within this class of "barely hanging on," a light of awareness was flickering. Secretly and quietly this awareness swelled: the promises were not being responsibly met.

The first decade of the twenty-first century saw the unraveling of these predictions for the unification of the species by economic redistribution. The fantasy dreams of this now universal model of human social organization were beset by puzzling inner contradictions. The gradual drift of power to the state had sucked away the productive wealth of the independent sector via taxation and the redistribution of this wealth to the supposed needy. But in the process it was taking a good chunk of this "surplus wealth" for its own parasitic perpetuation. The universal Western debt crisis of 2012–2013 had finally uncovered the inevitable shoals of factual reality. As billionaire Warren Buffett noted, "When the tide goes out we will know who is swimming naked."

For a moment, the end of cheap fossil energy became the efficient cause of this dissolution. In the United States it collapsed government subsidized housing and stimulated a vast mobilization of debt to maintain the social equilibrium. In Europe it was much the same cause: vast debt, a sinking banking system, all exacerbated by the rigidities of a unified monetary system, the euro. This experiment in "universality" had still allowed each member nation to engage in its own pluralistic ethnic level of fiscal irresponsibility.

The banking system, deeply complicit in this debt crisis, had to be saved, all while the system of wealth production was incapable of maintaining the economic growth that could have saved Europe from its "philanthropic" dividing up of the people's pie for the benefit of its various "crony" capitalist renters. What would be left for redistribution to those internal and international dependents from this long ephemeral wealth spigot remained to be seen.

The additional challenge which now faced the formerly wealthy West was, as noted above, the entrance of China and India, amongst other nations, into this productive competition for jobs and trade surpluses. The low wages and high skills of these peoples now were matching the productivity of the 35-hour-week French worker, a nation in 2012 in which 57% of its gross domestic product was governmentally derived, supposedly by taxes, but in reality by the issuance of debt: $233 billion to be refinanced in 2012. Further, during the first twelve years of this new century, 800 million people, mostly from the "third world," had been added to the planet's demographic surplus.

Something had gone wrong with this nineteenth-century vision of a universal redistributive prosperity for humankind. The twentieth century had produced unprecedented horrors in pursuit of this egalitarian vision, to a great extent the destruction of its intellectual elite. The twenty-first century had shown that the vision, the model, the social reality that had been predicted, was tragically in factual, scientific error. There seemed not to be enough redistributed brainpower remaining to gain rational control over the future.

And yet, as we look back at our horrifically misapplied vision of species-wide unification, in its human societal and cognitive exemplification, aren't we on the cusp of this inevitable evolutionary vertebrate reality?

## · 1 3 ·

# NATURAL SELECTION OF HUMANITY

*Psychology can tell us what is.*
*Evolution tells us why it is.*

## Breakthrough Dynamics

The planet earth has provided a variety of opportunities for living forms, counter-entropic mobilizers of external environmental energy sources, to then explode into life dominance and engrave their presence onto the records. Multicellular forms succeeded the simpler entities. Much later, vertebrate migrants coming ashore c. 400 mya found vast open land spaces to move out into, diversify, and then compete selectively. The genetic imprints of evolutionary successes, living forms going back several billion years, provided the potential variability for the building of the new.

Primates, c. 60–50 mya, while still holding back in the race to take advantage of a larger brain, diurnal sensory processing, omnivorous diets, and placental birthing adaptations yet found a vast opening on the surface of the continents to pause, consolidate, and thence make their adaptive and selective moves. So too there was the simultaneous decision by some mammals to go back to the seas, or even fly off to distant horizons. It cannot be predicted what kind of homeland opportunities this planet will provide for the seemingly ever-new combinations of genes awaiting phenotypic exemplification and nature's ever-variable selective nod of approval to "make it" in the sweepstakes of living forms.

The dynamic patterns leading life towards domination, diversification, competition, eventually substitution, and then extinction, have taken place over and over again with those more adventurous multicellular forms. The originating primates were conservatives. They gambled on versatility of behavioral options, mostly staying out of the way, a larger brain to communicate danger and opportunity, thus developing no great predatory or defensive morphologies and behaviors that might have alternatively worked for them.

By the time we arrive at the Miocene period, c. 25 mya, it is probable that a small semi-bipedal anthropoid was peeking through the high grass to negotiate the territory. Still omnivorous and by now semi-predatory in terms of small-animal feasting, as well as berry-, fruit-, and nut-picking, it had by then carved out a long-lasting and "fruitful" adaptive niche.

And because this grouping was mostly of ground apes moving around to find opportunities, the usual diverse racial and then species differences developed over many millions of years. There was always a tendency for opportunists to go whole hog into an adaptive specialization. As we move through the Miocene time zones the monkeys will have already peeled off, the lemurs and tarsiers left behind. The disappearance of the open country African apes, c. 15–12 mya, and the return to the ground of the baboon (an Old World monkey) tell us of the flow of opportunity and disaster that predated the appearance in numbers of the early hominids, ancestors of *Homo*. Those surviving African apes, the predecessors of gorillas and chimpanzees, had by this time long fled into the jungles of west Africa, becoming ever more specialized away from the adaptive press of the proto-hominids.

With a bigger brain, a growing body size, aggressive confidence, and no natural predator enemies, these proto-hominids spread out in numbers and species, finally beginning to make their evolutionary statement. In all probability, by the time these hominid forms revealed themselves in the paleontological record, c. 5–3 mya, they were long diversified into several genera, many on the road to extinction, as the brainpower of one genus, early *Homo*, began to assert itself, selectively.

## Competition and Selection

As species/races of a form of life begin to expand into their opportune ecology, they inevitably begin to compete. This can become violent. More often it is a subtle behavioral or morphological advantage that begins to tell. Distant exemplifications of the type can remain intersterile and "fight" to the death for their adaptive sweet spot. Or, as is often the case with large free-ranging mammals, they can remain interfertile even while maintaining or exemplifying very different phenotypes, e.g., dogs. Modern humans are such examples. And it is probable that at a certain point in the evolution of proto-*Homo*, this interfertility became the norm of the victorious genus.

Thus while we find great phenotypic variation in all the early types of *Homo* evolving into *erectus* and then *sapiens* typologies, an inevitable process of intra-generic and intra-species competition occurred. All of these fossil exemplifications of *Homo*, some from c. 2 mya, would have all been completely competent and successful anthropoids if it weren't for the most successful variants of *Homo*.

There can be no doubt that the disappearance of all the earlier forms of hominid life was precipitated by the pressure of newly minted brainy and aggressive hominids. The exact push—who drove whom to extinction—we cannot know; our fossil record is still unclear. But the pattern of ever-bigger forms of *Homo*, with ever-larger endo-cranial capacities, tells us that the pattern of selective dominance over the land surfaces for this form of life is, and probably will always involve, the human brain and its intelligence potential.

The world was "much bigger" several million years ago, and humans ran into each other with less frequency. Thus the selective inter- and intra-specific dynamics were much more placid. Moving forward, the historical geographic races of *Homo* became subspecies because they interbred at close quarters and thus developed a modest distinctiveness at a distance from other proto-racial groups. As they moved out of Africa, certainly by 2 mya, they spread out and multiplied/diversified, yet these originating differences translated mostly on the subspecies level. Too much genetic consanguinity over the eons had determined that the final surviving racial prototypes of *Homo* would interbreed into modernity. The Australids were perhaps the most extended geographically, from Siberia west and east into southern and eastern Asia.

The creation of *Homo sapiens sapiens,* Cro-Magnon, c. 300–200 ka BP, exploded a wholly new set of dynamics. There should be no question that all of the existing racial forms of *Homo* have since been reshaped by the outflow of this new genetics, thence catapulted over the *sapiens* Rubicon even at a distance from its originating center in Eurasia. The discovery of earlier discussed, and very primitive, dwarfed Australid type human fossils on an Indonesian Island, Flores, they who disappeared some 18 ka ago, corresponds in time to the similar disappearance of the more advanced Caucasoid Neanderthals of Eurasia some 40 to 27 ka ago.

The pressures of the new genetics from a distance could allow for the slow reshaping of the human form. Wherever still existent and stagnant subspecies of humans have faced newly introduced and radically cerebralized and always aggressive moderns, the outcomes have been immediately disastrous for the more vulnerable humans. The Australid Tasmanians and Capoid Bushman are more recent exemplifications of this selective trend.

## Our Sociobiological Reality

The powerful cultural realities of human history have given rise to a number of "sociality only" views of human nature, a great break with traditional Darwinian categories of human evolutionary dynamics. However, the advances in biological understanding, the expanding knowledge of genetics and molecular biology, have given rise to new evolutionary thinking under the title of "sociobiology."

Most recent sociobiological writing has attempted to revive traditional selective evolutionary categories: the struggles between alpha males for female partners and many babies; the seeming altruistic kin affiliations and behaviors of familial, co-religionist or ethnic genetic sharers. And of course as we search for these underlying behavioral dynamics that ostensibly have positive selective consequences for the sharers of such behaviors and their genetics, problems of prediction between theory and fact have tended to intervene and conflict with all necessarily deterministic models.

A claim for a scientific principle or law should not have exceptions, counterfactual exemplars. And this is the problem. There is no supposedly mammalian principle of adaptive or selective behavior which applies to human "cultural behavior," always and everywhere. And as we know there is no ostensibly human kin behavior that is not momentarily violated. We are exposed to a constant parade of historical and contemporary fratricides, patricides, civil wars between common nationalities, even co-religionists, even that most abominable act, the killing of one's own children. These behaviors have taken place, and are today rationalized all for supposedly explainable cultural reasons. And that, of course, is the rub. Human culture always seems to intervene in canceling out our belief in supposed deterministic adaptive/selective biological behavior.

But this fact does not entitle us to declare ourselves "sociological creationists," as the Stalinists and Maoists once claimed. Humans are still products of the planet's biological evolution. *Homo sapiens'* supposed cultural and social behavior is still determined by the fact that we are part of this ancient naturalistic process. Our understanding of these realities still has a way to go.

Certainly we are guided by our genes in terms of behavior. And to an extent our murmuring mammalian heritage does factor in. We do favor our own biological kin when we recognize them. Instinct, smell, doesn't help here. When we are altruistic we act so only in cognitive ways, choosing, or not, for "altruistic" reasons, to help strangers very different from ourselves. After all, what is "altruism"? A Nazi killer could claim it in defense of the purity of his "*Vaterland und Volk.*"

In terms of gender behaviors in humans, there is major sexual dimorphism in the human heritage, as with the lion or the wolf; but with us there is a basic difference. The human female was rarely a hunter, or a fighter. She is bound to her many dependent neonatal offspring for the major years of her maturity. Males are Ice Age programmed to bring *home* the bacon, hunting, fighting, competing. Hominid females are needed, and thus shaped, physically and psychologically, for the task of caring for their dependent young. The evolution of *Homo*, as we have earlier described it, required a long period of prenatal care that limited physical activity. The delicacy of both the female body and the delicate newborn required much community cooperation and separation of responsibilities for a successful birth of a normal, healthy infant.

Note that human sexual dimorphism is a product of several million years of hominid evolution and the fragility of the neonate. It is interesting to witness the evidence that in many of the rediscovered graveyards of the Cro-Magnons, we find a high number of very young females and often, the remains of their newborns. This testifies to the fragility of the process of reproduction amongst advanced *Homo sapiens sapiens*, and the supposition that the role of the midwife was early on a critically important female function.

The cortex dominates all social behavior. There is no mammalian behavior that cannot be contravened by a cortical decision—infanticide, fratricide, patricide, even the destruction of one's own tribe or ethnicity—if the cortex demands it. Consider that sexual behavior in all vertebrates is intended to create and raise the young to reproductive maturity. Then explain celibacy, homosexuality, through traditional sociobiological models! This is difficult. Of all our mammalian relatives, only humans can say *no!*

Our sociobiological expression is in fact rooted in our brain neurology, our symbol-creating intelligence and its embedded impact on human evolutionary destiny. Behaviorally adaptive changes within the generation are dependent on the brain's cultural analysis of danger/opportunity, and a sense of the future survival chances of the social intra-breeding group, band, or ethnicity. This sense of futurity, and the causal analyses that shape decisions of the social group, are supervised by the cortex, the thinking brain. It can now always veto the seemingly traditional instinctual imperatives of vertebrate/mammalian adaptive drives. But then humans will have to face the selective consequences.

## Intelligence: The Selective Dimension

The murky origins of the Cro-Magnons do not give us clear evidence of their role in reshaping the hominid clade. The hypothesis is that their great genetic deviation from traditional hominid development and morphology may have taken place in a northern crisis zone c. 300–200 ka BP. Obviously small populations must have been involved. And it probably took another 100 ka for the intergroup social selection of high-intelligence individuals to slough off the weaker "sisters" in the naturally rigorous selective Ice Age environment.

The evidence of the Skhul and Qafzeh fossils c. 100 ka BP in Israel argues for Cro-Magnon genetics being passed down, intermixing in a Neanderthal social and toolmaking environment. One small hurrah for a few Cro-Magnon hunters who got lost on the way. Their genetics started a trend, small as it was at first. Even some 50 k years later in Mladek, now the Czech Republic, we see hints of this interbreeding: Neanderthal brow ridges, robust bone structure—yet here were humans with large endo-cranial capacities using a well-defined Cro-Magnon technology.

Then there is the reported and the mysterious appearance of Cro-Magnid-type tools in west Africa, dated hypothetically to c. 90 ka BP. No skeletal fossils, just tools. Carleton Coon's analysis of the racial origins of the Negroids argues for a Caucasoid (Cro-Magnid) intrusion into west Africa before 30 ka BP, possibly resulting in the reshaping of these ancient jungle people to raise them up to the *Homo sapiens* level. Here the pygmies of this region add a fascinating and DNA-deviating element to the question.[1] It is this analysis that allowed him to argue that morphologically, Caucasoids and Negroids were the most similar of the races.

These wandering tendrils of human migratory curiosity were probably absorbed even at the distant boundaries of the Australid clade. We have discovered advanced skull types in northern Australia, also c. 90 ka BP, which seem more modern than subsequent, nearer-in-time exemplars in other parts of Australia. In New Guinea we find contemporary aboriginals, apparently well-nourished redheads, in the highlands of this great island. Then consider the Caucasoid, Cro-Magnid fossil found in Washington state, dated c. 15–10 ka BP. When and how did he/she get over here, and how much Cro-Magnid genetics is now intermixed into the other more Mongoloid Native American geno-phenotypes?

Remember, c. 200–100 ka BP there were many different morphological incarnations of *Homo*, probably reaching back to the level of *Homo erectus* and *Homo ergaster*, if not *Australopithecus*. "They ain't around anymore." How did this great morphological and cultural revolution take place? Then the world was empty. Small groups of racially diverse humans still retaining their ancient morphologies were thence impacted by a few oncoming Cro-Magnid hybrid types. Over a period of 100 ka, much wandering and subspecies genetic intermixing could have taken place. New hybrid forms were created, now more functional since having partaken of the Cro-Magnon genetics. Still, they carried with them the attributes and original racial markings of the ancient group.

Consider that much more interbreeding of racial and ethnic groups has taken place in the past 100 ka. Given the two or three centuries during which the modern Europeans, descendants of the Cro-Magnons, made their way aggressively en masse, moving around the world, colonizing, exploiting, enslaving, but also inseminating, these once-sharp racial differences have continued to fade. And considering that high intelligence, the morphological and the neurological substrate of our behavior is selectively powerful, given the test of hundreds of millions of years of increasing brain dominance, the hybridization and positive social selection of humans with the genetic of high intelligence is hardly a threat to the future of this species.

In sum, the reality is that the modern incarnation of racial uniqueness is very different from what it was some 100 ka BP. Today all members of the human species are at the least *Homo sapiens*. However we may be justified in arguing that many humans today representing all the ancient racial characteristics carry the phenotypic intellectual potencies of the genetics of Cro-Magnon, *Homo sapiens sapiens*.

As noted above, with regard to the Tasmanians in the nineteenth century and the Bushman today, when large numbers of advanced or aggressive human newcomers enter the geography and culturally settled ecology of more ancient human types, the results can be genocidal. This can also be the case with the introduction of new animal or plant types into settled ecologies. With regard to the Neanderthals, for example, the Cro-Magnons lived at arm's length with these Caucasoid peoples (Neanderthals) in Europe for about 20 ka. It is not clear that specifically aggressive actions of the Cro-Magnons did them in. Rather, as with the Tasmanians and the Bushman, it is the cultural advances of the new people, their way of life, more efficient, even to the point of reducing the economic and social potency of the originals, which can lead to lost fertility and the concomitant capacity to bring the young to reproductive maturity, this the selective desideratum for survival.

In our own time the genetic advantage of highly intelligent human beings has been overlain by cultural-psychological factors. Instead of perceiving these brainy *Homo sapiens sapiens* as uniquely and highly selective additions to our nation or the world, we see them as scientists, entrepreneurs, politicos, lawyers, professors, or as Jews, Igbos (Nigeria), Tutsis, Armenian Christians, Bosnian Muslims. These descriptions now embody a series of ideological semantic transformations. They now become exploiters, bourgeoisie, capitalists, enemies of those who live down the street from them who work at less elevated levels of value and reward.

The only way we can shield them from genocidal destruction by the majority who can use a few highly capable "quislings" to destroy their own (Heisenberg in Nazi Germany), is by understanding cognitively, and under the power of the law, the need for a society to cherish these intellectual contributions for the good of all. We have had in the twentieth and twenty-first centuries so much genocidal destruction of intellectual talent, transformed into hated exploiters destined for annihilation, that it is difficult to understand how the contemporary sociobiological model of Darwinism makes any sense of these events. Cultural symbolic elements deep down in the human psyche have overlain the raw reality of intellectual differences, transmuted them into ethnic and social-class warfare, such that any rational observer from Mars would predict the eventual suicide of modern civilization.

## Cultural Selection

The world environment changed radically with the retreat of the glaciers, c. 12–10 ka BP. The opportunities in the southern climes, especially around the Mediterranean littoral, acted as a magnet for the eager and cortically endowed refugees from the over-forested hunting grounds of the north. The literate civilizations which were subsequently created in those several thousand years of economic and social reconstruction, settled agriculture, mixed farming, and craft industries eventually brought about the urban revolution and economic specialization and reshaped and presented wholly new selective conditions for the human species.

The natural selection of the species was now not centered on the ancient movement of the Cro-Magnid genes in terms of the displacement of borderline *sapiens* groups. Now natural selection focused on the civilizational thrust of the descendants of the Cro-Magnids. Their very success in moving outward from the Eurasian homeland inevitably created new hybrid ethnicities in the border lands of north Africa, India, even northeast Asia. Over time, as tribal migrations gave way politically to national states, the intra-specific competition shifted to a within-nation ethnic jostling for power. Within-nation instability and international competition and warfare that has developed in historic times does not seem to have been a significant factor in the days of the late Pleistocene Cro-Magnid intergroup cultural relations.

We can hypothesize that the five or six thousand years of readjustment to a post-Pleistocene (12–5 ka BP) world of modern seasonal climatic conditions allowed for semi-peaceful, noncompetitive movements into a new underpopulated cultural ecology. The most recent five-thousand-year period has seen a more intensive competition of cultures and nationalities, more brutal wars, and the occasional intervention of the super-cortical attempt to regularize the natural intellectual/symbolic competition for dominance within humankind, the law and peace. Notice that in recent times the brutality of wars and genocides has not necessarily been derived from those ancient genetic human differences of race and ethnicity. We kill for purely symbolic cultural rationales, seemingly irrelevant to the discursive consequences for the future of the species.

Basically, the reason for this horror is that we have not as yet been able to bring the realities of meaning as to our human nature to the fore. In short, we do not as yet understand the underlying dynamics of human evolution.

The intra-specific nature of human competition for survival and dominance has shifted to the symbolic cultural level. This involves trade and population expansion as well as war. Rome expanded its ethnology only so far: north to the borders of the Alps, in Italy, south to Sicily. But it also, through military ingenuity and endurance, geographically expanded its societal symbolic structure of laws, trade, technology. It helped that it built on the already universal cultural hegemony of the Greeks. It thus created an international civilization, only partly speaking the Latin tongue, but bound together by the cortical power of Roman militarism and the law that eventually made all members Roman citizens.

## Natural Selection in Our Time

Rome decayed symbolically. No natural resources drying up, plenty of mercenary Franks and Goths to fight for Rome, no lead-pipe poisoning in the city. The cause: tired internal cultural values and external energetic Germanic invaders to the north. The winner, Christianity, was an Eastern mysticism that evoked a deeper human sensibility than the crass vulgarity and ugliness of imperial warfare and pagan moral degeneracy.

The world of the medieval was still open demographically in terms of the human ecological impact. The twelfth-to-sixteenth-century rediscovery of the ancient Hellenistic treasures of knowledge was linked to very diverse and politically weak European political/military entities. Quickly revealed was the ongoing conceptual fertility of high human cortical intelligence, here the ancient Cro-Magnid heritage. Then, five hundred years of explosive human expansion and change. These five most recent centuries have remade the selective conditions for our survival.

The recent European wars, often shrouded in the symbolics of religious and ethnic rivalries and the push for dominance, are an example of the selective battle for intra-specific domination through the sixteenth to twentieth centuries. This intra-European struggle for domination took on a life of its own after the defeat of medieval Islam. An increasingly indolent and impotent Islam gave rise to the perception that the human world was Europe alone. Victory on this continent, Europe, meant becoming alpha in the world itself.

The horrors of the first half of the twentieth century have led to a conceptual "superego" intervention in this perennial evolutionary cultural struggle. The post–World War II coming together of the European Union is an example of a cortical/political decision of a people, the Caucasoid Europeans, and North America, to form a union, now extending beyond these continents, a post-Roman, post-Christian vision of a universal panmictic profile of the human race. True, the decision temporarily left some Europeans out: Russia and some of its allies, not yet participating in the cortically activated political system of the European Union.

As with all decisions in the post-literate world of humanity, deeper sociobiological thrusts for cultural domination can be tactically modified by cortical considerations of prudence and opportunity. Why, for example did two hated enemies, Hitler and Stalin, come to a momentary truce after their division of Poland in 1940? In the post–World War II period the Europeans embarked on their misdiagnosed utopian vision of unity with the third world. It was partially an invitation to "come to Europe" plus trillions to be spent through the UN, World Bank, IMF, ECB, plus much bilateral and philanthropic aid.

In this exhausting attempt to raise up the world to European standards, one can concomitantly raise the question as to whether this altruistic effulgence essentially undermined the Europeans' ability to maintain their own dominant sociobiological position. Here, once more presented to cognitive analysis is a paradox that is rooted in the human cortex, a cortex that is liberated from and unrestrained by mammalian instinct. How do we know what altruism or seeming self-interest serves the survival of our own "selfish genes"?

Scarcity inaugurated a new human transition in the twenty-first century. The heavy demographic footprint of humankind was now linked to energy-resource depletion, here including ever-scarcer precious water for agriculture and basic human needs. What had changed in this transitional interval was the fading need for unskilled human labor. The race for techno-economic dominance had created conditions that no longer required an early-twentieth-century industrial model of advanced productivity. No longer would nations have to merely show their military muscle (intelligence) to gain economic and political advantage.

The northeast Asiatic nations and a once-defeated Germany, even while bereft of its high education/intelligent one percent, the Jews, would now show the world that science, technology, and surplus value productivity had become the desideratum for the economic and social victory of high-intellect nations. The dream of an internationalism that was universal in its encompassing of equal inputs and equal outcomes in the traditional Eurasian vision of civilizational values and achievements had dissolved with the concomitant undermining of the dominance of the euro.

The question before humanity was how this technological and intellectual advantage would translate into power. Standards of living would now be purchased through a balance of population with natural resources, these either found at home or purchased in trade. Scientific achievement and educational dominance, would inevitably lead to general military security, especially from those nations and peoples who would need and want more.

A new dynamic of natural selection is beginning to reveal itself as each nation's leadership, facing the challenge of attaining demographic and energy/resource viability, confronts choices remaindered from recent ideological infatuations. Can they still govern while giving away a portion of their own middle class's economic and social viability to the nonproductive dependent within its borders, or to those failed nations beyond? Failing societies will see their populace suffer and become ever more dependent on the ever-thinner porridge of support from the international community, the haves. Eventually will they not be forced to "voluntarily" rein in their population growth or by the determinism of nature have it reduced, in tragedy?

## Perspective

Today, the Europoid West, including North America, is losing its inner cohesive optimism, while yet indulging their ideological innocence. In eastern Europe and in the northeast Asiatic nations there is a silent but greater awareness of the current realities of social selection, and they strive to take advantage of the cognitive dissonance of the deluded.

Cognitive recognition of the underlying significance of cortical intelligence and its educational institutional instrumentalities can create a new ball game for the world community. Then, all ethnicities-nationalities could rise up to the challenge and make serious efforts to channel their intergenerational demographic dynamics towards the upper end of the Cro-Magnid IQ-educational scale.

As all nationalities reach for the alpha domain of intellectual prowess, there will gradually occur a lessening of the traditional intra-specific tensions within the human species. Ethnicity, cultural pluralism, and the fruits of non-discursive symbolism still rule the roost as human institutional societal changes are quieted down to manageable institutional governance and legality. The world seeks peace and sustainability.

A new European-style union could be put into place for the entire human race. The ancient racial differences within humanity are even now being blended into the panmictic dynamics of an interbreeding super-species. New structures of symbolic innovation will always emerge, requiring clarification and analysis from the standpoint of *Homo sapiens sapiens'* evolutionary heritage and destiny.

## Note

1. Coon, C. (1962). *The origin of races*. New York, NY: Knopf; Coon, C. (1970). *The living races of man*. New York, NY: Knopf.

## · 1 4 ·

## REALITY SUPPRESSED

… The more perceptive the senses are of differences, the larger is the field upon which our judgment and intelligence can act.—Francis Galton, 1883

### Millennial Revolution

Images that tell a story; tipping points into a world of new rules; the end of old assumptions.

a) An old British film, post–World War II, symbolized what had happened during the war to the old set of values: Colonel Blimp, preparing for the war games. His brigade of Greens against fellow Blues. This training battle was to begin at midnight. Blimp at 10:00 p.m. in his bath, humming in lubricious warmth. Soon to come, a Spartan meal and then into uniform to meet at 11:30 with his Greens. Suddenly the door to the bathroom is flung open. Three officers with blue armbands burst in, waving their pistols. "Colonel, you are under arrest, a prisoner of war." "What the devil is this—war begins at midnight!" "Not anymore, Colonel."

b) Again England. Outside the city of Bath, at the Roman ruins. Here an ancient city luxuriating in its benign ecology. For many hundreds of ancient years it had prospered under the comforts of *Pax Romana*. In the contemporary museum stands an inscribed stone declaration to the citizens of this ancient city, end of fourth century. It is a message transmitted from faraway Italy, the emperor now virtually besieged in his northern redoubt, Ravenna. A reply to a presumed appeal. Paraphrased: "We cannot help you, our legions in Gaul are stretched too thin." The cause of the crisis in "Bath": Germanic tribes have crossed over into Britain from the north and are descending on *Londinium* and other southern towns such as Bath. There is to be no military resolution here.

The Roman Britons, long citizens of these parts, with sadness, pack up their portable belongings, abandon their lush gardens and inlaid mosaic terraces. Off by ship to *Armorica* (Normandy/Brittany), where the Gaulish allies of Rome will presumably protect them. Lives, a world, abandoned to the unanticipated, the unplanned.

c) Another image: even further back in time. Envision the funerary paintings of the Romanized citizens of Egypt, first century CE. Here again wealth, comfort. Picture the ships of trade, plying the waters of the Mediterranean then up the Tiber to the city of Rome itself, one million folks, four months' supply of grain to this metropolis from the wealth of the Nile. The population of ancient Egypt was then in the four to six million range.

Jump forward 2,100 years, to the Egyptian revolutions of 2011–13. A people newly committed to democracy reveling in their ancient historical heritage, the greatness of the civilization that Egypt once was, once more struggling against primitive ideologies. Again, consider the resource requirements of modern life along this ancient river, now threatened by upstream dams in what was once barely inhabited Nubia (Sudan, Ethiopia). Wonder about the singular challenge today of feeding and governing the existing population of Egypt, c. 85 million, in chaos.

d) "In the ten years ending in 2009 U.S. factories shed workers so fast that they erased almost all the gains of the previous seventy years; roughly one out of every three manufacturing jobs—about six million in total—disappeared."

Joke from cotton country: The average mill [textile] has only two employees today: " … a man and a dog. The man is there to feed the dog; and the dog is there to keep the man away from the machines." Adam Davidson, *The Atlantic*, December 20, 2011.

## Civilizational Transformations

One can understand the radical reassessment of the nature of social justice that began to form in the nineteenth century. Science had suddenly created the conditions for the preservation of fragile life at birth, and it was beginning to extend life into maturity. In addition, there was work in the mines and factories of the West. Great infrastructure projects developed with the new modes of transportation and communication. The world, which had been moving in psychologically positive directions of social and political reform, now was confronted with a new socialist dialectic which ended contemporaneously in assertions of oppression and exploitation.

Having undercut the intellectual rationale for the old medieval order and created visions of individual liberty and intellectual and entrepreneurial freedom, we heard instead the slogans of class warfare, ever-new divisions between the haves and have-nots. And so it went for another two centuries. Humans did not stop pouring out from the fertile womb of the dynamic technological world and its twin, scientific medicine, producing ever more "have-nots."

The twentieth century, with two world wars, innumerable genocides, and the *Holocaust*, aimed primarily at the successful middle classes, scarred this new utopian landscape. Yet the momentum continued, ever-recurring demonological accusations of oppression, now increasingly ethnic and racial. The world was coming face to face with the vastly increasing populations of the partially-Cro-Magnid peoples in the "third world." Even while the rich became richer, the poverty-stricken segments of our world remained inertly cemented in, primarily by their own despotic leaders. No longer do we see the old European and North American colonial exploiters. Rather, natural-resource "entrepreneurs" newly arrived from geographies to the east.

Everywhere in the West, including Europe and North America, the utopian vision of the nineteenth century was, "equalize by fiat, a gun if necessary." Within the nations, and throughout the world, the twentieth-century vision was of a world divided: the evil racist exploiters and the victims thrust down into the cold, dark basements of societies.

There was only one utopian solution: to rectify through the force of political and military action. This worked for a time in both Europe and the United States. Vast wealth was redirected politically and an industrial middle class did emerge, but only until the piled-up debts suffocated the political machines of redemptive social welfare-ism. In the socialist/communist world this gnostic search for evildoers eventually led to the buildup of vast genocidal, totalitarian, political/military machines, eventually to crumble internally and be thrown over by a new breed of heretical political revolutionaries. Sadly, in Russia and its satellites, and in China and its followers, the vestiges of authoritarianism still remain.

Unquestionably many saw this general civilizational debacle coming. But every great cultural tradition has a good percentage of those with a vested interest in maintaining the momentum of what makes life easy and graceful for those wielding the instruments of power. Here both private and public institutions play the same symbolic games and carry forth similar allegiances. Except, one day nothing works anymore, and the most vulnerable find leadership groups that engage, as once did Marx and his followers, in a process of ferreting out the exemplars of these ideological systems of power, to show the world that they "wear no clothes."

## The Irrelevance of Race

The Marxist/Leninist/Maoist revolutionary visions of the model of exploiter/exploited were developed in the context of European and Asiatic populations. Marx himself was skeptical of the capacity of the African Negro to attain the intellectual/industrial model of European and the North American Caucasoids. And Mao saw in his Chinese Han ethnicity a superiority that would eventually dominate Asia, at the least. Under the press of these totalitarian ideologies, European and North American liberals suffered under a self-imposed guilt. The enormous gap in socioeconomic development between the Europoids and other less-developed peoples of varying racial and ethnic origins became the secular equivalent of original sin.

It seemed to most universalist liberals that the obvious reason for this international maldevelopment in "people of color" relative to the well-off Cro-Magnid Caucaosids was clearly a case of momentary historical evolution brought about by European and American colonial exploiters, the slave trade being an important element in this armorial ideological rationalization. It made little impression that some people of color had already—1905, Japan versus czarist Russia—defeated a European power. But of course Marx would have chuckled, as he believed Russia was far below the bar of being an industrial equal with the other Europeans.

Neither did the Japanese attack on the United States, as well as their final defeat culminating in two atomic bombs, change the view that it was all colonial exploitation and ongoing segregation and prejudice that was the crucial element in these international disparities of civilizational development. Moving forward sixty-seventy years later into the twenty-first century, the Japanese (once bulldogged by Admiral Perry, 1857), the Koreans, Taiwanese (both for long under the heel of the Japanese), Singapore, Hong Kong (once colonial adjuncts of Britain), as well as mainland China, once dominated by almost all of Europe, were all exploding in industrial, technological, economic power, and cultural advancement.

Is it possible, then, that these disparities are not necessarily inherently racial or caused by demonological Caucasoids? The factual answer is both yes and no. As we have earlier noted, the great human evolutionary divide came with the as yet mysterious origin of Cro-Magnon, possibly 300–200 ka BP. They were Caucasoids, predecessors of the eighteenth-century Europeans and North Americans. But so were the more traditionally primitive Neanderthaloids, also residents of Europe and Asia. And truthfully there probably are, as we have earlier noted, Neanderthal genes floating around as recessives in the Europoid Caucasoid populations.

The northeast Asiatic dominators of the current international economic scene are not pure Mongoloids, not more advanced descendants of *H. erectus pekinensis* of paleontological fame, 500 ka BP. The ancient Mongoloid clade was a relatively isolated one living in the general region of Beijing. More widespread was the Australid subspecies spread out from the mid-Pacific to Pakistan. Coming to the scene a bit later were the Cro-Magnid-Caucasoids from Europe and west Asia, an ongoing geographical movement east for at least the past hundred thousand years, both of Neanderthals and Cro-Magnons. "Sadly," the Mongoloids were genetically swamped by these other two races. Pure racial exemplars of "Peking" man have not been about for many thousands of years.

But with the infusion of Cro-Magnon genes, these descendants, who also have within their genoplasm a good proportion of Australid genetics, these mixed-race genes advanced all throughout Asia. The only "pure"-blooded exemplars of the Australids are the remnants in Australia, a few tribes in New Guinea and elsewhere in isolated geographies. But even here, as noted, we find non-nutritionally-challenged exemplars with red hair. There are remnant Negrito type Australid aboriginals in the Philippines, India, and other tropical hiding places. Throughout Asia respective populations have a mixture in varying quantities of the genetics of the above three races. The Chinese, Japanese, and Koreans are thus triracial hybrids. In fact the Japanese and Koreans speak languages that are distantly related to Hungarian, Finnish, and Estonian. These relatively recent genetic combos have wandered east in the past two thousand years.

Note that the Indian subcontinent, invaded by Caucasoid elements five thousand years ago, originally held a large Australid population. In the tropical south, to survive is to have dark skin. But the dark skin of the present populations of these three nations, India, Pakistan, and Bangladesh, is a genetic mixture of the two groups, one indigenous from at least a million years ago, the other intrusive in the past several thousand years. The two interacting populations were very different intellectually and culturally, leading to divergent sociopolitical solutions, including the caste system started in Hindu India by the Sanskrit civilization of the Caucasoid (Cro-Magnid) Indo-Europeans, c. 2000 BCE.

Of the other two other evolutionary and geographical races of humanity, Negroid and Capoids, the purity factor can here also be questioned. Sadly, because such biological diversity in an interbreeding species is always to the good, sometimes purity doesn't work. The Capoids, as with the Australids, are a disappearing race. Once they dominated all of Africa. They may have also been related biologically to another wandering out-of-Africa group, the distant Mongoloids. As with the story of the Koreans, "Japanese who stayed home," the Capoids could have been the Mongoloids who didn't travel. We see evidence of Capoid art and genetics throughout North Africa; their art is seen in Spanish caves, where these Capoid/Boskopoids once encountered the Cro-Magnons, and with disastrous results.

Then, an apparently newer racial group, the Negroids, started to vigorously spread east and south out of their west African homeland. They and newly migrating Europoids eventually pushed the Capoids into their last redoubt, the Kalahari Desert. Simultaneously Caucasoid migrants crossed the Strait of Gibraltar, and others came around the eastern edge of the Mediterranean to Egypt, and the south and west of Africa, subsequently absorbing these Capoid elements. Today the Bushmen are a disappearing remnant; the Hottentots, a hybrid Capoid-Negroid ethnicity, also are radically diminished in number.

As we noted in the previous chapter, Carleton Coon, one of the great scientific anthropologists of the twentieth century, believed Negroids to have been a product of an ancient Caucasoid intrusion into tropical west Africa sometime after c. 100 ka BP. Those mysterious Cro-Magnon-like tools found in the jungles of this region dated not long after this timeframe. But the fossil evidence still eludes. Coon also believed that the two races most closely related were the Caucasoids and the Negroids. Today, Africa is a pastiche of racial elements, not too different from the diversity of Asia.

Note that the Tutsi of Rwanda/Burundi, a tall, once migratory cattle-raising people, speak an Amharic language similar to the Ethiopians; the latter are Caucasoid in origin, but since enfiladed by significant Negroid migrants from the southwest. In South Africa there are large hybrid Bantu/Europoid/Indian groups. North Africa has its ancient Capoid-Europoid elements, but also a large and more recent immigrant enslaved Negroid population absorbed into Islamic universality. And of course this latter amalgamation is true of the once-Caucasoid populations of the Near East, which are today completely hybridized with Negroid genetics originating from this medieval slave trade.

The United States is also an exemplar of a hybridized society. The estimate is that the African American population has approximately 20–25% Caucasoid genes, plus a small admixture of Native American and Hispanic genetics. The growing Latino population is a mixture of its original European Spanish, then Indian (Mongoloid, Australid, Caucasoid) and African genetics absorbed into the Caribbean and other Latin American populations. Within the North American Caucasoid population some estimates argue for a c. 5% Negroid admixture, so-called "mulatto" hybrids having passed into the "white" population.

Given that the non-European genetic element in that continent approaches 10%, and now with a higher birthrate, the homeland of the Caucasoid race is rapidly becoming hybridized with the rest of the world. And of course, this goes for humanity in general. As we will point out below, this heritage of subspecies differences is real, but it is a passing element of humanity's history.

In evolutionary terms, strong selective factors tend to allow one racial clade to become momentarily dominant, to have its genes spread throughout the adaptive domain of the larger species until the species itself becomes panmictic, a universal or near-universal blending of genetics that fits the species into the selective requirements of the ecology. The geographical barriers in the human species have long been dissolved through modern technology. Traditional primate biological drives will eventually, three or four hundred years hence, create a predominantly random racial genetic profile for humankind.

## The Intelligence Factor

We are in a transitional stage in human evolution. We still have to live and come to terms with our evolutionary past as we attempt to prepare for our future. There should be no doubt that the revolution in human morphology, which allowed for the creation of our modern international civilization, began with the birth of Cro-Magnon. Cro-Magnon happened to be endowed with the phenotypic attributes of modern Caucasoids. They, as with the more primitive Neanderthals, were northerners. They were "white" people.

The critical element in this revolution in morphology was that enormous bulging skull cavity enclosing a passionately inquiring cortex. Because of the dangers to the female, this enormous skull by big-brained neonates exiting a morphologically ancient hominid birth canal, it is probable that Cro-Magnon and its descendants stand at the edge of morphologically selective functionality. More brain bulk could under ordinary circumstances—vaginal birth—destroy the female. Today, a brainier neonate might be possible via C-section. The genes of Cro-Magnon have now wandered far. Humans do like to travel: basically for curiosity, secondarily for conquest and sex.

A large cortical brain created the possibility for abstract thinking, organizing sensory experience into symbolic structures of thought that in almost every aspect of human sensory experience attempts to universalize these experiences into laws. Thus literacy was created by the Sumerians for their international economic trade. This technology, *literacy*, spread rapidly to other ethnicities that were ready for it. The Chinese were late into the world of the power of the written word and the abstract mathematical theorem. Their literacy came from the west, the hybrid, probably Persia-originating horsemen. These migrants gave China the clue to the powers of abstract thinking, planning, communicating the ideational power that produced a Confucius, Lao Tzu.

There is no question but that this power of mind, abstract intelligence, put the Caucasoids on the side of historical and geographical dominance. But they did pass their genes onto many other peoples. In the process, as we see in India, China, Korea, and Japan, the cerebralization of society allowed for the creation of competitors to the West. Also, within each ethnic domain of our world, and throughout history, what a nation or a people did subsequently as a matter of social policy, either consciously or unconsciously, to nurture or destroy this heritage of Cro-Magnon intelligence, determined their power as a people or a nation.

Ideology can counter and then nullify the dynamics of increased cerebralization, the capacity of a nation to rise to intellectual, moral, and economic greatness. The twentieth century is the prime exemplar of humankind's paradoxical ability to choose beyond the constraints of instinct, sadly, stupidly.

Some peoples have come into the zone of cerebralization later than others. They were remnant survivors of *Homo sapiens sapiens*' surge, but that does not mean that they are forever condemned to living in the shadow of the "white" man. Tell the Asiatic Indians and Chinese that. They will laugh and point to modern-day Greece, the modern inheritors of the greatest civilizational achievements in literate history.

As pointed out in the previous section, the ancient racial divisions are passing into history day by day. Today there are real ethnic divisions, peoples and nations who want to live apart, within their borders. Their capacity to flourish, or wither, will depend upon what they do with their intellectual capital—degrade or enhance it. Here social and political policies based on factual reality or fanciful ideologies will determine outcomes. Our universal knowledge has brought us to the point where we now can consciously determine our fate.

## Suppression

In the late nineteenth century in England, Francis Galton, polymath cousin of Charles Darwin, grandson of the groundbreaking scientist/philosopher Erasmus Darwin, was bedeviled by the seemingly intractable educational aptitude differences within the traditional English population. This population had grown mightily during the century, mostly from the agricultural and industrial proletariat. Galton attempted to create empirical research tools for evaluating what he and others at the time were now hypothesizing as biological differences in intellectual abilities.[1]

Unlike his cousin Charles, Galton was not a tightly focused genius; he ranged over a wide span of scientific issues. However, similarly to the epochal breakthrough of Charles Darwin, Galton carved out an analytical and research vision for the future study of human aptitudes and abilities. In the first decade of the twentieth century, Alfred Binet and Theodore Simon were commissioned by the French government to create tests for young children that might predict their success in the traditional elitist educational climate of that country.[2] No minority racial groups were part of these European research efforts, with the exception that Galton had taken an interest in the abilities of the impoverished Jewish and Italian children in the London slums. He saw these Jewish and Italian children in the East London schools as having abilities that exceeded what one would expect given their low socioeconomic status. He also photographed them to provide additional anthropometric data for his research.[3]

These beginnings of the scientific study of intelligence shortly led to an explosion of research. A follower of Galton, Charles Spearman, created the theory of factor analysis and the concept of *g* for general intelligence. This research became one of the foundations of the psychometric analysis of human abilities. His first paper outlining his research methods, in 1904, was published in an American psychology journal.[4] This research perspective rekindled the study of eugenics, the improvement of the human race in terms of health and social behavior, a very stormy area of study in the late nineteenth century.

Concerned with the indigenous Caucasoid populations of Europe and the United States, the eugenic concept for the improvement of the human race, physically and mentally, was highly popular amongst the early twentieth-century left-wing elite. Harold Laski and J. B. S. Haldane, in England, and Margaret Sanger, in the U.S., were leading proponents. The rise of Hitler and fascism in Europe, and the smoke screen of race improvement that fascists used to destroy the highly creative and productive Jews of Europe, put an ideological hold on such idealism, especially as the psychometric movement was finding significant differences in g-factor intelligence tests and their educational embodiments between the races and ethnicities. Hypothetically, this was estimated to be causal in the differential vocational and economic outcomes evidenced in modern society.

However, under the cover of the ideological view that all human intellectual differences were environmental, sociological, and historical, the practice of eugenics was demonized as racist and psychometric testing began to go underground, transformed into the SAT and other euphemistic testing applications. The world is yet awash in such tests, almost always searching for the underlying *g* of abstract intelligence and the consequent predicted abilities for high civilizational professional achievement that it could herald.

In the Soviet Union, the communist denial of the biological element in human behavior led to the genocides ordered by Joseph Stalin. Here came the slaughter of millions of intellectuals or the successful farmers of the Ukraine, the Kulaks. The study of "Mendelism" was done away with, the talented academic leadership sent off to the "gulag." The environmentalist ideas of Stalin's heroes, Michurin and Lysenko, practically destroyed Soviet agriculture. This vision of sociopolitical creationism however made its way, more benignly, but equally disastrously, into the West.

Those in the West who argued for the biological rooting of human intellectual achievement were seen as implicit racists and suffered the professional consequences of marginalization and expulsion. The power structure could not envision the eventuality that the surplus wealth of the West would disappear as a result of zealous redistributionist and social welfare policies—ultimately, dysgenic programs.

The hope today has to be that the irrevocable factuality of this social and economic decline in the West will allow for the entrance of a smidgen of rationality in social policy making. Here we must exclude from this warning and hope the more pragmatic northeast Asiatic peoples who have suffered, as with the east Europeans, their own share of ideological insanity. Given our ancient heritage of Cro-Magnon intelligence, the prediction has to be that the world will eventually allow the morning sun of truth to finally enter the windows of an awakening generation of the ever-inquiring young.

## Notes

1. Galton, F. (1869). *Hereditary genius*. London: Macmillan.
2. Binet, A., & Simon, T. (1916). *The development of intelligence in children* (E. Kite, Trans.). Baltimore, MD: Williams & Wilkins.
3. Galton, F. (1883). *Inquiries into human faculty and its development*. London: Macmillan; Galton, F. (1888). Co-relations and their measurement, chiefly from anthropological data. *Proceedings of the Royal Society of London, 45,* 135–145.
4. Spearman, C. (1904). "General intelligence," objectively measured and determined. *The American Journal of Psychology, 15,* 201–292; Spearman, C. (1927). *The abilities of man: Their nature and measurement*. New York, NY: Macmillan.

# PART III—OUR TWENTY-FIRST CENTURY AND BEYOND

## · 1 5 ·

# CONDITIONS OF INTERNATIONAL SURVIVAL

### Twenty-First-Century Adaptive Shift

From the standpoint of our evolutionary knowledge of the pulsations of expansion and decline of the larger taxonomic units involved in evolutionary change, as well as species and races, the sub-categories of the larger evolutionary exemplars, our recent five hundred years on a roll of expansion and multiplication is not atypical. All life forms tend to take advantage of even momentary adaptive opportunities for a possible surge into dominance. Their movement is explicable as an attempt to preempt an ecological, morphological, or behaviorally adaptive niche, and grow in both size and in number.

It is only when restrictive conditions enter their life space that these forms of life tend to specialize into the possibly positive ecological setting, or shrink in both number and size to fit the limitations that time, events, and nature have now thrown their way. Genesis and the Joseph story in the Hebrew Bible said it all, a warning to mankind at a time when the issue of breakthrough demographics and economics was not a tipping point survival issue for the international community, as it is today.

High cognitive, abstract intelligence was the key to the survival of the neotonous Cro-Magnons in their struggle against the icy, late Pleistocene winds. Probably it was an interregnum of moderating weather, as with today, that brought them westward into the heart of Europe where they met their ancient recidivistic Neanderthal relatives. In spite of the renewed descent of the glaciers, they adapted to and flourished in this rich hunting, fishing, and berry-picking environment. They expanded in numbers over a thirty-thousand-year period eventually pushing the Neanderthals into extinction, not without some genetic assimilation between both groups. In the meantime these wandering, exploring genes had made their *sapiens* mark at great distances beyond this new and fecund homeland, Europe/west Asia.

The rhythms of civilizational advance, regression, and transition that have followed, slowly adding to *Homo sapiens sapiens'* knowledge of, and predictive control of, the worldly environment, was to give this mammalian clade a great adaptive thrust forward with the distillation of the scientific method, a product of the Renaissance unleashing of the human mind to freely think and analyze without the ideological supervision of institutional religious mysticism. The five hundred or so years of advance into our human ecology has now hit its dialectical endpoint. The inner contradictions of this sometimes-chaotic thrust forward should have been understood better by our elites by virtue of the experience of the twentieth century's horrific human bloodletting.

We now have entered a twenty-first century made emblematic by additional inner contradictions in our seemingly adaptive suzerainty: international terrorism, endless wars, overwhelming human poverty amidst localized plenty, the drying up of our heritage of plentiful and cheap natural resources. We will eventually come to the headline conclusion that there may now be an end to economic growth, and thus a finality to the hope for a luxurious, universally high standard of living for the human masses. *Humankind: batten down the hatches, half-speed ahead.*

## Illusion

Those who are in power, who draw the rewards of the status quo, even when this status quo is disintegrating around them and ordinary people are hurting, will never say: "Folks the game is up, this is the end of the track. We have to negotiate our way onto a narrower gauge, and all, including ourselves, presumptive leaders, will have to thin down, put on the hair shirt and suffer the challenge."

It's tough to give up the perks of privilege. Classical Rome in the West was on the edge. It hung on for over one hundred fifty years before ceding history to Constantinople. For the contemporary international community it will be a shorter transition, but an equally revolutionary one. It finally hit us in the first decade of the twenty-first century. Global oil production peaked around 2005–6, and we in the West soon slipped into an ongoing recession. The blame was the housing bubble here in the U.S. and everywhere. But the jobs were disappearing, the robots and computers flourishing. These events took place well before the ever-rising prices for crude. The jobs were migrating to smart, cheap labor. And with it went the growth economy. The shoals of debt surfaced with the outgoing tide. The bond vigilantes licked their lips. Beware, the 2015 oil glut is an epiphenomenon.

The disbelief, the anger, the awareness that the populace had been led by charlatans was reflected in the demonstrations, pathetically empty of dynamic, as the people reluctantly admitted to the truth. They had been taken. From early 2012 the world had looked on in schadenfreude as the thieves who led the Greek people and who subsidized their free lunch holiday for a decade with Euro debt fought against telling the people that they were really socioeconomically incompetent and poor as church mice, as an ethnicity and as a nation.

Naturally, the ideological dream of wealth redistribution through debt accumulation under the illusion of having real economic productive growth dies hard. The meetings all over the West, the central bankers, striving hard to negotiate the salvation of the system, discussions, of course over filet mignon, continued unabated until the poor suckers, meaning the tax-paying citizenry, in one convulsive breath would blow away this ideological smoke screen.

Naturally, these events would take time to spell out their ultimate international consequences. The depletion of natural resources linked to the ever-expanding numbers of the needy would require a few more years to explicate its full force, the worldwide recession to evolve into a permanent global depression. The crisis to come would eventually evoke from the masses, a silent-lip articulated implication, *triage*. The educated citizenry, those holding on to the ever-sinking life rafts of hope in the current system, at some point would come to the realization that the revolutionary moment had arrived. They would have to adapt to this new reality in the modern lexicon, *scarcity*. Thus has arrived the revolutionary concept from which the new international world of 9.5 billion oncoming humans would henceforth be built.

## The Millennial Twenty-First-Century Transition

Lessons from the Hellenic-Hellenistic transition are instructive. The mainland Greeks had lived in stony poverty, struggling with the barren land to raise barley and oats. Then, in their transforming industrial heyday, the grape and olive arrived. But their surge into prosperity came not from the raw materials. These poleis became economically competitive in the international market by the beautiful ceramics that their artists created for the wine and olive-oil export trade. The Romans lived in a richer ecology and were able through their more methodical economic and military efforts to sustain their wealth and power for centuries. The Roman thrust beyond their home town into the quest for international military suzerainty never matched the cultural achievements of the Greeks, and they knew it.

An exemplar of the awakening of the Greeks to their implicit powers to stave off a more wealthy and numerous enemy, to raise and organize disciplined armies and navies, is given in the following story that appears towards the end of Herodotus's chronicling of the end of the several Persian wars of the Greeks:

> A story has got about that Xerxes [479 BCE] on his retreat from Greece left his tent with Mardonius [the Persian commander killed in the battle of Mantinea, by a united Greek army of mostly Spartans, but also Athenians. This battle finally forced the Persians back into Asia]. When Pausanias [Greek/Spartan commander-in-chief] saw it, with its embroidered hangings and gorgeous decorations in silver and gold, he summoned Mardonius's bakers and cooks [captured in battle], and told them to prepare a meal of the same sort as they were accustomed to prepare for their former master. The order was obeyed; and when Pausanias saw gold and silver couches all beautifully draped [for the sitting], and gold and silver tables, and everything prepared for the feast with great magnificence, he could hardly believe his eyes for the good things set before him, and, just for a joke, ordered his own servants to get ready an ordinary Spartan dinner. The difference between the two meals was indeed remarkable, and, when both were ready, Pausanias laughed and sent for the Greek commanding officers. When they arrived, he invited them to take a look at the two tables, saying, "Gentlemen, I asked you here in order to show you the folly of the Persians, who, living in this style came to Greece to rob us of our poverty."[1]

The important lesson here is that a free people, empowered by their love and aspiration for national integrity, can indeed destroy an enemy built on misappropriated wealth, leading an army of servile mercenaries. From the poverty of material opportunity can come greatness of mental, and then physical, achievement. The Greeks had, before this series of wars with the Persians, already excelled in sculpture, ceramic arts, poetry, and in music. The Athenians had created an architecture of wooden beauty on their Acropolis, recently (480 BCE) burned down by Xerxes. This "city on high" would soon be rebuilt with marble and gold. Except for the Macedonian parvenus, Philip and Alexander, the classical Hellenes did not thrust for international military honors.

The world can be rebuilt in beauty and plenitude, beyond the twenty-first century. But first it must come to its rational senses, face up to the instrumentalities of institutional disintegration which we have created over the past century and a half. The test of *Homo sapiens sapiens'* evolutionary viability lies in our corporate capacity to take advantage of our cerebral cortex's capacity to think factually, empirically, to secularly analyze the factors impinging on our destiny. Only then could we set out on an international venture to live within the parameters of our bio/social nature and the earth's capacity to accommodate our presence.

## Conditions

*1. High Intelligence*
This, the necessary condition for all policy-making decisions. The capacity for high, critical, intelligent thinking-things-through depends not merely on the power of an elite to will its decisions, but for the masses themselves to have the capacity to discipline their limbic system emotions and be able to live by the principle of the law. The intelligence that flowed out of the Cro-Magnon brain and is now distributed unevenly, internationally, is not exclusive to any racial or ethnic group. Our conjoint intellectual competency will eventually define our species. Today we are, in brainpower, a mixture of *Homo sapiens/ Homo sapiens sapiens*. Eventually we will become truly panmictic: intellectually integrated in quality, but also ethnically diversified.

*2. Rationality*
We humans have always lived and thought through our embedded views of reality. When we deviate from the best empirical understandings of our world and selves we inevitably undermine our viability, as individuals and as social members of a political entity. Today we are challenged by the highest intellectual embodiments of knowledge derived from our skills in the sciences. We need to use our unencumbered brainpower within our political nationalities, but also internationally to confront the growing challenges to the secular middle classes.

The brainpower off of which rational policy making is derived is wanting, within most nations, and cumulatively, internationally. The result is the wafting of the bitter incense of ideology, sometimes secular, sometimes religious. Humans, emotionally driven, will fall into either mode. In high-intelligence nations such as Nazi Germany, its ideological infatuations destroyed a people, and their morale. Yet with a decent remnant of high intelligence still remaining in its populations, an intellectual and emotional reversal came into being. Sixty-five years later its people flourish. The same reversal could apply to the former Soviet Union and communist China, and their satellites.

In other parts of the world, in the Arab Islamic nations for example, the situation is more questionable. Will they be able to throw off their religious veil, which has separated them from the more progressive nations of the north and east? Then there is Israel, which has prospered by first exiting its socialist mantra. Secondly, it must face a conflict with its own ultra-Orthodox medievalists, even while under the gun of tragic and retrogressive Islamic terrorism.

For many nations of the West, social-class, intellectual, and educational differences undermine their futures. These differences leach into an enormous economic separation between haves and have-nots. In our own time these widening class lines derive from ideological delusions about the uniformity of human educability. As a consequence, policies have been instituted that widen the national social gap in each successor generation. This ideological chimera has now been exploded, even if this fact has as yet not been brought to our vision of reality. The social policies that subsidized and thus created these underclass minorities, now becoming national statistical majorities, need everlasting support from a shrinking independently productive segment of society.

There is a sad irony in our current human evolutionary state. The crowning jewel of our human nature, our high cortical potentiality, has been obfuscated by our mammalian emotions, here by an elite that should have known better. First, this intellectual elite misdiagnosed the problem of uneven social and economic advancement in these ostensibly progressive democratic societies. Seeing the problems not improve, especially in their non-majority Cro-Magnid minorities, and under emotional pressure, they engaged in a massive debt-ridden redistribution of the momentary national wealth in the hope that impoverishment would magically disappear.

Having bloated the numbers of poor of all racial and ethnic groups, through this process of subsidization and redistribution of what once was an enormous surplus wealth accumulation by the cognitively productive, these nations were now up against the wall. By the beginning of the twenty-first century this surplus wealth was gone, the nations all drowning in a sea of debt, the productive sector of society shrinking in size and means. No longer could this vanishing wealth be redistributed, especially under this incubus of debt. At the very least, interest on the debt would have to be paid. The prognosis for the amount and percentage of interest on this debt was *not* down!

The only conclusion that can be gleaned as a message for the future is that the leadership was not merely irrational, but was playing for its own momentary sociobiological advantage. Oddly, this advantage was not necessarily characterized by biological fecundity. It had co-opted assent by the psychologically vulnerable productive majority, through ideological/mammalian intimidation.

However, for the so-called advanced nations of the new international West (Europe, North America, northeast Asia) the numbers of mostly equally competent "have-nots" is such that the rational philosophical basis of domination by this misconceived sociopolitical elite has been undermined, and probably for the duration of the century. The suffering of the uneducated impoverished within the developed world will only increase. Tragically, the weak nations of the third world who ostensibly benefited from this redistribution are today ever more vulnerable to their own strong-armed intimidators, and the new colonialist predators from afar.

Irrationality in policy has led to weakened intellectual, scientific, and economic capabilities in these now debtor nations of the Europoid West. Hopes for the spread internationally of democratic institutions have not been helped in the misguided aspired road towards human equality. Instead of building on their home-based intellectual capital in order to secure both the material and social benefits of science, these nations have undermined and wasted it. Their philanthropic immigration policies are exemplars of this establishment's self-serving "nuttiness." Ironically, in once-colonialized northeast Asia, this ideological disease has not yet spread. They do not search far and wide for educated and wealthy foreigners to bail them out.

If we are to resolve the enormous crisis that awaits humankind in the twenty-first century, we will need to sweep away the debris caused by the ideological insanity of the twentieth and twenty-first centuries under which Cro-Magnon's intelligence has suffocated. These centuries have resulted in the debasement of our intellectual capital and our rational profiles. If intellectual potentiality is the necessary condition for human progress, then rationality in public policy making is its sufficient condition.

## 3. Demographic Discipline

Here is an exemplar of the current international irrationality and policy impotence. This is the lack of a serious secular debate about the ongoing and crushing weight of our bloated international population. There is no awareness in our international elites that the hope for achieving an egalitarian economic resolution to the current sadness rests on the solution to the heavy weight of masses of humans on this planet. Even the ecologists shy away from placing overpopulation first on the challenge to our dying ecology, its potentiality for inducing a vast climate, public health disaster, not to speak of making our planet barren of most other living forms.

At the moment the rationale for doing nothing is the slogan that populations will level off as higher economic possibilities motivate even presently poor humans to practice birth control. This is happening in the developed West, now including East Asia, and even segments of the Islamic world. Another argument for not acting to decrease our international population uses Europe and Japan as case studies for denial. It is purported that these nations will not have enough vigorous hands to support, economically and socially, the growing percentage of the aged.

The propaganda further argues that larger populations provide jobs for the great mass production, entertainment, and retail industries. Rarely stated is that smaller industrial components rarely throw off as much wealth for the plutocratic managers of vast enterprises, here especially including the powerful financial conglomerates.

Truthfully, one does make a wager with the future in calling for an international population shrinkage of significance. This wager of warning takes into account the present and oncoming shortage of the raw materials that have propelled the past several centuries of population expansion and economic growth. Given present statistics, 7-plus billion humans going on to 9–9.5 billion by 2050, there must be included in our calculus of possibilities the dangers of severe climate incidents, desertification, earthquakes, floods, even a disease pandemic spreading beyond the control of present medical capabilities. Such a crisis could produce a wipeout of populations beyond the rescue capacity of the formerly affluent. The impact on the sociopolitical psyche of humankind of such catastrophes could be millennial.

The first obligation of each nation, after defense of the people, is to plan for and put into policy a steady-state internal national structural relationship between population and resources. Especially important are energy production levels sufficient to maintain some element of middle-class life. The world will eventually have to face up to the reality that some nations and peoples cannot manage their population growth even given current international medical levels of disease and death control. What will happen? Either nature's forcible triage or external direction and guidance will inevitably be applied to lower population levels.

At the same time one can hope that every nation will be obligated to raise its intellectual levels to a worldwide norm of modern scientific, advanced technological, and civilizational institutional life. The old "romance" of the primitive sheepherder or "friendly cannibal" in faraway places is being replaced by starving populations desperately seeking migratory access to middle-class welfare benefits.

National/international wisdom: plan for, institute policies for, the expectation of the *worst* to come. Hope for the *best*.

4. Energy
In 2016 there is still doubt as to whether the planet has reached its peak of oil production, the lubricant for the luscious middle-class life of the West. That the rise in the price of petroleum and its refined by-products from the period 2005–6, when a production peak seemed to have been reached, did not stimulate an increase in production commensurate with this rise in price, did not discourage the halcyonic views of the peak-oil naysayers.

The increasing rise in price coincident with scarcity, given that we avoid an international economic calamity, will at some point early in the twenty-first century create one dimension of the crisis. There is no limit to the items processed from petroleum, natural gas, and coal by-products: agricultural fertilizers, pesticides, medicines of all sorts, plus innumerable products that we consume or use in daily life. We will all be poorer for this evolving event. The question is: who will get what, and by what means?

Clearly the threat of war by nations armed to the teeth with the most terrible weaponry will, of necessity, have to be resolved by a compact between the most powerful. Africa and South America most especially will be in contentious play. The Middle East will also look to "big brother" to protect its various autocracies and semi-feudal regimes. Which "big brother" it will be will be decided by those with powerful military machines, but also those with the deepest pockets.

It is doubtful that forms of renewable energy will provide for the needs of a modern society, at the least for many generations to come. To be realistic we must presume that over the next decade there will be an international scramble to secure for the various nations fossil-energy deposits necessary for economic viability. We know that there are great deposits of natural gas embedded deep within the earth in shale deposits. Not merely in the United States, now in Europe and soon throughout the world, these deposits will for a moment add to known fossil-energy supplies supplementing traditional petroleum, now being steadily depleted. The question: for how long, and at what price will we be able to compress this gas into gasoline?

Shale natural gas deposits will help to soften the decline in fossil energy and mitigate the price rise and thus the inevitable worldwide tax on consumption. At the most optimistic, this would merely add a few decades before the day of reckoning for the survival of our contemporary technological civilization.

If we pray passionately enough to the scientific establishment, some energy miracle may come forth to support the nine or ten billion people who will be living on this planet in the next half century—hydrogen power, wind, sun, nuclear? The price of energy nevertheless still will surely soar, and autos and homes will be miniaturized. The great question concerns the consequent political and cultural condition of humankind as we proceed through the twenty-first century.

Certainly no nation or group of nations will walk away untouched by this slowly churning disk of scarcity. However, as the big boys carve out resources for themselves from the weak, inevitably large portions of the world's peoples will be in serious danger. Again, and inevitably, there will have to be international action to ward off the worst. The concretia of tragedy in one part of the world has a tendency in this modern age to quickly spread to the complacent.

Through the relative price immediacy of the threat of energy shortages we may be able to build a consensus to also bring population into balance with nature and long-term worldwide ecological health. An international accord as to fossil-energy conservation and balances of use could allow the world the time needed to attempt to find renewable and other transformative resources that could lead to a steady-state world ecology for humankind. Here lies the dream for transitioning into a rational balance with nature and our hoped-for survival through the millennia.

In the above discussion the emphasis has been on the most positive of the possible responses to the as yet unacknowledged reefs that could sink this international ship. Given our heritage of irrationality, bad outcomes are more likely. We must yet focus on the possibilities inherent in Cro-Magnid intelligence and rationality.

## Note

1. Herodotus. (1954). *Histories*. (A. de Sélincourt, Trans.). New York, NY: Penguin, 1954.]

## · 1 6 ·

## UTOPIA INTERDICT

UN Population Predictions: May, 2011
World: 2050 = 9.3 billion; 2100 = 10.1 billion; (2013 = c. 7+ billion)
Africa 2100 = 3.6 billion, (2011 = c. 960 million)
Nigeria 2100 = 730 million, (2011 = c. 240 million)
China 2100 = 940 million, (2011 = c. 1.330 billion)

### Challenge of the Century

No one at the beginning of the twentieth century could have predicted either the events that took place after 1900, or what the world would look like at the end of 1999. Certainly 1999 was a better year than the intervening events of the twentieth century. Yet in a short period of time, little more than a decade and a half, 2000–2016, a wholly new prognosis for the future of humankind would be suggested.

Recall that in 1900 the world population was in the range of 1.8 billion people. In 2000, this population had exploded to 6.2 billion people, even while several hundred million humans had been killed in a variety of wars, two worldwide, many genocides, the *Holocaust*, plus untold other sad events.

These figures alone denote an epochal evolutionary event for our evolving panmictic species.

In any forecast or prediction of the future, one cannot but include the so-called "black swan" occurrence: rare, unpredictable, beyond our mental imagination. The best one can do is to argue from the evidence of the human past, the theoretical and empirical realities of *Homo*'s venture upon this planet and the nature of this biological creature's impact on himself, the world of living things, even the physico-chemical environment that has sustained his presence for the several million years of the existence of his genus. Thus we exclude the unpredictable natural events, mostly unhappy, that might alter our vision of the future.

In the preceding chapter we have laid out the basic challenges for the future of humankind in terms of 1) intellectual potential, 2) rational policy-making, 3) demographic discipline, 4) energy resources.

In the following sections we will lay out the short vision responses to these challenges in the diverse politico-ethnic regions of the world, here leaving an analysis of the United States for the following chapter.

## Europe

The traditional economic rule for national governments is that the people are taxed fairly, enough to encourage enterprise and produce requisite tax wealth. In moments of stress the federal government can issue debt to cover the emergency, this debt to be paid back promptly. This was basically what economist John Maynard Keynes suggested as the world was undergoing the depression of the 1930s. The next several decades of the twenty-first century will see all the nations of Europe struggling to pay back old as well as new debt. These nations as with the United States are facing up to what in reality is a deviation from what Keynes thought the role of the state to be in its relationship with the private economy. Except for a few states, such as Russia, with a relatively small demographic footprint in terms of its geography and great natural resources, the challenges will be enormous because of this deviation from rational political responsibility.

There is in Western Europe a new demographic profile, the immigrant minorities from beyond. Their birthrates are high, and their assimilation into the Western educational and cultural profile unenthusiastic. Were the new European minorities to continue their high birthrates, here subsidized by the various on-the-ground social welfare benefits, Europe could be in deep trouble a few decades down the line.

Contained to a minority presence below 10% of the populace, the democratic ethos of the Europeans and their high Cro-Magnid intellectual and educational profiles should eventually bring them into a stable relationship between population size and resource availability. It will be a different Europe than what we have seen in the past one hundred fifty years. Fewer wars, less socialist welfare mythology, perhaps even a return to Renaissance creativity and leadership, a time when materials were expensive but human intelligence and labor innovative.

With the dispersion of modern communication and transportation, it is to be doubted that in a time of scarcity the cartel agreement between the political autocrats and the kleptocrats, as in Russia and Belarus, can long continue. A slow evolution towards Western democratic forms would hopefully take place. On the other hand, given a severe turn of economic events, populist tyranny from the right or the left could also rear its head. The conditions for long-term stability in Europe today exist, even if the dream of the governmental-sponsored welfare/debt growth model is forever gone.

The model of the EU and its possible expansion has been dealt a possible death blow by the events of the years 2011–2014, when a number of nations required severe bailing-out by the European Central Bank and the International Monetary Fund. These several states expanded their debt far beyond their productivity and capacity to repay. The EU had no power over these fiscal excesses. Culture and the non-discursive traditions do still reign, as the north: Scandinavia, Germany, Netherlands, and Austria still maintain an economic sanity while the southern nations—Greece, Italy, Spain, Portugal, but also northerners Belgium and Ireland—sprint for the edge of the cliff. One recalls an old Austrian proverb: "Every nation should have a southern neighbor."

This is not to say that Europe will again fragment into competing societies, always at the brink or over the edge into suicidal wars, as in the twentieth century. Merely that either a very tight universal discursive economic (budgetary) control will be established over the economies of the several states, or that some will be off on their own to experience stark declines in their standard of living. The lesson of Greece may imprint on international memory.

Also disappearing from the European scene will be the freedom to migrate across borders. First, non-Europe immigration will wane. Non-Europeans are already stigmatized by ultra-nationalist groups from Britain to Russia. Second, intra-European migration, complements of the current EU integration regulations, will probably end. Each nation will likely begin to cultivate its own non-discursive cultural and national visions, including language, religion, social values, and most importantly their intellectual profiles, which makes all things possible, or impossible.

## China/Northeast Asia

One postulates that Chinese political autocracy exists for the purpose of transforming China into the leading economic, technological, scientific pseudo-capitalist nation in the world. The general acceptance of this autocratic political environment, with its state-engendered bureaucratic forms of corruption, is already in question. The Chinese people, as with their northeastern Asiatic brethren, the Japanese and Koreans, are Cro-Magnid educable, intelligent, and frothing to become the middle-class superiors to their Europoid brethren.

Eventually the dominance of the Communist Party will wither. But it is doubtful, even with a declining Chinese population imprint, slated to be below the present 1 billion, 350 million down to c. 940 million by 2100, that it will allow for a more localized province-wide democratic environment, given the discursive need to manage almost a billion people of one ethnic nationality (90% Han) in one contiguous geographical area.

The population of this region is large and full of potential political instability. However, the example of the Japanese people during World War II, the terrible human losses, fire bombings, atom bombings, the recent 2011 earthquake, the tsunami, and nuclear meltdown, all revealed a potentially peaceful and disciplined populace. The process of economic retrenchment and the probable redistribution of wealth to these ethnically unified peoples should ensure social stability. One suspects that North Korea will dissolve politically and unite with South Korea in an arrangement different than the total integration of West and East Germany, but yet add to the power of Korea, economically and sociopolitically.

Mao's original enforced one female–one child policy was an accepted voluntary program for the Chinese people. However, this commitment has recently been liberalized. They have the discipline and the desire to rise up economically. As with the Japanese and the Koreans, who are also self-maintaining a low birth rate profile, these populations throughout the twenty-first century should decrease, all while the intense skilled labor profiles and their technological/scientific abilities should allow them to compete productively with the Europeans.

It is important to note that all three ethnicities are related. Similarly, as with the European heritages, they contain within themselves the genetics of Cro-Magnon. They will probably gather themselves together and offer an EU type of relationship with their neighbors to the south and west. Already there are Chinese outposts in Hong Kong and Singapore, but also in Indonesia, Malaysia, the Philippines, and Russian Siberia. The natural resources of Russia and central Asia can be purchased with the productive industrial wealth of these three major ethnicities, hopefully peacefully. And of course, with the trillions in dollar cash, the Chinese are busily reinventing the concept of economic and political colonialism, now without the need to import slave labor.

Finally, the issue of intellectual capital and policy rationality is crucial to the solving of problems as they occur over a century-long period. As noted, these national entities are ethnically, thus educationally, homogeneous. This in itself places into solubility the necessary, if not the sufficient, precondition for any long-term non-ideological problem-solving stance.

## Middle East

We here include North Africa. And it is a very iffy region for surviving deep into the twenty-first century. The oil will be significantly depleted by mid-century. The demographic condition of this region is in the main horrifically congested. Egypt, for example, has the Nile as its only resource. But Sudan and Ethiopia will be contesting for this liquid gold with their own dams at the tributaries (Chinese finance?). At one time Egypt, with five million people, fed itself for a year, and also exported to the city of Rome, with one million people, four months' worth of food grains. Today it has eighty-five million yearning to be free and prosperous. Relatively under-educated, as are their other Islamic confreres, this region produces little that the world wants except oil; Allah's momentary gift of rent.

The Saudis, Iran, Iraq, and the gulf states have several decades' worth of oil, and in good supply. They are overpopulated and need to import food and purify their water. They also have needed the United States to protect them.

China and its neighbors need lots of oil, have the money, and soon the military wherewithal to contest for this precious lubricant.

Though there are contesting signs of an awakening from medieval autocracy and theological confusion, there are few signs of real intellectual capital potentialities that might auger for the production of a self-sustaining middle-class and then the creation of real democratic institutions supporting such a middle class. Once the domestic need for domestic oil blotters out the export potential, certainly before mid-century, the fun should then begin in earnest. That is, if their economic-social profiles have not earlier begun to disintegrate in anarchy and blood. The signs in early 2016 are not good.

Iran is the only one of these nations that has shown any enthusiasm for secular independence. Regretfully they are now imprisoned by theological/military insanity. Once this incubus is thrown off, as it will be, the Persian people will have to bring their population numbers under control. Under Islamic legal traditions this can be done. They have a rich heritage and potential, the only non-Arabic state in the region, and the one with the most long-term hope for democracy, secular science, and the creation of a modern self-maintaining middle-class society.

Israel is in the Middle East, surrounded by hostile Arab neighbors. Ironically, the Jewish state's greatest threat for the moment is the non-Arab Iranians. It was a Persian king who once allowed the Jews to reclaim their ancient capital, Jerusalem. Now the mullahs want to destroy it. Israel is an exemplar as to how high intellectual capital leads to high educational, then to scientific/technological leadership in the world, all while maintaining democratic institutions, producing an independent middle class. Yet it has had to lose much blood to survive the ongoing attempts of annihilation by neighbors who hate and fear what it represents. It is yet Western and internationally competitive in its civilizational standards.

But Israel has an internal Muslim population increasing demographically relative to the existing Jewish majority. By mid-century, given the continuity of current birth/death rates, Arabs will constitute about one-third of the population of Israel. This does not include the Palestinian territories, which are tragically overpopulated and presently on international life support. Of course as Arab oil depletes, the loose monies for aggression will dry up. And Israel is the only nation in the region with the knowledge wherewithal to be able to arm itself independently, exporting technology internationally on a sustaining level. In addition it has recently discovered vast natural gas fields offshore.

Thus if there is no possibility for real love between these national/religious entities, there could come a time when a concord of the type that exists today between Jordan and Israel would yet lead to an unenthusiastic peace.

For the Arab world in general, there has to be pessimism. Most probably they will not revert to an economy of the camel. Their intellectual demographic and resource profiles augur little hope for the successful establishment of middle-class democratic institutions, a la Europe, nor the technological economy that could support it. Without such wealth, their options for aggression and war will be limited. International supervision by the wealthier more stable powers will be an ongoing necessity. But there will probably be little effort to rescue them from their own fate when all the chips must be tabulated.

## South Asia

Pakistan, India, and Bangladesh epitomize the dilemmas of third-world ascent and survivability. In 2016 it is clear that as Islamic states, both Pakistan and Bangladesh suffer for the Muslim world's intoxication with Islam, and the debilitation that Islam represents in their spasmodic thrust for modernity amidst scarcity. Both nations are overpopulated and under-capitalized, educationally and productively. Bangladesh, itself living in a delicate and dangerous ecology, with rivers now flooding over treeless hills and plains, is threatened with being washed out to sea, probably condemned to life support at the lowest manufacturing margin levels in the world economy.

Pakistan is riven by class warfare, tribalism and fundamentalism. The future here is bleak. Pakistan does contain within its population productive minds and a once highly educated, modern elite. They have mostly fled to greener pastures. Can one see hope for this put-upon people? Hope requires the rational throwing off of the medieval and regressive Islamic fundamentalism that is choking this people. Is there enough Cro-Magnon intellectual/educational capital in Pakistan to respond to the lures of modernity?

India is unique: now as populated as China, and vulnerable to the control that China exerts over the south-flowing waterways out of their Tibetan highlands, from the Indus to the Mekong. India has an able upper-caste elite that is responding to the intellectual challenges of the twenty-first century. But the population is probably not as uniform as is China's in terms of intellectual capital. The Indian elite now exploits the industrious capacities of its modernizing population and the nation grows unevenly in wealth. At some point its fragile democracy will have to face up politically to the inevitable maldistribution of wealth that augurs. Eventually energy constraints will cause economic growth to slow, and the Indian people will awaken to the reality of its debilitating heritage of caste and population density.

## Third World: Africa, Latin America, Southeast Asia

Africa: not much hope, continent-wide. Western philanthropy has well achieved its goal in lowering death rates and raising birthrates. Population densities are soaring, and food and mineral production, including oil, is well under the control of the new colonialism. The food issue will never fade away. In contrast, the natural resources will eventually be gone. Both Nigeria and Angola, for example, will soon show significant oil depletion profiles. If the political criminal/terrorist situation descends to utter anarchy, the foreigners will once more depart. In a time of worldwide resource scarcity, someone will come to the "rescue"—who?

Latin America has a few hopeful outposts. Here the intellectual/educational capital and the political controls are centered in the indigenous elites, mostly European in origin. Perhaps under-populated Argentina, Uruguay, and Chile, mostly European in ethnicity, can survive. They have the best natural resource/demographic profiles. They also have an educated popular majority. They will have to adjust their political programs to mimic what the former east European nations are doing: roll back the autocratic economic and social programs, and institute free market patterns, while maintaining the rational democratic voice of the people.

Brazil is run by a European-originated elite in a mostly mixed-race nation, with heavy concentrations of underclass desperation. Their population is increasing rapidly. But! Brazil has enormous natural resources, a vast hinterland of possibilities, and untold offshore oil reserves. For most of the twenty-first century it should be able to keep political anarchy away from its doors as it exploits this cornucopia of wealth.

The rest of Latin America is a deep dark question mark. Most of it could turn out to be another Venezuela, populist tyrants destroying the potential that a free market has to offer given its indigenous, exploitable fossil-energy reserves. Whether Latin America will become Castro- or Hugo Chavez–like, sputter under military control even as it maintains a surface democracy as in Ecuador, still authoritarian in reality, is difficult to predict. But when one puts together population growth and natural resource retrenchment without the backup of major indigenous technological or educational resources to earn its way in the world, the prognosis cannot be positive.

But wait. The critical issue will always be centered in the available intellectual and educational resources. Recent events in even drug crime–scarred Mexico hint at a hopeful denouement. Careful economic discipline, a growing educational profile, lowering birthrates, a work force improving in skills, and a combination of Cro-Magnid European and indigenous hybridized talent may land Mexico and other Latin American nations on their feet.

## Transition to *Triage*

The facts of national and international civilizational survival are simple and clear. Reduce your population footprint to balance out the resources, human and natural, that can allow for a modern middle-class life. Five hundred years of international growth have, however, blunted our flexibility, and the wisdom required to adjust to a new reality. Oddly, Mao perceived this for China. That is why he ordered, and his successors and the people in general have mostly continued to maintain, this discipline of one female equals one child. The northeast Asians and the Europeans have the mental sagacity to know this. Unless you are very rich, but only as long as you have a sustainable economic profile, you can raise in a modern way only one or two children.

Nature has its own timetable. It is highly likely that it will inflict its own rules in shaping the tough oncoming profile for human life before leadership will acknowledge the requirements that nature itself imposes. And thus we will be in for some very difficult moments in this century, and not only those caused by raw starvation, and other natural disasters. As societies decline we will see more of the kind of terrorism and anarchy that we presently taste. The international intellectual profile of our species is not yet attuned to the rational social disciplines required to survive the "seven years of severity."

For large parts of the world, the next ninety or so years are going to be horrific. While the times are good, we can tax ourselves a bit more, send to the weak and backward some of our plenty, hopefully to induce them to recover and become productive and competent. This is the ancient way of mammals, human philanthropy here extrapolated from our love of our own. The cortex here is nurtured by our blood flow.

But what happens when the plenty is no more, and we are struggling to feed and clothe our own? Then we start asking differing kinds of altruistic questions. We will begin to examine the causes of human failure even while we weep over the consequences of deep suffering. The question will be, why they, and not us? Why did our people not collapse? One suspects that a new stage in international policy will have begun. Reward those who have limbed to the challenge, taken on their responsibilities. Will it come to *triage*, when secular eyes settle on perpetual failures, individuals, families as well as nations?

Sadly, it need not be. The educated leadership of the world could first of all stand forth and admit that the path to survival is to use our evolutionary heritage, the cortical power of cognitive analysis and prediction. The factual reality is that nature has granted *Homo sapiens sapiens* this adaptive potency in order that the species should look forward in time to the consequences of our decisions, to both survive and flourish.

## · 17 ·

# THE UNITED STATES IN TRANSITION

Ben Bernanke may be bullied into raising interest rates, when he should do no such thing. There will eventually come a day when the Federal Reserve Board should tighten—but that day is years away. ... Our economic policy should be concerned with jobs, jobs, and jobs.—*Paul Krugman (Nobel Memorial Prize in Economic Sciences), The New York Times, May 11, 2011.*

## Our Dominant Twentieth Century

Even by 1900, a historian could argue, the United States, still in formation, was the dominant power on earth. We now "owned" the Western Hemisphere, politically, economically, and of course militarily. Our industries were modern and working overtime. Energy resources with the oncoming use of petroleum were seemingly infinite. Our writers, musicians, artists, were amongst the avant-garde in the West. Soon we would be decisive in winning the First World War for the allies against the central powers. The Second World War was even more clearly a victory for the American industrial, technological, and military machine, against fascism.

The United States also led the West in turning back a new totalitarianism, Soviet communism. It led a revitalized West, now including the democracies of

West Germany and Japan, in turning China away from Maoist madness into a state capitalist politically authoritarian society, so much more in tune with the ways of the free-enterprise West. Even Russia and her former republics were enticed to become pseudo-participants in the democratic vision of the victors.

The exploding masses of humans in the impoverished "third world," now rid of colonial "oppression," were invited to join the West, which now engaged in an explosion of redistributionist philanthropy. The vision was to create a universal democratic, technological egalitarianism amongst this exploding mass of non-Europeans in our world. Here, the United States was a leader in offering vast amounts of wealth to both its indigenous poor, but also to the needy around the world.

The vision amongst the victors of the Second World War was reconciliation, democracy, limited capitalism, much welfare-safety-net support by the state, and a deep ideological conviction that all humans on our planet had the inner educational potential and the sociological right to attain equality of condition. The wealthy, now centered in a few nations, led by the United Nations, anchored in the United States and mostly supported by the United States, would guide the world towards a utopian social democracy peace amongst humankind.

The United States at the end of the twentieth century was indeed the leading voice for democracy, scientific, secular liberalism, a beacon of prosperity and hope for humankind. And the immigrants, educated and uneducated, were breaking down the doors to be part of this benevolent and ever-hopeful nation.

## The Twenty-First. Whose Century?

Entering upon the second decade of the twenty-first century, however, a new situation seemed to be developing under a suddenly anxious American nose. There were still masses of Americans that were living on the edge. Great industrial cities such as Detroit and Cleveland were a shell of their former prosperous working-class ethos. Most of the industrial heft of the U.S. had decades since been migrating to northeast Asia, some to Europe, even our vaunted automobile industry. What were left were mostly the import factories from Japan, Korea, and Germany.

The terrorist attack of 2001 reinforced a picture of hatred of a powerful secular America which, in spite of its philanthropy, still saw much of the Islamic world left behind, even with their well-saturated oil wealth. And of course political expediency led the United States into a quagmire of twenty-first-century wars in Afghanistan and Iraq. Besides much precious life sacrifice, the wealth of the nation was seriously dissipated. It was a weaker nation economically than after the earlier inconclusive and losing twentieth-century conflicts in Korea and Vietnam.

This was in essence a profligate society when it came to government intervention in order to attain the dreams of the left, equality of condition. Lyndon Johnson's "Great Society" used the tragedy of eighteenth- and nineteenth-century African American slavery, and then segregation in the South, as a vehicle for this radical egalitarian thrust, redistribution of wealth, affirmative action, and racial, ethnic, and gender quotas to funnel education and jobs to recipient groups of the government's choice. This panoply of government taxation as it was to be redistributed to the "needy" classes set off an avalanche of illegal immigration of poor uneducated people from the bottom classes of Latino and Caribbean nations.

The internal and external redistributionist philanthropy of these past fifty or so years has continued with unabated passion. However, in 2008 there occurred the proverbial "straw that ... "A spike in oil prices, up to an unprecedented $145 per barrel crude, became the precipitating event that unraveled what now was revealed to be the pseudo-prosperity of the preceding decades. First the housing "bubble" imploded. The banks, intimidated by the redistributionist illusions of the power players, had underwritten billions in basically fraudulent loans to masses of homeowners who, in a down-draft economy, could not now meet the tab.

The Western nations in general, following the ongoing *weltanschauung*, had themselves been creating a similar debt time bomb. And when it went off, the entire interrelated Euro-American gamble that the ideological overseers had set into place came apart. Simply there was no creation of wealth from the independent productive institutions of the Western nations to equal the debt obligations that the governmental and financial leadership had taken on to lull the masses into obeisance. The "banksters," national bureaucracies, international redistributionist organizations, the UN, all had participated in an under-the-table compact to ensure the maintenance of their extra cut of the pie, extracted from the working middle classes. While the banks, their workers, and stock holders crashed, the individuals of management in these institutions rode away with enormous personal fortunes, millions and billions, extracted as bonuses, to be untouched by the law.

Seemingly the center of productive wealth creation had been transferred from the United States and much of the Western Hemisphere—perhaps resource-rich Canada is the exception—to northeast Asia, Japan, South Korea, the Chinese ethnicity throughout Asia, and to a lesser extent to a now-awakened India. The travail of West and Central Europe and the United States in the first decade and beyond of the twenty-first century clearly revealed evidence of a permanent shift in the power center of gravity. It all plumbed down to how much cash would be available, debts to be paid. Japan, yes, debt-ridden, but largely to itself.

## Economic Symptoms of Decline

While seemingly in better straits than most of the west Europeans burdened down by anemic productivity and massive debts, the collar of the euro, the United States could momentarily inflate its debt out (QE I, II III, etc.) of the looming well. But in the long run it faces deeper challenges. An increasing proportion of the population has been distanced from their former quasi-middle-class lifestyle by the shrinkage of our industrial model, now mostly ensconced in Japan, South Korea, and China.

In 2012, an election year, the call, as noted in the Krugman quotation cited at the beginning of this chapter, was "jobs, jobs, and more jobs." The question was and is, are these to be created jobs, governmentally subsidized "jobs," or true entrepreneurial private-sector work? In this critical year of transition the true unemployment/underemployment rate was closer to 16% or above, if one counted those discouraged from seeking work or existing on part-time or minimum-wage jobs. This rate was close to Spain's 2012 more than 20% rate, the highest in a major European nation, although the skeptics whisper about the untaxed "underground economy." Back home, the long-term prognosis for the return of the old-time high-paying American jobs of the 1970s was pessimistic.

The creation of private-sector work is dependent on a richly innovative entrepreneurship in the society, what we had in the 50s, 60s, and 70s of the twentieth century. For almost thirty years the United States has seen middle-class wages in stasis. Here, a true decline in the American standard of living, hardly mollified by the vast growth in wealth of the upper 5%.

The Timken Steel Company of Canton, Ohio, is benefiting from the increased use of steel in the American oil and gas industry, especially with oil in the $90–$100-per-barrel range in 2012. Thus it is expanding, building three facilities at a cost of close to $300 million, here including a building of twenty-six stories. The rub however is that these new facilities will not require many new workers: " … automation in the new buildings most likely meant that few if any jobs would be added."[1]

These technological changes have hit those at the bottom of the educational ladder. To compensate for this stagnation and the increasing desperation of the ethnic minorities at the bottom of the income scale, the U.S. leadership chose the route of debt. By early 2016 this debt was almost touching $18.5 trillion. There were varying political perspectives on this situation of over 100% debt to current GDP, the latter encompassing government spending, of which over 40% was deficit expenditures. One's perspective was dependent on one's political orientation. Thus "liberal" Democrats, Paul Krugman variety, saw the need for continued government stimulation (spending-debt), plus stimulative taxes on the super-rich until the independent economy would begin to produce jobs.

Conservative Republicans and "Tea Partiers," the libertarian wing of the Republican Party, saw the United States as being on the brink of bankruptcy and insolvency, considering the looming entitlements payouts for Social Security, Medicare, Medicaid, and now, "Obamacare." In this "entitlement society," they saw America heading towards socialist dissolution.

A significant policy problem for the liberal point of view was that the structure of the present, heavily subsidized governmental redistribution programs was built on a tax structure in which the very rich were already heavily subsidizing this liberal vision. The top 40% of household income in 2006 already paid more than 99.2% of the federal taxes for that year. The top 20% of households paid 67% of the federal tax receipts. The top 1% of household incomes in 2011 paid 40% of total federal income taxes.

Over forty-six million households paid no federal income taxes, many receiving redistribution funds from the federal government. In addition, 30% of American households were receiving checks from the federal government for support, child care, or earned income credit. Here we do not include the monies that were paid out for Social Security, Medicare, Medicaid, or disability.

The question that worried even political liberals was how long the U.S. could continue running these vast fiscal deficits without destroying the currency and inflating the cost of all imports (our negative trade deficits, current account), thus completely shutting down our ability to support the ever-increasing numbers of the needy.

## Societal Symptoms of Decline

A nation's economic profile does not exist in a vacuum. There are many social elements that give life to the economic facts. The United States as an entitlement society did not come out of nowhere. Initiated in the darkness of the Great Depression by FDR, World War II rescued the economy. The explosive post-war industrial advance of the economy, pretested by our wartime productivity, and the shadow of a residual underclass and a racially segregated South stimulated President Lyndon Johnson to re-initiate major governmental involvement in racial/ethnic and social institutions, education, jobs, etc.

These "Great Society" programs, begun in the mid-1960s at the time of the apogee of American industrial dominance and wealth production, were continued into the twenty-first century by a political leadership of varying points of view, including supposed archconservatives such as President Richard Nixon. It is ironic to note that the consequent productive, economic descent of the United States began in the mid-1970s.

The "Great Society" social vision fostered by all major political and academic communities expected that with a punishable ban on discriminatory practices involving race, ethnicity, and gender, and an explicit involvement by governments at all levels in "affirmative action" practices and quotas in jobs and education, these existing differences would gradually dissolve. All citizens were not only to be legally equal, but they were to be seen as substantially similar in intelligence, educability, and character. The need was to root out those "evil" human practices that had held back all politically identified groups needing redress.

The predictive success of this great national gamble to create a substantive egalitarian society is given in the statistics provided by this self-same government. In 1958, the United States, with a population of 175 million, had an illegitimacy rate of 5%. By 1969, with a population of 201 million, this illegitimacy rate had doubled to 10%; by 1980, our population had increased to 227 million and the percentage of children born to unmarried mothers reached 18%. In 1999, our population now soaring to 278 million, the illegitimacy rate had likewise soared to 33%. In our own day, 2016, with a population, now including all aliens, to have reached c. 330 million people on board the fifty states, the illegitimacy rate was over 40%. By all sociological accounts, children born into dependent single-parent families are destined to a lifetime of poverty.

Most galling to advocates of the "Great Society" vision was the monumental increase in illegitimacy by the two most vulnerable minorities, those who were the ongoing focus of these redistributionist programs. The African American illegitimacy rate had risen steadily to its 2013 rate of more than 72%. The Latino illegitimacy rate was then c. 55%. A vast population depended on food stamps, close to 50 million in 2016, plus a variety of welfare programs, housing, and remedial education. There now were terrifying drug and crime statistics, plus a growing dependency amongst the supposedly advantaged whites.[2] The "Great Society" experiment had succeeded in shifting the social structure of the United States ever more downward from its former middle-class base.

These trends are not a vice of one nation alone. It is part of the redistributionist, equality-of-condition ideology of all the Western nations. In France the percentage of children born to unmarried mothers is very high. However, amongst the indigenous European population in that nation, this is a consequence of a cultural stylistic element. There, fathers still take responsibility for the rearing of their biological children. They are not anonymous sperm donors.

Concomitantly, the wealth that inflated the American ego created another stylistic sociological movement. There was discouragement of upper-class men and women from marrying to raise families and producing those well-provided youngsters that might have bolstered the nation's cultural and economic future. Feminism amongst the educated young females during these several generations led especially to the shrinking birthrates amongst highly educated women. Equality with men now meant that all privileged ears were listening to the siren song of sexual freedom, careerism, and high economic achievement during these halcyonic days of economic expansion. It echoed especially loudly in the halls of ivy. This modern parasitic elitist vision of "me first" was of an America not-to-be.

In 1986, research already revealed that amongst the highest cadres of female corporate executives, all beyond child-bearing ages, 54% had no children. Rome went through the same phase, much satirized by male Roman writers during the several centuries of its greatest worldly power. In the case of modern America two factors, large expansion of the birthrate at the bottom of the social ladder and few births at the top, have coincided with weak competitive economic productivity at the mid-levels of our economy and a shrinking of the indigenous creative talents at the top.

The University of California system, having seen a decline in the preparation of its oncoming student body, is even now struggling with the demand for affirmative racial and ethnic quotas. Like other leading public universities, it has begun to institute a strictly merit-based admissions policy. California, in addition to having a large indigenous population of the impoverished, now grapples with the additional social and financial burden of absorbing vast numbers of uneducated and illegal aliens. On top of this, it must finance one of the most vaunted higher education establishments of any state in the union. At risk is the retention of their distinguished faculty.

One result of their newly initiated merit-based admissions policy is that at their most illustrious institutions, UCLA, Berkeley, Santa Barbara, etc., Asiatic undergraduates now constitute some 50% of the student body. Asiatic Americans, with a very thin demographic footprint, now dominate this educational landscape. This bit of factuality underscores the shift in the American gaze to the west, across the Pacific.

The Bureau of Labor Statistics in early 2012 related the unemployment rate of Americans over twenty-five years of age. Those without a high school diploma—13.8%; with high school diploma, no college training, 8.7%; those with some college or an associate's degree (two years), 7.7%; those with a bachelor's degree or higher, 4.1%. Here, an augur of our future.

## How Will We End the Twenty-First Century?

Given the evidence of human evolution and history, it is clear that the necessary precondition for a nation's civilizational flourishing, if not leadership, is the level of Cro-Magnon intellectual capital contained within its citizenry. The conclusion we must draw, from the decline of American leadership, is that the ongoing economic and societal drift downward must be laid at the ideological policy decision-making by its leadership groups. Some nations go under because of the terrible decimation in war or genocide of its best and brightest. Europe here is a prime example. The ancient Greeks, it can be argued, destroyed themselves in senseless internecine wars.

The United States elite put into effect policies developed from a cultural ethos that had the productive elements of the society subsidizing the raising of children of the poorest and least educated of its peoples, also encouraging massive illegal immigration of the uneducated for cheap slave-like labor. The saddest part of this trend is that the ideological force that caused this trend downward is still in place, in 2016. And thus, we must sadly look to a future in which present social dysgenic policies will continue, only then to count up the consequences.

The accumulated wealth of this nation will not disappear in a moment. Wealth is international today and the dominant classes will fight on strongly to protect their interests at home and offshore. Great Britain, long after its heyday, still has an established middle- and upper-class, and some glorious civilizational institutions and competencies at home, even though it teeters socially and economically at its own brink. Truth to tell, Britain has already lost that intellectual élan that moved it to its predominant nineteenth-century place.

It is difficult to see how a traditional classless democratic environment can continue as the social classes increasingly separate: a large majority politically vulnerable, poor and hanging on, an ever-smaller productive minority providing the waning taxable wealth. Inevitably there will be a turn to the autocratic.

One pathway towards autocracy would be for a populist series of elected demagogues targeting the affluent minority, with their consequent fleeing to more beneficent shores, probably welcomed momentarily by another kind of autocracy. Much of our industry is already headquartered on foreign shores, as corporate taxes in the United States are one of the highest in the world. In the 2012 presidential elections class warfare rhetoric was already thrown around, "more taxes on the rich."

An alternative to the populist egalitarian demagogic route to national impoverization, but equally authoritarian in nature, is a model characteristic of many Latin American nations. Here the privileged are protected by the army and the police, plus much propagandistic efforts to opiate the populace. In the United States, the power of Hollywood and the media, the current intoxication with soft porn, glamour people, and games, an alliance of the powerful and wealthy, given an alliance with the police and military, could calm the waters, keep the masses entertained and drugged.

A solution away from autocracy, given America's substantial (c. 50%) productive middle-class population is a gradual shifting of power away from the federal to the localities and states. What with a national debt approaching what Greece and Italy represented in 2015, and without the benefit of the ethnic and geographic integration of these societies, a nation such as the U.S. with a tradition of divided powers might see a push from a majority of the states, if not to formally secede, to attempt to devolve more power and autonomy to local communities and the several states. Indeed, this was the original intent of the American Declaration and Constitutional writings.

As people realize that they are paying more to the federal government than they are receiving, and given the probability that our national debt will cause a great rise in interest rates by the international bond vigilantes, there could be a sharp reduction in the powers of Washington, D.C., precipitated once more by a great depression. After all, the disintegration of the center once happened to ancient Rome, after a much lengthier period of wealth and *Pax Romana*. Check with the Soviet Union, end of the twentieth century.

This shift in political and economic responsibilities to the localities will also set off a psychological shift in the thinking of individuals and their communities. Here the non-discursive symbolism, the emotional affect rooted in limbic-system energy flows, will center their foci on distinctions in language, cuisine, literature, a sense of (*Texas*) history, religion, and art/music—all those culturally pluralistic symbolic values that can reshape the ethnic awareness of humans. These have been, and are, historic alternatives to the growth energy flows of the discursive universalistic symbols of human thought and their dominant institutions of culture.

In all, the twenty-first century could see both the weakening of centralized powers as well as a possible increase in local democratic governmental models. High energy prices and scarcity will themselves bring humans closer together. The other side of the equation computes the consequences of the current decline in intellectual capacity and the dominance of emotional symbolic drives, class warfare, the politics of charisma and narcissism. This latter, alternative trend could gift us with new forms of Stalinism and Maoism.

In a shrinking free economic model of life, it is inevitable that those on the bottom of the intellectual/economic scale will first and inevitably suffer the impact of triage. Long term, the inability to support and subsidize those members of the society incapable of modern high tech/educative productive labor will redirect the demographics of intelligence and educability upwards. And over time, a less intimidated populace will speak up. This is beginning to happen today in formerly totalitarian and autocratic nations. Time is a gift in and of itself. The proportional growth of an independent middle class will in and of itself move any nation away from autocracy and towards more rational and democratic public policy programmatics. In the long run we could look forward to a second wind for this nation and civilization.

## Notes

1. Schneider, K. (2012, April 25). As demand rises, Ohio's steel mills shake off the rust and expand. *The New York Times*. Retrieved from http://www.nytimes.com/2012/04/25/business/energy-environment/ohio-steel-mills-expand-to-meet-demand-in-energy-and-auto-industries.html
2. Murray, C. (2012) *Coming Apart: The State of White America*, 1960–2000. New York, NY: Crown.

# · 1 8 ·

# CATASTROPHE, RENEWAL, AND LAW

## Irrational Centuries

It takes great catastrophes over time to break the back of an entrenched cultural/civilizational/ideological model of life. It has happened many times. In recent history the world community has experienced the cancer of egalitarian/totalitarian visions of social existence in which ideology linked to modern technologies of national power has precipitated incomparably bloody wars and horrific genocides, concluding with one of the great stains against the sanity of the human race, the German Nazi initiation of the *Holocaust*. Here we saw the systematic and intentional destruction of over six million of Europe's finest Cro-Magnon-like minds, the European Jews.

The human brain, the Cro-Magnon brain that dominated in Germany, the Soviet Union, and communist China, freed from the instinctual genetic automaticity of fellow mammals/primates, was able to perpetrate such dysgenic acts. Nature would not have selectively and genetically allowed any of our animalian cousins to commit such a species-annihilating set of actions. It has happened before in human history: the vast genocidal destructions by the marauding, medieval Mongols. Further back we saw the fatal self-inflicted genocidal and dysgenic destruction of the Hellenic youth and their civilization. We again write about the civilizational excesses of seemingly educated peoples. One has to predict that these events will be seen as the defining "achievement" of the bloodstained twentieth century.

The twenty-first century may experience its own catastrophic crisis, hopefully with less suffering. Consider the ongoing surge of humans fattening our ever more bloated worldwide population; then, the soon-to-be shortage of fossil fuels necessary to sustain the lives of so many billions; finally, the terrorism, crime, and social chaos spreading across populations whose hopes for middle class rational security cannot be fulfilled. Will there be enough Cro-Magnon intelligence in the twenty-first century necessary to ward off the emotional, sub-cortical waves of passion that paralyze our political will? How long will it take, and at what price to world functioning, to bring only the external materialistic crisis under the control of disciplined communal actions?

The German and Japanese people were able to come back to democratic, rational political and philosophical life after their dalliance with brutal irrationality. How many other nations will be able to disabuse themselves of the counter-rational ideology that is currently leading the world community down towards chaos and catastrophe? Will the international community of our world in mid-twenty-first century have fewer or more vicious autocracies of the populist kind, or the oligarchic model?

The initial blow to fragile stability may likely come from a great material event: terrible drought amidst changing climate trends, global warming, even a recurring of the centuries of cold. We will need to succor vast populations whose economic base has disappeared. They, as is traditional in all the primates, will want out from their established homeland base, creating vast migrations. There will be some oil, natural gas, and coal for energy use. Probably we will have more nuclear reactors online in the next forty to fifty years. But scarcity will render the cost ever higher and bring economic growth to a final halt, if it has not already, in 2016, done so.

By mid-century the world will probably have imploded into poverty, a few better off than others. There will be two powerful intellectual/altruistic forces at work. One will call for a massive humanitarian shifting of the wealth from the complacent better-off, e.g., Russia, Norway, to sharply reduce their standard of living at least for the "keeping of the other folks down in their hometowns." The other emotional trend will focus on the need to allow some parts of the successful world to be a beacon of resurrection when the times of troubles have waned.

When these downhill events occur the natural first response will be to mend and patch, keep the system going, too many self-interests in control. Eventually when all fails, a new group of thinkers emerge from the cave—see Jerome or Ambrose for Rome, Adenauer for Germany, Galileo for Italy and the Enlightenment. But this time the crisis will be worldwide. It is anyone's guess whether there will be enough voices of reason in the United Nations or elsewhere to grasp the glimmering light of resolution.

## A New Vision of Reality

We have got to hope for a twenty-first-century oasis of political stability, middle-class economics, and a social platform for scientific and technological development. In the context of social dissolution, our expectation must be that the populist autocrats and the oligarchic generals will have no ability to join their ideas with ever-progressing science and technology. What destroyed Nazism, Stalinism, and Maoism, and what will destroy the modern welfare redistributionist state that thrives on mediocrity and the pseudo safety net, is the advancing power of high intelligence as expressed in science and technology. Autocracy represents a failure of the social system. Such failures cannot for long enlist their finest minds. The Nazis had their Jewish intellectuals flee, or they destroyed them. Stalin's scientists slept on the job, and Mao sent them out to shovel manure.

This essential cadre of humans has been instrumental in creating the modern middle-class style of life. They will eventually throw off the chains of both politically-correct ideologies in the West as they become self-aware of the significance of their own intelligence, the educational vision that should become the rule, the modus operandi for all of humankind. Take the Arab Emirates, today awash in oil wealth, deciding to go modern, inviting the brainy people to remake these small societies. They will be a beacon to Saudi Arabia and Iran. Most of all they will reshape the Western world and its intoxication with egalitarian mediocrity and decline. First we will have to win the oncoming war against dissolution in the twenty-first century.

What we are seeing in this world of the twenty-first century is essentially a struggle for victory of two basically antithetical populations struggling for dominance in shaping our culture and outlook for the planetary future. The major features of Homo sapiens behavioral motivations still derive from the sub-cortical limbic system of emotional energies. These mental attitudes are immersed in the symbols of ethnicity, religion, the psychology of envy, hatred of accomplishment, and suspicion of the natural leadership of secular educated intelligence. In contrast there are those who are productive Homo sapiens sapiens who are building on the values of cognition and knowledge. Ideology has blurred this basic irreconcilable duality. The productive minority is not yet aware of the implicit and explicit sociobiological conflict of these two subspecies, both neutral as to race, nationality, and ethnicity.

What we are experiencing today, and what is leading us towards worldwide catastrophe, is the heritage of an as yet uncompleted human evolution. Our eventual destiny is that of the most advanced model of Homo, that of the cognitive and artistic mentality of Cro-Magnon. One old-time academic phrased it thusly: "Even a professor of Latin literature can let his hair down, if he has any, and enjoy a night out at the burlesque. After all he has a body and mind that has interests below the neck. Sadly, most of those attendees in the burlesque theatre can't rise up to what is above their necks to an appreciation of Locke, Velasquez, or Beethoven."

The new intellectual class will in the end come into international dominance simply because we humans, Homo sapiens and Homo sapiens sapiens, have reached the demographic and resource limits of expansion of these respective subspecies and in their respective ecologies. The catastrophe that will circumvent the dynamic of the past five hundred years of a human economic growth and population expansion, and now the redistributive vision of humanity, will have collapsed. We humans will then live in an environment where material resources will be scarce. This will set off a desperate competition for what is available, but also a fierce scientific and technological search for both renewable sources of energy and new possibilities, such as in hydrogen. Both efforts will involve educational and intellectual skills and heft, indeed probably phasing into military/technological potential. Ultimately the demand around the world will be for every individual, as well as every independent national entity, to pull its own weight. World peace will require it.

This new world will be defined by steady-state economy on our planet, always to be in harmony with its fragile ecology. Yet, we must allow and provide mental and physical room for the *tychistic*, the unexpected, the innovative. Humans have to live in an ever-incomplete symbolic world requiring new meanings, a mental world forever in process.

## Survival: Demography and Intelligence

One can conjure up innumerable scenarios for catastrophe. Our argument is to suggest inevitable survival strategies if this human race is to achieve a measure of stability and longevity on this planet.

The strongest need will be to bring our demographic footprint into balance with the material resources necessary to the maintenance of the middle-class life that humans have enjoyed ever since complex urban life was established on earth by the Sumerians, five to six thousand years ago. Catastrophe will undo this quality of life quickly for large parts of the world: drought, earthquakes, volcanic eruptions, typhoons, hurricanes, insect infestations, medically unmanageable epidemics. Even today there are parts of the world where people still starve, are subject to epidemics, terrorism, slavery, and genocide, failed states and millions at risk. Such tragedy will surely increase as our worldwide resources and surplus wealth wanes.

A tyrant, Mao, instituted the one-child-per-female national policy for China almost fifty years ago. If anything, the Chinese population has continued to slowly increase. Most Western intellectuals and policy makers condemned the autocratic nature of this nationally dictated policy. Often, forced abortions and fines were instituted for those females and their spouses who through accident or forethought became pregnant for the second time. Most Chinese still think of their demography as an intolerable burden on their future. But there is a new lure for more workers in the momentary successful Chinese economic experiment. As always, the shortsightedness of a new generation of autocrats.

In Athens, c. 410 BCE, toward the end of the Peloponnesian War with Sparta, given the heavy losses of their finest young men in battle, the citizens are thought to have gathered together to consider their dire situation. A war was going badly, the future of the city-state itself was in question. The apparent solution: a vote to have all men still capable of siring children take on another wife, there being plenty of young widowed or unmarried young women without a possible husband. This is one explanation for Socrates in 399 BCE having, at age seventy, two young sons age, eleven and nine, and perhaps also an older wife and older sons.

In times of tragedy, when a nation or an ethnic group is at the brink of disaster or possible extinction, the minds of the leadership as well as the citizenry will tend to become sober, face up to difficult situations with only grim choices left and historically unseemly decisions in the making. Sadly, the contemporary Greeks, once more, are at the brink.

In the contemporary welfare societies of the West, one quick and rational solution might be to encourage births from that class of citizens able to raise their children to the highest levels of education and morality. On the other hand, it would be incumbent on the citizenry to discourage through law the conceiving and birth of children to those who are in the dependent classes, who are without the education, intelligence, and economic means to independently raise successful families contributing positively to the life of the nation. The independent classes here would transition from raising the children of poverty, to raising their own responsibly.

It is quite possible that in the most advanced societies, where a majority of the population is able to cope with and advance the leading modes of technology, science and productivity this transition to the level of *Homo sapiens sapiens* can be achieved through democratic processes of law and cooperation. In those areas of the world where poverty and more limited Cro-Magnon intelligence levels still predominate, and where in the early twenty-first-century populations are still exploding through the provided gift of modern medicine, leadership groups from international agencies, as well as from domestic origins, will have to resort to more aggressively persuasive techniques.

In a world where race should play an ever-smaller and more insignificant role in our concerns, we will over a period of centuries see an ever more intermixed population of a variety of heritages. It may then seem right to the leadership of continents and nations, in Africa, Asia, Latin America, and other parts of the impoverished world, to so introduce real human progress. Today we see cadres of Chinese workers, possible immigrants to Africa, exploiting the natural resources for the home country. These populations of male workers will act as men away from home always have acted, to find mates and pass their genes on and into the indigenous population. This is exemplified by the nation of South Africa, where we find mixed-race populations along with the existing African Negroid population and the Europoid minority.

In the long run there will be no racial exclusiveness in any geography of the world. It is not beyond the imagination to conceive of the disadvantaged peoples and nations of the world welcoming the introduction of modern techniques of artificial insemination to produce young of increased adaptive educational potentiality, if only for the economic advance that these children will create for family, community and national competence, eventually a middle-class life.

This is a process that will have a timeline of centuries. But if we move forward to create new and dynamic means for uplifting nations and peoples on all the continents that have been subject to colonialism and then have seen their fortunes as independent nations descend into terror and tyranny in comparison with the more advanced peoples of the world, we could anticipate such acceptance and then see real progress. Our goal should be the integration of the peoples of the world into an international community of true bio-social equality, not the fantasy world of guilt-ridden Western moral redemption through the spurious redistribution of productive wealth.

## Intelligence and the Law

When the time arrives that our world can be rebuilt on a rational material basis of small populations in balance with the resources bequeathed by nature, we must then assure ourselves that the very basic perquisites to peace, if not prosperity, must rest on the inner mental capacity of the human species. High Cro-Magnon intelligence is key. This is the ability to channel the passions of our limbic system, the ability to integrate our emotions with the neurology of the cortex, to meet the minimum criteria for rational analysis and discussion, no less the heights of scientific and philosophical inquiry. Without these pre-conditions there will be no future human civilization capable of guiding us through millennia of scarcity and challenge.

The model has to be what the Athenians achieved for but a century or so for themselves, here including a structure of law-guided democracy and a thirst for high esthetic creativity, as well-constituting a community open to a philosophical/scientific culture. Naturally, they didn't have the information that we humans have accrued in the several thousands of years that have passed over the horizon. They engaged in irrational wars of egoistic nationalism against their own kind. But so did the Europoids destroy hundreds of millions of their own kind from the sixteenth to the twentieth centuries, when they should have known better.

Another model, created on an almost tabula rasa ecological and social environment, was the founding of the United States of America. Its documentary assertions of secular rationality and strict adherence to the principle of limited governmental powers, freedom guaranteed for all indigenous political entities and voluntary associations, were a great landmark of history. It created, for but a century and a half or so of independence from centralized power, a respect for individual conscience, and its creative ardor. This was a vision of the future not bounded by the past. The core historical precept was an ongoing commitment to the people's law.

We cannot envision a democratic society without its underlying human component, individuals capable of thinking through the myriad, often complex issues of policy, a polity highly literate and informed. If one observes early twenty-first-century political behavior in the United States and elsewhere in the world, it is clear that the voting public is moved not by serious secular discussions of issues based on factual reality but often by emotionally manipulated ideological themes, mass-entertainment lures that blur the seriousness of the issues and the choices to be made. Here now exists a situation of seduced irrationality that inevitably catapults the United States and other pseudo-democracies into disaster. Unfortunately, the predicted worst is yet to come in the twenty-first and twenty-second centuries.

The methods for the achievement of human social equality have ranged from confiscatory taxation of the rich then redistributed by distant bureaucratic political overseers to the genocide of the dissident independent classes and their intellectual elites. Today, the self-serving oligarchs of power have created conditions for the inevitable socioeconomic descent of the mass. Could we create social conditions whereby there is relative equality of intellectual and educational potential, we might then establish conditions whereby tyranny can be kept at bay. The next step would be to reduce centralized powers, as Marx would argue, to envision the withering-away of the state.

First one has to promote policy pathways that will limit class exploitation. This can only be accomplished were we to raise the educational achievements of the mass to the highest uniform levels possible. Again, high Cro-Magnon intelligence is the necessary precondition for a world without hatred, envy, exploitation, and the social policy irrationalities that inevitably lead to bloody conflict. There is an old Cambridge, Massachusetts, aphorism: If you want to find the most diversity of mind and talent, take a peek at the Harvard undergraduates, all of high intellectual abilities, all with an amazing variety skills and interests.

We cannot know for sure what the long-term demographic carrying power of our planet will be. Naturally there will be fluctuations, perhaps from one billion humans up to two billion, and then down again to one-fourth that latter number. Here we will need a true United Nations, a rational, non-ideological cohort of Platonic "philosopher kings" of different ethnicities, but not different and incompatible ideologies as are today represented in that institution's almost comical antipathies.

Henceforth the world will need the rule of law exercised beyond the boundaries of nationalities and ethnicities. There will always be critical supra-national controversies, ambitions, and perceptions of factualities, here hopefully limited by a universal commitment to scientific secularity and moderation in dealing with cross-border discursive issues.

Critical to the success and usefulness of any international organizations assigned by its members to render on international issues will be a limitation on the powers of this international organization over its national membership. The limitation is essential to keeping the doors open for humans to be able to actualize their creative symbolic vision of the new. The decline of twenty-first-century Europe, given its earlier twentieth-century involvements in war, genocide, and statist welfare solutions, has revealed that security in one set of decades can lead to dissolution of this security in the next, merely through the flow of time and events. Take the League of Nations as an exemplar.

The trick in devising any "superego" organizational plan for humankind is to limit the conceivable disasters that go-it-alone nationalities may pursue, but not yet putting structural blockades in the face of the constant renewing and possible revolutionizing of our symbolic values and enthusiasms. The avoidance of catastrophe for the human species must depend on the ability of its constituent political units to pursue the future under the guidance of the laws of rational decision-making. Underlying this hope for better events in *Homo sapiens sapiens*' history is the requirement for humankind to maintain the capacity in all contemporary populations and in all nationalities and ethnicities, to respond to the need for the cortical analysis of issues of law.

# · 1 9 ·

# DESTINY

## Predicting?

There is nothing more hazardous than attempting to predict the future using our day-to-day map of understanding. What has been attempted in this essay is to outline the natural evolutionary forces that have played a dominant role in shaping the most modern forms of humans.

Cro-Magnon, the brainiest of our ancestors, lives on within all humans today, but in various genetic quantifications. What this apparently final evolutionary exemplification of humankind created in terms of cultural products that have come down to us over the millennia has much to tell us about ourselves. These prospects and probabilities ought to be definitive for all of our leadership cadres. The descendants of Cro-Magnon, whether in India, China, or Eurasia, did produce the great civilizations of history. These have defined what humans have and should continue to seek to attain.

What the Cro-Magnons achieved in their nonliterate civilizational life experiences will always act as a spur to humans in the future, those who have the brainpower to be interested in the symbolics of high civilizational achievement. Excepting a vast catastrophic event that decimates humanity, in the long run, humans will want to cherish high cognition and both the discursive and non-discursive symbolic products that highly intelligent individuals and their societies produce.

So, while we cannot predict how human society will configure in the next millennium or so, we can lay out the plan of human symbolic thought as it issues from a highly corticalized world community that eventually will come into being. As we have reiterated, this process of corticalization of the human species is ongoing and it will happen no matter the terrible or benign events of human history to come. Hopefully the demographic indigestion that we presently experience with plenty more to come, given its potential denouement, will open up human history to a more benign and creative phase.

## The Discursive Domain

The trend towards large agglomerations of political units, epitomized by the United Nations and the European Union, will continue. Our material and political destiny as a species depends on cooperation and pacification. The critical impediment is the fact that our attempts to unify and pacify are blockaded by enormous differences in intellectual and educational accomplishment and thus so too is the productivity of those basic material elements that contribute to the modern life. Even where there is real evidence of high intellectual, scientific competence, there are, as in Russia and other European nations, not to speak of China, real ideological differences in the controlling leadership.

Karl Marx's vision of world classlessness was to be accompanied by the withering-away of the exploitative state. The ultimate revolution in blood could only be brought about when a society achieved the most advanced levels of economic organization: industrialization. The inner contradictions afflicting the ruling classes in this ultimate stage of history would be the instrumental trigger to set off the final antithesis. Take this idea forward a century or two and we see that many parts of the world have not as yet achieved the scientific/technological level of economic life to produce the potential for classlessness or social equality in a world community in which individuals share and contribute in relative equal measure.

The United States has contributed to its own demise as a major player in the modern world by expanding its population base from the weakest segments of its educational/intellectual pool. As an ever-greater percentage of the population is unable to measure up to the intellectual productive requirements of the most advanced scientific/technological societies; the United States is tilting towards third-world dependency.

There will doubtless be a time in our future when the nations of the world will be able to do without the superego of supra-national world organizations. At the very least they will need to guide the various nationalities in making their respective decisions in the discursive areas of life. The material and social decisions of one nation or group rarely are innocuous when it comes to affecting the affairs of other nations and communities.

Eventually we all will be mandated as nations and peoples to keep our demography in balance with material resources and ecological stability. There will be arguments as to the factuality of the prognosis, given the constant dynamic of people and resources. However, the international community will vote, and all humans will have to listen. By then we will long have seen biogenetic and race issues pushed into our distant memory bank.

This free delegation to the international community of some supervisory/advisory responsibility will have as its main concern keeping this human species in all its cultural variants on an even keel with nature. By no means should it have the power to impede the natural symbolic creativity of its various ethnic, cultural, and national components. On the other hand, the discursive elements of thought flow back and forth into the non-discursive—ethics/science, architecture/art/politics, music/theology, and many other combinations and influences.

The issue of intellectual capacity, however, is not a cultural or ethnic issue. It strikes at the heart of our discursive possibilities for bringing about a rational and lawful world. There can be no cultural or religious choice here. Rationality is at the foundation of the ability of humans to make decisions on the basis of the law. Only a high, disciplined intelligence in any community can keep the tides of emotions, too often irrational, from sweeping human civilization into chaos and decline.

It is true that there is very little in human discursive life, from the mining of uranium to the organizing and justification of fair national or local elections, that does not have an impact on neighbors, whether close in geography or distant across oceans. This is why the "interstate commerce clause" in the American Constitution has been utilized to constantly expand federal jurisdictions and policies. But there has to be a natural limit to this kind of expansive controlling. Even in a world society of putative equals, we will have to scour the resources of humanity to find our universal philosophers: those having "souls of gold," hearts filled with discretion.

## Equality of Condition

From the time of the Hellenes, the struggles between democrats and oligarchs—among the Romans, the battle between plebeians and senatorial gentry, in both cases, communities of like ethnicity and intelligence—have continued. It is clear that, in all societies that are on the move—population growth, military and/or economic expansion, even cultural advancement—there are some who move faster into the opportune moment than others. When there is an advantage in having more of something of tangible value, there will be those who will be sharp and enterprising enough to get it. And it is never going to stop being this way.

However, there is a point in the evolution of any society, especially when the tide stops rolling in, when a society has to give inequality of outcomes a second look. The limits on monopolies or cartels, the legalization of workers' rights to organize into unions, were all justified attempts to level the playing field a bit. Then the question must be raised about a world in which human intelligence will have minimal grades between the higher norms of our time. How much difference in the symbols of value can we tolerate in order to assure internal social peace? At the same time we will have to consider the fact that there will exist the usual amounts of gene flow from generation to generation in which dynastic prominence is undercut by the principle of "regression toward the mean."

There will always be individuals who create value that the mass also values. And this fact of creativity will always give the creators a monetary and/or political position of power. It is right to consider that overwhelming wealth or power by any individual or group in the democratic community over time can constitute an excrescence, a cancerous growth that blocks the way for the normal human interactions of others less powerful or wealthy. This power and wealth also tends to impede the flow of the new, the next phase of value creation and accumulation. Usually it is governmental and bureaucratic power that does the stifling. It does not matter; the stiflers must be restrained.

In the twentieth and twenty-first centuries, a new form of social and economic exploitation has arisen out of the redistributive welfare state. Modern governmental bureaucracies have become a parasitic encrustation on society, taking their cut in this governmentally controlled economy. They take their cut from the productive classes, sending what is left, the government checks, down to the dependencies who keep them in power. And this is facilitated by the purchased votes of these classes in pseudo-democratic elections.

Most probably the democracies of the future, small in size and relative power, will not have dependent social classes that need perennial support by the highly educated productive citizenry. There may also be a new philosophical argument that the creative newly wealthy in a democracy should live modest citizen-like lives, not as oligarchic parvenus. They would donate their wealth to philanthropies of their choice, thus infusing the respective societies with innovative inputs that derive not from extortive, stagnant, self-serving bureaucracies, but from the creative individuals and groups themselves.

These creative innovators, having given their wealth away and contributed a new input of cultural initiative to the community, could then sit back in modesty with their self-chosen community and live unostentatiously as one equal amongst others. A medal or two might suffice. What we see in today's America, the ostentatious trappings of personal oligarchic wealth and power, is made possible because of the great discrepancies in intelligence/education, and the rapid advances in economics and technology, as well as the current explosion in population. These trends do benefit that 1% at the top of the economic/intellectual/educational ladder. As we all know, the basic principle of mass production is that even a penny profit per unit, given the masses of consumers, can add up to billions of dollars of wealth for the managements of such enterprises.

As world society shrinks in numbers and slows in its forward lurch, guided by our international and national "golden souls," there will be greater opportunity for the democratic voice of the communities of the world to be heard. In the discursive world of things of value, we will hear the voice of the democratic community of equals: how to live politically and economically, how to manage the transition from discovery to the productive distribution of new things. Non-discursive ideas, arts, even religious and moral concepts, will be far more difficult to control, and perhaps we should not, except when they themselves transition to the discursive realm as factors in the symbolics of politics and power.

In the end there will always exist differences in economic and social condition. The critical issue will be that these differences ought not, in the case of the high flyers or losers, be transformed into dynastic generational fixtures. Observe our supposedly democratic assemblies and note the nepotism and grabbing for family advantage, a reality that constantly bubbles into sociobiological reality. In the long run it is hardly possible that term limits will not be the norm for political service.

## The Centrality of Art

What has always excited paleo-archaeologists when they study the Cro-Magnons is the art: the overwhelming commitment by these people to the arts. Even the most basic tools of hunting seem to be infused with a deep esthetic sensibility. They are beautifully conceived and artfully constructed. Sometimes these tools warrant the question about utility. They are often too delicate for the seemingly practical purposes that were in the fabricator's mind.

The Cro-Magnons were settled throughout Europe, from western Russia to France and Spain, for over thirty-five thousand years. They were hunter-gatherers in a rich ecological area below the southern descent of the glaciers. Their lifestyle in the caves: hand-fabricating clothing from the hunted animals, trading for materials found far from their home sites, usually sending off their garbage and refuse to piles well distanced from their living quarters, and then attracting the scavenging transitional dogs. They seem not to have advanced technologically in their lifestyle during this long period, c. 35–30 ka, now called the Upper Paleolithic. Perhaps the exception is the real possibility that they domesticated the horse for riding-hunting purposes, the deer to be culled and eaten, the dog for garbage disposal.

The art of the Cro-Magnons permeated every aspect of their lives, from hunting and fishing to personal ornaments, painting and sculpture, all at the highest levels of artistic realization considering the materials and technology available to them in this period. By 35 ka BP, shortly after they arrived in Europe and traveled west, they were already deeply involved in the Aurignacian art and tool-making traditions. In the many thousands of years during which the Cro-Magnons dominated Europe, leading to the displacement and subsequent extinction of the Neanderthals, their art did not "improve." Rather, it evolved into other recognizable traditions: the Gravettian, the Solutrean, the final florescence of the Magdalenian coinciding with a final blast of cold; these plus other recognized, localized cultural traditions.

Richard Leakey has hypothesized that the Cro-Magnons artistic infatuation with the horse may have led to their invention of the harness and thus domestication.[1] They probably invented the bow and arrow as well as the spear thrower. Their handheld sculpted Venuses (10–12 centimeters), which they probably carried with them on their hunting expeditions, were modeled from pulverized bone and clay, then fire-hardened like pottery, all in the name of sensuous art.

Inevitably, humanity's evolutionary destiny will involve a slowing down of the aggressive creativity we have seen in the past five hundred years, the bloody complexities. The manner in which we have overshot the stabilization of our social (genocides) and biological (species extinctions) environment must lead to such a reevaluation. The probable stable cultural environment of our long-term evolutionary pathway opens up the probability that the swells of human passion will settle on the cultivation of intellectual art forms, quite a contrast to the semi-pornographic barbarism that today is called art/entertainment in our pulsating diversity of brainpower.

There will eventually come a time, possibly from the limits of scientific advance—e.g., Einstein's speed of light constant and other mathematical and logical blockades—that a different symbolic thrust of the human mind will be honored to allow for the needed "new." A highly cognitive world population divided into many small national and ethnic enclaves could provide for many eons of richly meaningful human existence. We could here expect diverse infatuating symbolic movements without the restrictive ritual and superstitious regulation that primitive cultures put into place to protect their narrow ecological settings for survival.

## Evolutionary Perspective

Uncontrolled and unpredictable events determine the destiny of every living form. Yet there is a history to all existing living creatures. These unexpected external events have had disparate impacts on all those creatures within the impact range of such novelty. It helps, when one looks forward, to turn and look back at the heritage and the nature of any line of living things. What had characterized their coming into living reality on this planet? And in particular, what can we say about the human move into dominance, and now our very fragile future?

In early 2012, a set of foot bones of an apparently newly identified hominid was found in Ethiopia.[2] East Africa contains a geology conducive to the preservation of such fossil material. Thus most of the ancient hominid ancestors of *Homo sapiens sapiens* have been found from Tanzania and Kenya, north. This creature, the Burtele Hominid, dates to c. 3.4 mya and is roughly contemporary with "Lucy," the early Australopithecine hominid first described by D. C. Johanson in 1974. However, this human creature's large opposable toe deviates from the Australopithecine humanlike foot structure and is characteristic of arboreal apes.

The new discovery again reveals the branch-like multiplication of humanlike beings recently being discovered at a time frame between 6 and 1.2 mya. The contemporary model of human advance is not linear but branch-like, indicative of a widely successful group of animals unchallenged in their exploration of a mixed forested-plains environment. Not all of these newly discovered non-ape "advanced" primates have as yet been unanimously welcomed into the hominid fold, such as *Ardipithecus kaddaba*, the oldest of a line of fragmented fossil material, here dating back from c. 6 to 4.4 mya. Some humanlike animals, as with *Kenyanthropus platyops*, 3.5 mya, give indications of a brachiating adaptation and only partial bipedal skills.

In specimens from 6 mya, we already see full-fledged evidence of non-chimpanzee-like anthropoids, thus giving additional evidence that the *supposed* timeline of separation of the lines leading to *Pan* and *Homo*, c. 6–5 mya, needs to be pushed back, perhaps as far as the c. 20 mya timeline between the ancestors of *Homo* and the ancestors of the modern apes, here including *Pan* and *Pongo* that this writer has proposed in earlier writings.[3] But the real evolutionary issue that points to the future of the human race is the reality that these now several generic lines of human predecessors, wholly competent in the selective struggles with other contemporary forms of life, have now disappeared. Also, those earlier members of our own genus, *Homo*, from c. 6–2.5 mya, are gone from this planet, as are the seeming last of these predecessors, the European/Asiatic Neanderthals, a mere c. 40 to 27 ka ago, and the hominids on the Indonesian Isle of Flores, some 18 ka BP.

Do not think that this process of the displacement of less-cerebral hominids has ended. Human evolution will not conveniently stop within the narrow centuries-old perspective of our own historical timeline. It should and will continue on, a process that has manifested itself for at least the past ten million years: ever-greater encephalization of the human skull, an ever-larger brain, and ever-greater mental powers of symbolic abstraction.

Thus it is that the transformative civilization revealed in the growth of science and technology, the general abstractive power of the culture that Cro-Magnon's descendants have revealed to our planet, will continue. We are yet a long way from being out of the woods in the ongoing intellectual competition and natural selection within this human clade. The brainy ones will eventually dominate and hopefully quietly relegate these recidivistic memories of the human past to history. Philanthropy and demography have for a historic moment placed this need front and center. Hopefully reason will operate to gently move nature's measuring ruler towards our species' cognitive and evolutionary fulfillment.

A momentary hiccup slowing this process would be a repetition of the self-delusionary ideology that contaminated these Cro-Magnon descendants in their twentieth-century genocidal destruction of their own most intelligent minorities, both ethnic and social class. No matter; the scattering of Cro-Magnid genes remaining behind in any surviving future populations will eventually reassert themselves. The continuing self-determining of the power of high human intelligence will once more show its effect in raising up the human race from the dust.

There will eventually come a time when the human species will, through adaptive opportunity, or selective pressure, dig deeply into its given ecological niche and achieve a permanent level of cultural and demographic stability, probably enforced discipline to live within its means. What this essay has attempted to do is to outline our short-timeline needs that necessitate a more stable contemporary adaptive plan.

This is why we need to go back and take another look at the evolution of our form of adaptive life. Here we will have found and presented to us these intimations of contemporary cognitive selection that is the basic story of human evolution. But also, we will discover the need to be moved by the immediate challenges to human survival: an overstressed environment and an ongoing history of terrible violence within this diverse super-species.

What it should mean to us human contemporaries is that the movement of human evolution has in these past two centuries gone off the track in a whirlwind of new symbolic stimulation, people, things, new geographical and temporal relationships. There exist laws of nature that we humans will always be subject to. We need to rediscover them, and then, obey.

## Notes

1. Leakey, R. (1981). *The making of mankind* (pp. 193–196). New York, NY: Dutton.
2. Haille-Selassie, Y., Saylor, B. Z., Deino, A., Levin, N. E., Alene, M., & Latimer, B. M. (2012, March 29). A new hominin foot from Ethiopia shows multiple Pliocene bipedal adaptations. *Nature, 483*, 565–569.
3. Itzkoff, S. (2000). *The inevitable domination by man.* Ashfield, MA/New York, NY: Paideia/Peter Lang.

# INDEX

## A

actinopterygians, 21
adaptationist fallacy, 95
adaptive
   behavior, 34, 42, 94
   brain-initiated exploratory trend, 48
   grooving characteristics, 86
   morphological and physiological
      pointers, 28
   niche, 23
   pathways, 13–15
   rubicon, 18, 22, 60, 157
   shift, 183–184
   solutions, 32
   survivability, 35, 95
   variable patterns, 36
   zone, 44
African/non-African separation, 82
African Eve hypothesis, 72, 82

agnathans, 19, 21
allometry, principle of, 60–61
altruistic behavior, 101, 150
Andrews, P., 52, 58
animal life, adaptations of, 13–24
animal symbolicum, 101, 133
anthropoid evolution,
      tradition of, 56–57
ape extinction, 66
arctocyonids, 45
Ardipithecus kaddaba, 232
Ardipithecus ramidus, 61
art, centrality of, 230–231
artiodactyls, 45
Associated Press, 60
Australopithecine, xiii, 49, 53, 61, 66, 67,
      69, 85, 231–232
Australopithecus, xiii, xxix, 47, 55, 61,
      67–68, 161
autocracy, 213–214

## B

Bach, J. S., 95
beacon of resurrection, 217
Beard, C., 41, 53
before the present (BP), 8
bilaterality, 15
billion years (by), 13
Binet, A., 177
bio-genetics, 6
bipedalism, 56–57, 59
birds, 18, 22, 28, 32–33, 46
black swan occurrence, 196
Bohr, N., 126
Bolk, L., 84
Boskopoid-Bushman, 77–79
brain, 18, 33–34, 215,
   behavioral revolution, 83
   complexity of, 99
   dynamics of, 35–36
   mobilization of energy and, 136
   size and power of, 67
   survival and the, 95–97
   structural differences in, 28
Buffett, W., 153

## C

Campbell, B., 56
Cambrian, 17
Capoid, xxiv, xxvii, 69, 77–80, 84, 158, 174–175
carved antler bones, xxii
Cassirer, E., 96, 126, 131
catastrophe, 215–223
Caucasoid, xiv, xxvi–xxvii, 9, 70, 77–79, 82–83, 99, 107, 120–121, 143, 150–151, 158, 160–162, 165, 172–176, 178
cause, 125–126
Cavalli-Sforza, L. L., xxviii, 83
Cenozoic Paleocene, 45
cercopithecoids, 58
cerebral integration, 16

cerebralization, zone of, 177
challenges of the century, 196–196
chimpanzee/human relationship, xii
China, 119–122, 132, 153, 171, 173, 176, 198–199
Chordata, 42
civilization, 8, 108–109
   dynamics of, 115–122
   failed, 112–114
   international disparities of, 172
   material conditions of, 132
   models of, 111
   progress of, 109–111, 132
   transformations, 170–172
Cnidaria, 23
coelacanth, 22
Colbert, E., 35, 46
color vision, 44
comparative skulls, xiv
complicit exploiters, 150–151
cone system vision, 34, 44
Coon, C., 70, 160, 174
cortico-cortical
   analysis, 124
   connectivity, 44
counter-entropy, 135–136. *See also* humans
creationism, socio-political, 4–7, 9, 159, 178
creativity, pulses of, 132
Cretaceous, 21, 31, 35–37, 42, 44–46, 56
Cro-Magnon/ Cro-Magnids, xiv, xxiii, xxv, xxix, 7, 70–72, 77–87, 94, 96, 99–100, 102, 105–107, 111, 138–139, 143, 150, 157, 159, 162, 173–174, 176
   artistic mentality of, 218, 230
   burial traditions of, xix
   capacities of brain, 124, 215
   chronometric markings by, xvii
   civilization of, 132
   competitors and, 10
   cultural emanations of, 109
   genes of, 163, 199, 232–233
   heritage of, 164, 176, 179
   hybrid types of, 161
   inheritance of, 116

intelligence and, 166, 189, 197, 198, 216, 220
intrusion, xxiv
mind of, 136
minorities and, 188
origins of, 160
progeney of, 135–143
survival of, 183
technology and, 120
tools, xv–xvi, xxv
Upper Paleolithic, 82
venuses of, xviii
*See also* homo sapiens sapiens
crossopterygians, 21–22, 28
cultural
 behavior, 158
 relativism, 105–106
 selection, 163–164
 symbolic elements of, 162
culture, 96, 98, 100, 106, 108, 132, 158
cynodonts, 29, 31, 33, 36, 66

# D

Dart, R., 67
Darwin, C., 9, 126, 177
Darwinian perspective, 1–2, 5–9, 28, 42, 86, 101, 124–125, 158, 162
Dawkins, R., 97
Deacon, T.W., 85
de Beer, G., 36, 84
decline
 economic symptoms of, 208–209
 societal symptoms of, 209–212
de Duve, C., 21
demographic discipline, 190–191
denouement, 152–154
destiny, 225–233
deuterstomes, 15
Devonian, 18, 22
Didelphis marsupialis, 35, 37
Didelphis virginiana, 35
diminished state, 141

dinosaurs, 45, 66
dipnoan lungfish, 21
discursive domain, 126, 130, 226–227. *See also* symbolic
Dobzhansky, T., 95
dominance, 28
 adaptive, 86
 competition for, 163
 cultural, 165
 insectivores/primates and, 44
 sensory, 33
 techno-economic, 165
Dryopithecus, 68

# E

ecological
 change and, 43
 mastery of, 18–19
economic systems, 6
Einstein, A., 126, 231
Encephalization quotient (EQ), 35
endomorphism, 44
endothermy, 31–32, 43
energy, 191–193
entitlement society, 209
entropy, principle of, 13
environmental adaptations, 44
Eocene, 41, 45–48, 53
Eodelphis, 35
Eosimias centennicus, 41
equality of condition, 146–148, 152, 211, 228–229
eucynodonts, 33
eugenics, 6, 178
eukaryote metazoan animals, 42
Europe, 196–198
Europoid, 3–4, 166, 172–175, 189, 198, 220–221
evolution
 covert, 85
 hidden dimensions of, 27–28, 36–37, 43, 85

of tools, xv
social, 126
understanding of, 7
evolutionary, 4–5
change, 42, 52
comparisons, xxvi
descent, 54–55
dynamics, 1, 7, 19, 150
innovation and, 17
luck and, 86
natural forces, 225
perspective, 231–233
problems, 28
specialization and, 15
theory, 41–43
timetable, xi
Excoffier, L., 82
experience
dimensions of, 34
sensory cores of, 124
exploiter/exploited, model of, 172, 222, 228

## F

forms, of life, 14
free will, 98

## G

Gadow, H. F., 29
Galton, F., 169, 177–178
Garden of Eden, 83
genetic bottleneck, 81–83
genetics, 7, 42, 94, 150
genocide, 149, 152, 162, 171, 178, 195, 215
gibbons, 53–54, 57–58, 61
Gigantopithecus, 58
golden souls, 229
Goldschmidt, R., 27, 79
Goodman, M., 51
Gould, S. J., 27, 84
Great Society, 210

Greece, 116–117
Gregory, W. K., 35–36, 84
Grehan, J., 55

## H

Han Chinese, 121–122, 132, 172
haramiyids, 66
Hardy, A. C., 86
Harris, E. E., 82
Hedges, S. B., 42, 45
Heisenberg, W., 126
Hellenic, 116, 137–138, 140, 186, 215–216, 227
Herodotus, 186
heterochrony, 36–37, 83–84
Hey, J., 82
Hill, A., 61
Hitler, A., 165, 178
Hobbes, T., 140
Holocaust, 5–6, 149, 171, 195, 215
hominid, 37, 49, 53, 58, 66–67, 231–232
brain, 106
chimpanzees and, 72
dominating, 60
expansion of, 59
evolution, 55–56, 65, 98
Hominoidea, 47
Homo, xii, 42, 51–61, 65, 68, 85, 99, 218, 232
erectus, 68–69, 83, 161
erectus pekinensis, 173
erectus pithecanthropus, xiv, 61
ergaster, 67–68, 77–78, 161
evolution of, 159
florensis, xxiv, xxix
fossils of, 66
habilis, 67–68, 77
neanderthalis, xiv, xxvi
rudolfensis, xiii, 67–68
sapiens, 8, 99, 128, 136, 160–161, 218
sapiens Idaltu, 69–70

sapiens sapiens, xiv, 8, 28, 69–70, 77–87, 93–103, 133, 136, 143, 157, 159, 161–162, 167, 177, 184, 187, 204, 218, 220, 223, 231
  *See also* Cro-Magnon
hopeful monsters, 27, 79
Huizinga, J., 109
humans, 2
  ape divergence and, 47, 51–54
  competition, 164
  conditions of, 7
  counter-entropic process, 135–136
  creation of, 84
  equality of opportunity and, 10
  erectine, 81
  evolution of, 8, 163, 233
  gender behavior and, 159
  Judeo-Christian perspective on origins of, 5
  language and genetic relations of, xxviii
  materialists and, 100–103
  modern, 71–72
  nature, 107–109
  origins of, 56
  predecessor lines of, 232
  revolution of, 83–85
  size and, 57
  social equality and, 222
  sturm und drang of, 137
  superego organizational plan for, 223, 227
hybridization, xxiii, 51
hypermorphosis, 83–85

# I

ideology, 143, 176
illusion, 184–185
immigration, 212
inclusive fitness, 97
inequality, 3, 5
information systems, 34
instinct, 93, 95, 139, 176
institutional structural commitments, inner contradictions of, 110
intellect, 3, 8, 57, 160–162, 175–177, 187, 221–223, 227
  capital and, 199, 201, 212
  competition and, 232
  g-factor tests and, 178
  power of, 233
interstate commerce clause, 227
Irhoud, J., 77
irrationality, 189–190, 215–217

# J

Janis, C., 32, 48
Janke, A., 42, 44–45
Jerison, H. J., 28, 30, 35
Jews, 116, 118–119, 149, 152, 162, 165, 178, 200, 215
Johanson, D. C., 67, 231
Johnson, L., 207, 210–211
Jorde, L. B., 81–82

# K

Kabwe, 69–70
Kant, I., 4, 131
Kenyapithecus, 58
Kenyanthropus platyops, 232
Keynes, J. M., 196
Klein, 82
Klein, R., 59, 61, 79
Korzybski, A., 102
Krugman, P., 205, 208–209
kuehneotherids, 66

# L

Langaney, A., 82
Langer, S., 126, 131
laws, 125–126, 137, 162, 176, 215–223, 233
Leakey, L., 69
Leakey, R., 230

Lewontin, R., 95
liberal perspective, 1–2, 4, 209
life, 23, 214
limbic system, 17
literacy, 176
live bearers, 31
Lucy, xxix, 67, 231
Luo, Z-X, 42
Lysenko, T., 6, 178

# M

MacLatchy, L., 60
Magdalenian (Würm) glaciation climax, 81
mammals, 27–37
   evolution, issues in, 37–38, 44
   homoeothermic regulation and, 43
   morphology and, 66
   origins of, 29–32
man the play animal, 109
Maoism, one female-one child policy, 198–199, 217, 219
Marshack, A., 100
marsupials, 29–30, 32–34, 37, 66
Marx, K., 5–6, 126, 147, 150, 172, 222, 226
Marxism, 109, 143, 147, 172
mass production, basic principle of, 229
Matsuda, T., 61
Mayr, E., 24, 95
McKinney, M., 84–86
McNamara, K.J., 84–86
Mendel, G., 6–7, 178,
Mesolithic period, 107
Mesopotamia, 107–108, 112, 116, 118, 137
Mesozoic, 35
metabolic regulation, 28
Michurin, 6, 178
Middle East, 199–201

millennial twenty-first century transition, 186–187
million years (my), 17
million years ago (mya), 15
Miocene, 47–49, 53–54, 57–61, 65–66, 68, 156
Mladek/Predmost exemplars, 80
modernity, 70–71, 110
molecular
   analysis, 42
   controversies, 51–53
Mongoloids, xxvi, 78, 79, 161, 173–174
monkey
   ape/prosimian divisions, 53
   New World, 54, 59
   Old World, 53, 58
monotremes, 29, 35, 37, 66
moral vision, 9–10
Morales, M., 35, 46
morganucodon, 29, 35
Morotopithecus, 60
Morton, D. J., 56
Mousterian Neanderthal tools, xv, 77, 79
mtDNA, 81–82
mud burrowers, 15

# N

natural selection, 65–72, 155–167, 232
   competition and, 156–158
   dynamics of, 155–156
Neanderthals, xxiii, xxv, 9–10, 70–72, 77–81, 83, 85, 96, 105, 162, 173, 176, 184, 230, 232
Negroids, 160, 174–176, 220
neoteny, 83–84, 94
Newton, I., 126
non-vertebrate chordates, 15

## O

Oklahoma Land Rush, 54
Oligocene, 47–48, 53–54, 56–58, 65
optic-tectum, 43–44
orangutan-hominid connection, 55
Ordovician, 17, 19, 22
Oreopithecus, 58, 68
*Origin of Species*, 7
orthoselection, 18, 86, 93–95
outliers, 86, 94, 114
out-of-Africa Eve thesis, 82
ovoviviparous, 29–30
Oxnard, C. E., 56
oxyclaenus, 45

## P

Pääbo, S., 44–45
Paedomorphosis, 83–85, 94
Paleocene, 47, 53, 66
Pan, 232
Paranthropus boisei, xiii, 55, 85
Parapithecoideia, 54
Pauling, L., 51
Peramorphosis, 83–84
Permian, 20
    extinction and, 43
    variability of climate, 32
phenotypes, 36, 97, 157, 161
philanthropy, redistributionist, 206–207
philosopher kings, 222, 227
Pikaia gracilens, 15
placentals, 32–34, 37, 42, 45, 48, 66
    morphology of, 30–31
    reproduction and, 28–32, 43
placoderms, 19–20
Pleistocene, 47, 68, 71, 78, 81–82, 86, 94, 163, 183
plesiadapiforms, 45, 47
Pliocene, 47
political
    emancipation, 140–141
    leadership, 111

Pongo, 232
Portmann, A., 84
power
    assumptions of, 3
    brokers, 150
    center of gravity, 208
    manipulations of, 8
    principle of limited government and, 221
    shifting of, 213–214
prey-predator relationships, 59
primates, 41–49, 83, 155–156
    identity and, 54
    timeline and, 46–47
primeval humanity, 77–78
Proconsul, 47, 57
Propliopithecoideia, 54
prosimians, 41, 46
Proterozoic "Riphean," 19
proto-
    amphibians, 21
    apes, 54, 58
    hominids, 46, 54, 56–61, 65, 67
    homo, 57, 157
    mammals, 29, 31, 66
    primates plesiadapids, 44
Ptilodus montanus, 35
Public Library of Science, 53
punctuated equilibrium, 27
Purgatorius, 44

## Q

Qafzeh, xxiii, xxv, 70, 79–80, 160

## R

race, 172–175, 220
Raff, R. A., 85
readaptation, 59
radical nerve net symmetry, 15
Radinsky, L., 31–33
Ramapithecus, 54, 58

rate gene alterations, 84, 86
rationality, 7, 139, 187–190, 199, 227
Rattus norvegicus, 35
redemptive social welfare-ism, 171
reality, 2–4
    evolutionary change and, 8, 154
    new vision of, 217–218
    social selection and, 166
    sociobiological and, 150, 158–160
    suppressed, 169–179
regression toward the mean, 228
relationships, structure of, 126, 136–137
relief venus sculpture, xxi
religion, 130–131, 137
religio-obscuranist controls, 5
remembrance carving, xx
renewal, 215–223
reptile neural retina, 34
revolution
    millennial, 169–172
    power structures of, 151
Richards, M., 82
rodents, 45
Rogers, A. R., 81–82
Rome, 117–119
Rousseau, J-J, 146–147
rules, world of, 169

## S

Sangiran 17, xxiv, xxvi, 69
Sarich, V., 51–52
scarcity, 185, 197
Schultz, A. H., 56, 84
Schwartz, J., 55
scientific method, 139–140
secondary altricality, 84
secular
    analysis, 124
    insanity, 150–152
    modernity, 136
    rationality, 221
selective, 5–6, 33–34, 43

ecological and environmental
    variability and, 23
pressures, 86
reproductive efficacy and, 8
stress, 81
values, 125
selfish gene, 97, 165
sensory integration, 34
sequential organizational hypermorphosis, 83, 85
seven years of severity, 203
Silurian, 18, 30
Simon, T., 177
Simpson, G. G., 45–46
Sinoconodon, 36, 37
Sivapithecines, 54, 58, 61
Sivapithecus, 58
Siwalla, B., 20
Skhul 5, xxiii, 70, 79–80, 160
Smith, A., 141, 147
social
    change, 141–143, 149–152
    dependency, 5
    policy initiatives, 3
    unification, 10
    welfare initiatives, 6
socialism, 6
sociobiological controversy, 97–98
South Asia, 201–202
Spearman, C., 178
social justice, nature of, 170–171
species-wide unification, 154
Spinoza, B., 140
Stalin, J., 6, 110, 159, 165, 178, 214, 217
Stebbins, G., 47
Stern, J. T., 56
Stringer, C. B., 52, 58
structural and behavioral variability, 86, 94
structures of meaning, 96, 133, 143
Sumerians, 107, 111, 116–117, 176, 219
superego intervention, 164
supersymmetry, 126
suppression, 177–179
survival

challenges to, 233
democracy and intelligence, 219–221
international conditions of, 187–193
new world of, 102
symbolism
cultural rationales and, 163–164
discursive forms of, 123–125, 133, 225–226
dynamics of, 103, 105–114
non-discursive forms of, 123–125, 127–129, 151, 166, 225–226, 229
politics and power and, 229
relationships and, 145–146
structures of information and, 124, 167
thought and, 123–133
vectors of, 123–125
systems of thought, 96–97

# T

taxonomic categories, 23
taxons, 15
teleost, 21, 30
tetrapods, 30
therapsids, 29, 31–33
therian morphology and behavior, 32–34
thinking, intellectual foundation for, 126, 141
third world, 143, 150–153, 171, 189, 201, 202–203, 206
Thorndike, E., 98
time, 17, 37, 177
Tishkoff, S., 81
Tobias, P., 61
Torroni, A., 82
totalitarianism, 151, 172
transition to land, 19–22, 28
triage, 185, 203–204, 214
Triassic, 32–33, 35–37, 66
tribosphenic molars, 32
triconodon mordax, 35, 37
Turkana (Kenya) boy, 68
Tuttle, R. H., 56
twenty-first century issues, 206–208

tychistic, 99, 218

# U

unified field theory, 125–126
United States, 205–214
universal
causality, sense of, 125–126
cultural hegemony, 164
humanity, dream of, 145–154
model of human social organization, 153
redistributive prosperity, 154
universality, 132–133, 153
unresolved super-species, 133
utopian
interdict, 195–204
perversion and, 148–150
social democracy peace, 206
vision and, 171

# V

vertebrate, 14–15, 42
adaptations, 57–58
brain and, 16–17, 94
history of, 23, 65
plans of, 22
survival of, 22–23
systems of, 16
vision of the victors, 206
viviparity, 30–31

# W

Walls, G., 34
Ward, S., 61
wealth, 111, 185
weltanschauung, 207
white people, 5, 70, 120, 175–177, 211
Wilson, A. C., 51–52, 71–72, 81–82

Wilson, E. O., 86, 97
world classlessness, vision of, 226
World War I, 5, 151
World War II, 2, 5, 149–151
   post-, 110, 165–166, 169
Wray, G. A., 42

# Y

yin and yang, 131–133
Yoder, A. D., 41–42, 53

# Z

Zuckerkandl, R., 51